Conspicuous

How Modern Luxury Redefined Craft, Clout, and Culture

Karina Vunnam

Creative Nudge Press

Conspicuous: How Modern Luxury Redefined Craft, Clout, and Culture
Written by Karina Vunnam
Copyright © 2025 by Karina Vunnam
All rights reserved.
Published by Creative Nudge Press, LLC
First Edition, 2025

For permission requests
Creative Nudge Press
2108 N St
Sacramento
contact@creativenudge.net
ConspicuousBook.com

Library of Congress Cataloging-in-Publication Data
Vunnam, Karina
Conspicuous: How Modern Luxury Redefined Craft, Clout, and Culture / Karina Vunnam
978-1-966193-24-1 (paperback)
978-1-966193-25-8 (hardback)
1. Fashion—Social aspects
2. Luxury goods industry
3. Consumer behavior
4. Brand management
5. Popular culture

Printed in the United States of America
10 9 8 7 6 5 4 3 2 1

Contents

Author's Note

Conspicuous draws on extensive research across consumer psychology, history, sociology, business analysis, and cultural studies to explore luxury's transformation. To create a seamless reading experience while maintaining academic rigor, I've developed this work with two guiding principles:

ON CITATIONS AND RESEARCH

Throughout this book, I've integrated insights from numerous sources including academic journals, industry reports, interviews, news articles, social media content, and historical accounts. Citations appear as superscript numbers in the text, with full references listed by chapter at the end of the book. This approach maintains scholarly integrity while preserving narrative flow and visual aesthetics.

My research has been comprehensive, drawing from both traditional academic sources and contemporary digital media to capture luxury's evolution across different eras and perspectives. This blend of sources allows for a multidimensional view that encompasses both quantitative analysis and qualitative human experience.

ON NARRATIVE APPROACH

To bring luxury's rich history to life, I employ vivid storytelling techniques throughout the book. Historical scenes have been reconstructed based on documented facts and research, with sensory details and dialogue added for narrative richness. These reconstructions aim to immerse you in pivotal moments rather than simply describing them.

All direct quotes within these historical narratives should be understood as creative reconstructions unless specifically attributed to published sources through citations. When a quote includes a citation number, it references an actual documented statement; unattributed dialogue serves to illustrate the spirit of the era in a compelling format.

Similarly, contemporary consumer experiences sometimes represent composite examples that capture authentic patterns revealed through research, even when not attributed to specific individuals. These narrative techniques bring abstract concepts into tangible, relatable focus while remaining true to the underlying research.

This dual approach, rigorous research paired with immersive storytelling, allows Conspicuous to be both intellectually substantive and genuinely engaging. My goal is to respect the factual foundation while creating an experience that resonates emotionally, making luxury's complex transformation accessible to all readers.

Introduction
The Eternal Migration

There was a time when stepping into a boutique felt like stepping into a temple. When a logo whispered a promise I desperately needed to believe. That time has passed. I didn't lose the magic; I carried it with me, until I no longer needed it to tell me who I was.

Some evenings, I still open my closet and reach for my Bottega Veneta Knot, its intrecciato woven metal mesh catching the light like moonlight on water. The gunmetal knot lock gleams as my fingers trace the precise pattern of the weave. This structured clutch, a piece I rarely carry but frequently admire, transcends mere accessory. In it, craftsmanship alchemizes industrial materials into art, creating beauty through deliberate elevation. The object carries no obvious logo, no shouted declaration of its origin, yet to the educated eye, it announces itself instantly through its distinctive technique and impeccable execution.

I rarely carry this clutch out into the world. It sits in my closet, an expensive object that serves almost no practical purpose. Yet when I hold it, examining how the light plays across its metallic weave, I still feel a whisper of what once captivated me so completely about luxury: the human ingenuity, the artistic vision, the exquisite attention to detail that transforms ordinary materials into extraordinary objects.

The magic I once felt stepping into those hushed boutiques hasn't entirely disappeared. I still see it reflected in the eyes of young women emerging from Chanel or Louis Vuitton, clutching their precious shopping bags with reverent hands, their expressions transfigured by the belief that they've acquired not just an object but a piece of something transcendent. I recognize that look, the belief that this purchase marks a threshold crossed, an identity claimed, a transformation begun.

This dissonance, between my faded enchantment and their vibrant belief, initially puzzled me. Had luxury changed, or had I? The answer, I discovered, was both. The magic hadn't vanished; it had migrated, following ancient patterns that have repeated themselves throughout history. Luxury's spell, like water, seeks its own level, flowing from vessels that can no longer contain it toward new expressions that preserve its eternal promise: specialness, distinction, transformation.

This migration isn't unique to our era. Since humans first adorned themselves with shells and feathers, the markers of status and beauty have followed predictable cycles of emergence, expansion, dilution, and rebirth. What began in royal courts, where monarchs employed in-house artisans to craft exquisite objects for their exclusive use, gradually shifted to specialized houses serving nobility, then to merchants serving the wealthy, and onward through each democratizing wave. At each stage, as one form of luxury became accessible to more people, new expressions emerged to maintain the essential distance between the ordinary and the extraordinary.

What defines luxury across these transitions? At its essence, luxury represents the deliberate elevation of the necessary to the exceptional. We all need clothing, but not cashmere woven from the throat hairs of Himalayan goats. We all need shelter, but not marble-clad penthouses overlooking Central Park. We all need transportation, but not hand-built automobiles with lambswool carpeting. Luxury transforms functional requirements into experiences of beauty, craftsmanship, and meaning.

The democratization of luxury, the gradual expansion of who can access these exceptional experiences, carries within it both promise and paradox. The promise lies in the expanding circle of those who can experience beauty and craftsmanship beyond mere functionality. The paradox emerges when this expansion inevitably dilutes the very exclusivity that gives luxury its psychological power.

This book explores this perpetual tension through the most dramatic luxury transformation in modern history: the journey from craft-focused ateliers to global conglomerates, from intimate boutiques to Instagram ubiquity, from inherited wealth to installment plans. It examines how different business approaches from LVMH, Richemont, Hermès, and Chanel shaped global luxury consumption alongside the parallel rise of social media, influencer culture, and new financial models that democratized luxury access.

The story unfolds across three acts:

ACT I - THE MAGIC EMERGES

The first act explores luxury's captivation of our collective imagination, tracing our emotional connection to these exceptional objects alongside the strategic creation of heritage narratives by the houses that produced them.

ACT II - THE MAGIC PARADOX

The second act examines the fundamental tension at luxury's heart: how brands expanded to meet growing desire while attempting to preserve the very exclusivity that fueled that desire initially.

ACT III - THE MAGIC MIGRATES

The final act follows the evolution of both consumers and brands as the magic migrates from democratized luxury toward new expressions of exclusivity, craft, and meaning.

This journey unfolds through a unique dual perspective, alternating between "Us" (the consumer experience) and "Them" (the brand strategy). Each chapter shifts viewpoints, creating a dialogue between desire and design, emotion and economics. Through this alternation, we see both sides of luxury's transformative power: how it changes those who consume it and how it's changed by those who create it.

The Dior fashion house serves as our archetypal example of luxury's cyclical nature. From Christian Dior's revolutionary "New Look" that restored Paris as the global fashion capital after World War II, through the excessive licensing that nearly destroyed the brand in the 1970s, to Bernard Arnault's masterful resurrection that became the template for modern luxury management, Dior's journey contains all the elements of luxury's eternal pattern in microcosm.

What makes our current moment unique isn't the cycle itself but its unprecedented acceleration and global scale. What once took generations now unfolds in years or even months. What once affected only the privileged few now influences billions through social media's democratizing lens. The fundamental pattern remains the same, but the velocity and visibility have transformed dramatically.

As luxury cycles through its eternal phases, it reveals deeper truths about human desire, status, and identity. Why do we seek objects that transcend mere function? Why does exclusivity matter so deeply in our pursuit of meaning? How do we balance the democratic impulse to expand access with the inherent scarcity that gives luxury its power? These questions have no simple answers, only the continuing dialogue between those who create luxury and those who consume it.

For me, the journey began with that Bottega Veneta clutch, a piece of artistry masquerading as accessory. Perhaps you remember your own first encounter with luxury's promise, the moment when an object transcended its physical properties to become a talisman of transformation. Or perhaps you're still awaiting that moment, curious about the forces that create desire so powerful it compels millions to spend beyond their means for objects they don't strictly need.

Wherever you stand in your relationship with luxury, this story belongs to you. Even if you've never bought a designer piece, you've felt the pull of magic, status, or belonging in some way. Because luxury, at its heart, isn't about leathers or logos, price points or profit margins. It's about the human yearning for meaning beyond necessity, for beauty beyond function, for enchantment in a world that often seems determined to dispel it. The vessels change, but the magic remains, perpetually migrating, eternally renewed.

ACT I
THE MAGIC EMERGES

We Discovered the Magic

They Sold Us Their Legacy

"Luxury is in each detail."

— Hubert de Givenchy

Chapter One

The Dream Factory

T he box was orange. Not just any orange, a particular shade that existed nowhere else in the natural world, as if it had been mixed specifically to signal that whatever lay inside was exceptional. I'd seen this color before, of course, on magazine pages, in films, clutched in the manicured hands of celebrities as they exited private jets. But this was different. This box was mine.

My fingertips traced the slightly textured cardboard as the boutique fell silent around me. The sales associate had tied the coffee-brown ribbon with practiced precision, each motion part of a choreography designed to amplify anticipation. When she finally slid the package across the counter with both hands, palms upturned in a gesture almost religious in its reverence, it was like a crown being passed down.

"Enjoy your Hermès scarf," she said, her smile warm but professional. "It's a beautiful first piece."

First piece. The words hung in the air between us, implying a journey just beginning. I hadn't purchased a simple square of silk; I'd bought

entry into a world where objects transcended their physical properties
to become talismans of achievement, discernment, arrival.

That's the thing about luxury in its golden age throughout the late
1980s to early 2000s, it sold itself as much more than the sum of its
materials. We bought not only the products but the story, the heritage,
the promise of transformation. And God, did we want to believe.

It's easy to dismiss this as materialism, as empty status-seeking. But
to do so misses the profound emotional alchemy that luxury brands
mastered during this era. They understood that humans have always
sought beauty, meaning, and transcendence through objects. From religious artifacts to royal regalia, we have long imbued physical items
with significance beyond their functional value. What luxury brands
managed to do was democratize this experience, slightly, selectively,
allowing more of us access to objects that felt sacred, special, transformative.

Walking into a luxury boutique during this era meant crossing a
threshold between ordinary life and something elevated, separate, almost sacred, a kind of modern liminal experience. The architecture
itself announced this transition, limestone facades, marble floors, soaring ceilings. Once inside, a sensory shift enveloped you immediately.
Outside might be chaotic, traffic noise, crowds, unpredictable weather,
but inside was controlled perfection. The temperature remained ideal,
lighting meticulously designed to flatter both customers and products.
The scent was distinctive, either the house's signature fragrance or
simply the rich aroma of fine leathers and fabrics.

Products were displayed like sacred objects, often a single item presented on a pedestal or shelf, spotlit to enhance its aura. Sales associates moved through these spaces as both acolytes and guides, possessing an unhurried confidence unlike the commission-driven hustle
of mainstream retail. They created time for conversation, for storytelling, for education about the maison's history and techniques. We
internalized these stories, becoming repositories and evangelists for
the lore of our chosen brands. We discovered the language of luxury,

terms like "patina," "atelier," "artisan," "heritage," that allowed us to discuss these objects with the reverence they seemed to demand.

"It takes a single artisan forty hours to craft one Birkin bag."

This oft-repeated claim about Hermès's iconic handbag exemplifies the narrative that luxury houses wove during their golden age, a story centered on human hands, meticulous skill, and time-honored techniques. Whether entirely accurate or somewhat mythologized, such statements served a crucial purpose. They elevated luxury objects from expensive commodities into something approaching art or artifact, justifying their extraordinary prices through the romance of human craftsmanship.

We absorbed and internalized these narratives eagerly. Something deeply appealing resided in the image of a white-coated artisan in an atelier, bent over a workbench that hadn't changed in a century, using tools and techniques passed down through generations. In a world increasingly dominated by mass production and automation, the idea that our purchases were still crafted by human hands, one at a time, felt extraordinary, even noble.

The luxury houses nurtured this perception carefully, opening their workshop doors just enough to tantalize but not enough to demystify. Hermès would occasionally allow film crews into their ateliers, showing artisans carefully selecting leathers, measuring with traditional tools, hand-stitching with the distinctive saddle stitch that machines couldn't replicate. These glimpses behind the curtain functioned as a form of "luxury porn," allowing us to vicariously experience the creation process and feel more connected to our purchases.

The narrative of hands wasn't just about aesthetics or quality, though those were certainly emphasized, but about time. Luxury brands stressed the hours, sometimes hundreds, required to create their products. This time investment stood in stark contrast to the efficiency-obsessed modern world. In luxury's golden age narrative, slowness became a virtue, patience a component of perfection. Patek Philippe's famous slogan captured this perfectly: "You never actually own a Patek Philippe. You merely look after it for the next generation."

What made these stories so powerful was their foundation in truth. Behind the polished marketing existed authentic craftsmanship, skilled artisans, and established traditions of excellence. Hermès saddles were indeed handcrafted by master saddlers; Louis Vuitton trunks were actually constructed by artisans using traditional methods. The magic of luxury's golden age lay in how reality, which was perhaps enhanced by storytelling, still predominantly matched the myth.

As one customer explained in a 2011 Wall Street Journal interview, after waiting eighteen months for her first Kelly bag, the emotional investment became so strong that price increases during the wait hardly mattered.

This calculated waiting game exemplified luxury brands' profound understanding of human psychology. They orchestrated desire through strategic inaccessibility, transcending simple product sales. The waiting list emerged as one of luxury's most powerful tools. Whether for an Hermès Birkin, a limited-edition Rolex, or access to a Chanel couture fitting, these lists stretched across months or years. They transformed acquisition from ordinary transaction into quests, a demonstration of patience and devotion.

Beyond formal waiting lists, luxury brands cultivated what might be called "the perfect distance," a calibrated space between desire and attainment. Products needed to be visible enough to create aspiration but not so accessible that they lost their mystique. This balancing act manifested in everything from price points to distribution strategies. A brand might offer small leather goods at entry-level prices while keeping their signature items at much higher thresholds. This created a "luxury ladder" that customers could climb over time, each purchase bringing them closer to the ultimate acquisitions.

Certain objects transcended their physical form to become cultural shorthand, instantly recognizable symbols that communicate without words. The Hermès Birkin and Kelly bags, the Chanel 2.55 flap bag, the Louis Vuitton Speedy, the Cartier Love bracelet, these weren't just expensive accessories but totemic objects loaded with social meaning and emotional resonance.

Popular culture played a crucial role in elevating these items from exclusive designs to universal symbols. *Breakfast at Tiffany's* maintained powerful influence through the decades, establishing the Tiffany blue box as an emblem of romance and aspiration. Holly Golightly's reverence for Tiffany & Co. as a sanctuary, "a place where nothing very bad could happen to you," connected luxury beyond status to emotional security and self-transformation.

By the late 1990s, television had become an equally potent force in shaping luxury desire. *Sex and the City* revolutionized how specific designers and items entered public consciousness by integrating them directly into character development and plot. Carrie Bradshaw's shoe obsession, particularly her devotion to Manolo Blahnik, became central to her character. The Fendi Baguette bag, featured in a pivotal robbery scene, became such a phenomenon that the company reported substantial sales increases for styles highlighted on the show.

What made these media influences so powerful was their ability to create emotional narratives around luxury objects. We didn't just desire a Fendi Baguette; we desired the confident femininity and New York sophistication that Sarah Jessica Parker's character represented. We weren't just coveting an Hermès scarf; we were reaching for the effortless elegance and timeless taste that Grace Kelly embodied.

For many of us, luxury purchases evolved into a form of self-creation. The items we selected spoke volumes about who we were, or more accurately, who we aspired to become. A Cartier Tank watch might signal appreciation for history and understated elegance; a Gucci Jackie bag might suggest fashion-forward thinking and cultural awareness. We selected these identity markers carefully, often gravitating toward brands and items that reflected aspects of ourselves we wished to amplify or qualities we aspired to develop.

Luxury's golden age was global in scope but experienced through distinctly cultural lenses. The same brands and objects were desired across continents, but the meaning attached to them varied significantly according to local contexts. This period saw the initial flourishing of a truly international luxury landscape, with heritage European houses expanding their reach while adapting to different cultural sensibilities.

In Western Europe, particularly France and Italy, luxury consumption was often characterized by understatement and insider knowledge. European consumers frequently displayed what sociologist Pierre Bourdieu called "cultural capital," the ability to make refined distinctions that weren't obvious to outsiders. Status was often communicated through quality and details recognizable only to those "in the know" rather than through obvious branding.

The American approach to luxury during this period reflected the nation's characteristic optimism and belief in reinvention. While appreciating craftsmanship and heritage, American consumers often embraced luxury's transformative promise more explicitly. There was less emphasis on family tradition or inherited taste and more on the ability of luxury to signal personal achievement and success.

Japan pioneered Asian luxury consumption, developing a distinctive relationship with European brands that combined reverence for tradition with attention to detail that sometimes exceeded even the originating cultures. Japanese consumers demonstrated a deep appreciation for craftsmanship and the philosophy behind objects. A Japanese customer might examine the stitching on a leather good or the finishing on a watch movement with extraordinary scrutiny, valuing technical perfection alongside heritage.

As China began its emergence as a luxury powerhouse in the early 2000s, its initial approach reflected both traditional cultural values and the psychology of a rapidly developing market. The concepts of "mianzi" (face) and social standing strongly influenced purchasing decisions, with visible luxury items serving as important markers in business and social relationships. Early Chinese luxury consumers often showed preferences for recognizable designs and visible logos that clearly communicated brand identity.

At the heart of luxury's golden age lay a remarkable transformation, not just of raw materials into exceptional objects, but of ordinary commerce into profound emotional experience. Leather, metal, fabric, and stone became something more than the sum of their parts through luxury's emotional alchemy.

The physical transformations were real and tangible, the quality difference between luxury materials and their mass-market counterparts was genuine, observable, and functional. But the more powerful alchemy happened in our perception. The same physical object, presented in different contexts, would trigger vastly different emotional responses. A silk scarf acquired from a department store conveyed different meanings than the identical design purchased at a Hermès boutique, unwrapped from the orange box with ceremonial care.

Through carefully orchestrated experiences, luxury brands imbued their products with meaning that transcended functionality or aesthetics. A watch became a milestone; a handbag became an achievement; a piece of jewelry became a legacy. We weren't just purchasing objects but moments, memories, milestones, and markers.

The most profound transformation, however, was in self-perception. Luxury goods didn't just signal status to others; they altered how we saw ourselves. The Burberry trench wasn't simply weather protection; it was a uniform for the international, cosmopolitan life we envisioned. The Jaeger-LeCoultre watch didn't just tell time; it was a daily reminder of the successful, accomplished person we were working to become.

What made luxury's golden age distinctive was that the emotional alchemy was supported by authentic quality and craftsmanship. The transformed perceptions were grounded in genuine excellence. The Chanel bag actually was meticulously crafted by skilled artisans; the Patek Philippe watch truly did represent generations of watchmaking expertise. The magic wasn't manufactured from nothing but built upon a foundation of tangible superiority.

This period represented a moment of perfect tension in luxury's history, the traditional houses had opened their doors just wide enough to welcome a new generation of appreciators but not so wide that the exclusivity was diluted. Distribution remained limited enough to maintain mystique; production volumes were controlled enough to ensure quality; marketing was sophisticated enough to create desire without overexposure.

The craftsmanship narrative aligned with actual production methods. The retail experience reflected the care put into the products. The price, while premium, still maintained some relationship to the cost of materials and labor. The exclusivity, while real, still allowed for new entrants and aspirants. Every element reinforced the others, creating a self-consistent world that felt both rarefied and authentic.

Yet even as we reveled in this golden age, subtle signs of change were appearing. The major luxury conglomerates were consolidating, acquiring independent houses and gradually standardizing operations. Limited production runs of Dior sunglasses, once made entirely in France, began to include components manufactured elsewhere. Distribution was extending beyond the exclusive flagships to department store concessions and duty-free shops. These changes were incremental, almost imperceptible at first, but they represented the early stages of a transformation that would ultimately alter luxury's fundamental character.

What made this brief moment so remarkable, and so fondly remembered by those who experienced it, was that it represented a perfect confluence: traditional craftsmanship meeting modern global business before the tension between exclusivity and scale became unmanageable. The dream remained intact, the promise still matched the reality, and the emotional and material aspects of luxury existed in harmony rather than contradiction.

Chapter Two

The House That Legacy Built

P aris, 1854. Rain tapped against the windows of 4 Rue Neuve-des-Capucines as a single oil lamp cast dancing shadows across the modest workshop. Louis Vuitton's calloused hands moved with quiet authority over a wooden frame, his scarred fingers revealing decades of devotion to his craft. At thirty-three, each mark on his skin told a different story, a slip of the knife here, the pressure of canvas-stretching there, a physical ledger of thousands of hours mastering trunk-making. Tonight, he was completing something revolutionary: a flat-topped trunk that would transform how the wealthy traveled.

Vuitton's hands moved with rhythmic precision, stretching gray canvas across the wooden structure. His thumbnail tested the tension, firm enough to prevent wrinkling during use, yet not so tight it would warp the frame. This knowledge resided not in manuals but in his body, acquired through seventeen years of apprenticeship under Monsieur Maréchal, Paris's premier box-maker and packer.

The trunk taking shape reflected a mind constantly solving practical problems. After years observing how dome-topped trunks, designed for stagecoach travel where water runoff was essential, became impractical as railways expanded across Europe, he reimagined the form entirely. His flat-topped innovation allowed for stacking in railway carriages and steamship holds, adapting perfectly to the changing world of modern travel. Every detail, from the waterproof canvas to precision-fitted brass locks, represented not mere aesthetic choice but a functional solution to specific transportation challenges.

Each brass lock was hand-fitted, tested repeatedly, and secured with materials that would endure the roughest journey. This obsessive focus on security wasn't abstract; Vuitton understood intimately that his clients would transport their most precious possessions in his creations. Their trust was earned through meticulous execution of every detail, from hand-stitched leather handles to interior compartments lined with handmade paper, each calibrated to hold specific items safely immobile during the jarring movements of travel.

By the time dawn broke over Paris, the trunk stood complete. Louis Vuitton ran his hands over his creation one final time, feeling for any imperfection. The sign outside his workshop made a simple, confident promise: "Securely packs the most fragile objects. Specializing in packing fashions." In this small space, in these skilled hands, the foundation of a luxury empire was being laid, not through marketing campaigns or brand strategies, but through the authentic mastery of materials, the solving of real problems, and an uncompromising standard of excellence no factory could replicate.

The mythology of luxury today often obscures a simple truth: the great houses began not as fashion statements but as problem solvers. Their founders weren't visionaries dreaming of global empires but practical craftspeople addressing specific needs with exceptional skill. Their early businesses existed in an ecosystem where craftsmanship wasn't a marketing narrative but the fundamental basis of reputation and survival.

Louis Vuitton's journey exemplified this pragmatic beginning. Born to a working-class family in eastern France in 1821, Vuitton left home at fourteen, traveling on foot for more than two years to reach Paris. Upon arriving in 1837, the sixteen-year-old secured an apprenticeship with respected master trunk-maker Monsieur Maréchal. For seventeen years, Vuitton absorbed the intricacies of his craft, learning to create boxes and trunks that would protect the elaborate wardrobes of the Parisian elite during the rough journeys of the era.

By the time he established his own workshop in 1854, his hands contained nearly two decades of accumulated knowledge. His innovations emerged as responses to concrete problems: flat-topped trunks addressed railway storage issues; his waterproof canvas prevented damage from rain and humidity; his systematic use of uniform compartments made packing more efficient. The legendary quality that would become synonymous with his name was no abstract concept but the practical necessity of creating products that could withstand the punishing conditions of 19th-century travel while protecting valuable contents.

Twenty-five miles north of Paris, in 1837, the same year Vuitton began his apprenticeship, another craft-focused enterprise was taking root. Thierry Hermès established a modest harness workshop in the Grands Boulevards quarter, dedicated to serving European noblemen with high-quality wrought harnesses and bridles for their carriages. Like Vuitton, Hermès came to his craft through years of apprenticeship, spending sixteen years mastering the trade before establishing his own workshop.

The extraordinary quality of Hermès's work wasn't simply decorative but essentially functional. In an era when a poorly made harness could lead to dangerous carriage accidents, his meticulous attention to material selection, stitching strength, and fitting precision addressed matters of literal life and death. Each stitch of an Hermès harness was double-sewn by hand using waxed linen thread, creating seams that would not fail even under the sudden strain of a startled horse.

Perhaps the most revolutionary of luxury's founding prob-
lem-solvers emerged decades later. Gabrielle "Coco" Chanel's entrance
into the rarified world of Parisian fashion in the early 1900s was driven
not by aspiration to create status symbols but by a pragmatic desire to
address women's actual needs. Born into poverty in 1883 and orphaned
young, Chanel learned sewing at the convent where she was raised after
her mother's death.

When Chanel opened her first shop, Chanel Modes, at 21 Rue Cam-
bon in 1910, her simplified hat designs directly challenged the elaborate, heavily trimmed millinery of the day. Her approach was radically
functional, creating hats that actually stayed on while walking or riding
in open cars. By 1913, she had expanded to a boutique in Deauville
where she began selling clothing made of jersey. This seemingly simple
material choice proved revolutionary, offering women ease of movement, comfort, and practical elegance in place of the restrictive corsets
and impractical designs that dominated women's fashion.

In each case, Vuitton's trunks, Hermès's harnesses, Chanel's liber-
ating designs, the foundation of what would become legendary luxury
brands was laid through solving specific problems with exceptional
skill and innovative thinking. Their early reputations were built not
on marketing narratives or aspirational branding but on the genuine
superiority of their solutions, recognized first by the discerning clients
who experienced these advantages directly.

The founders themselves embodied this integration of practical
problem-solving with exceptional execution. They worked directly
with materials, engaged personally with clients, and continuously refined their techniques based on real-world feedback. Their innovations
weren't developed in marketing departments but emerged organically
from intimate knowledge of their craft and deep understanding of their
clientele's evolving needs. This authentic foundation, where performance preceded prestige and function informed form, would provide
the legitimacy upon which generations of luxury mythology would
later be built.

In the gleaming flagship stores of today's luxury landscape, it's easy to forget that the great houses began as workshops, physical spaces where materials were transformed by skilled hands into objects of exceptional quality. These ateliers served as more than production facilities; they embodied a distinct economic and organizational approach that differs dramatically from modern corporate structures.

The workshop model created natural limits on production that translated directly into business realities. When every harness required days of meticulous handwork by skilled craftsmen, output was inherently constrained. An Hermès workshop might produce only a handful of complete harnesses in a week, with each representing dozens of hours of skilled labor. This wasn't a limitation to be overcome but the fundamental basis of the business; quality and volume existed in a balanced relationship, with the former prioritized whenever the two came into tension.

Rather than seeking to maximize units sold, these early luxury workshops operated on a higher-margin, lower-volume model. A Louis Vuitton trunk might cost 250-400 francs compared to 80-120 francs for standard alternatives, a premium justified by superior protection of contents worth many times the container itself.

When Charles-Émile Hermès took over from his father in 1880 and moved the workshop to 24 Rue du Faubourg Saint-Honoré (where the flagship remains today), he maintained this workshop-centered model even as he expanded the business to include retail sales. The proximity of production to sales wasn't just logistical but philosophical; clients could see, hear, and smell the craftsmanship behind their purchases.

In the growing Hermès atelier of the late 19th century, leather selection transcended supply chain logistics to become a sensory dialogue between craftsman and material. Master leather artisans at Hermès developed remarkable tactile sensitivity, able to detect subtle variations in thickness, grain patterns, and natural characteristics that would determine each hide's optimal use. This meticulous selection process, where craftspeople would often close their eyes to better feel the leather's qualities, became foundational to the house's reputation for extraordinary quality. The tradition continues today, with Hermès artisans still trained to identify leather characteristics through touch.

Hermès cultivated relationships with specific southern French tanneries, exercising first selection rights and typically claiming only 15-20% of available hides, those meeting their exacting standards for grain consistency, thickness, and minimal natural flaws.

Every morning in Louis Vuitton's Asnières workshop, young Georges Vuitton began by inspecting poplar planks drying in the yard. His father had taught him to tap each piece, listening for the resonance that indicated optimal moisture content. Wood properly seasoned for the required four years produced a distinctive tone recognizable only to those whose bodies had absorbed this knowledge through repetition and mentorship. This represented practical quality control; wood with excessive moisture would warp when exposed to varying humidity during travel, while overly dried wood would split under stress.

This philosophy extended beyond selection to transformation processes. At Hermès, leather tanning wasn't outsourced but integral to creation. The house developed proprietary techniques for achieving specific textures, colors, and hand-feels, understanding these qualities weren't merely aesthetic but functional, affecting how leather would wear, age, and respond to use. The now-legendary Hermès leathers, Box Calf, Togo, Clemence, emerged as specific material expressions developed through this deep engagement with the substance itself.

Louis Vuitton displayed similar material obsession in developing his signature waterproof canvas. Recognizing leather's limitations for travel trunks (heavy, susceptible to water damage), he experimented extensively to create a treated canvas both lightweight and durable, water-resistant yet flexible enough for wooden frames. His original gray Trianon canvas evolved through more than forty iterations, with Vuitton testing each by subjecting it to simulated travel conditions, soaking in water, abrading against rough surfaces, exposing to intense sunlight, before achieving the optimal balance of properties.

The material philosophy infused every component. Brass fittings were engineered for durability and security rather than mere decoration. Georges Vuitton's development of an unpickable lock system in 1886 exemplified this holistic material approach; security wasn't a feature added to a product but integral to its conception, with each component designed for optimal performance over decades.

These houses distinguished themselves by recognizing materials as dynamic substances evolving over time. Hermès embraced and celebrated the patina developing on natural leathers through use, seeing this not as deterioration but as the material recording the owner's life, a chronicle of journey and experience that enhanced rather than diminished value. An Hermès bag at twenty years wasn't degraded but matured, achieving character impossible in a new piece. Louis Vuitton trunks similarly gained character through travel, each scratch and sticker telling stories of places visited and challenges overcome.

This philosophy created an entirely different relationship between price and value. The premium commanded by these goods reflected the extraordinary care in material selection, the time invested in proper preparation, and the expertise required to transform raw substances into exceptional objects. When clients paid multiples more for a Hermès harness or Louis Vuitton trunk, they acquired not just prestige but tangible material superiority that translated into performance advantages, greater durability, superior functionality, enhanced beauty, and the pleasure of interacting with materials shaped by genuine masters.

To enter the Louis Vuitton workshop in the 1870s as a client was to step into a relationship entirely unlike modern luxury retail. There were no salespeople separate from craftspeople, no marketing department distinct from production. When an American heiress arrived with her unusual request for a special trunk to transport exotic birds between seasonal residences, she spoke directly with Georges Vuitton, who would not only design but help construct the piece.

Three weeks later, when she returned to collect her commission, Georges personally demonstrated every feature of the finished trunk, explaining the ingenious ventilation system disguised within the Vuitton monogram pattern and showing how the compartments could be adjusted as her collection grew. This wasn't transactional customer service but a creative collaboration between maker and client, where the resulting object embodied not just craftsmanship but deep understanding of a specific individual's requirements.

This direct connection between maker and client formed the foundation of traditional luxury's service model. When Charles-Émile Hermès took over his father's workshop in 1880, he maintained meticulously detailed records of each client's preferences, requirements, and past purchases. The legendary "client books" at Hermès captured not only measurements and orders but intimate personal details.

The physical spaces reflected this relationship model. Before the era of flagship boutiques designed primarily as brand showcases, luxury houses operated from workshops where production and sales coexisted. At Louis Vuitton's original Asnières facility, clients would walk through areas where apprentices stretched canvas over frames, where brass fittings were polished to perfect sheen, where leather handles received their final stitching. This transparency wasn't a marketing technique but simply the reality of businesses where making and selling were integrated rather than separated.

These relationships often spanned generations, creating continuous threads of understanding and service. A single client family might maintain a relationship with a luxury house spanning a century or more. This continuity allowed for a depth of knowledge and relationship impossible in the transactional model that would later dominate retail.

The service extended far beyond the initial sale. When a Louis Vuitton trunk arrived at the Asnières workshop in 1947, accompanied by a letter from a British aristocrat, it told an extraordinary story. Purchased in 1912, the trunk had been aboard a ship requisitioned during World War I, survived a torpedo attack that sank the vessel, and somehow washed ashore in Portugal. After changing hands multiple times, it was spotted in a Lisbon antique shop by a family friend who recognized the nobleman's initials painted on the side. Despite thirty-five years of extraordinary abuse, including extended submersion in seawater, the trunk's frame remained intact, and its original locks still functioned.

Claude Vuitton, Louis's grandson, personally supervised the trunk's six-week restoration, preserving its battle scars while making it functional again. This wasn't mere repair but resurrection, treating the object not as a disposable product but as a companion with its own biography, worthy of care and renewal.

This intimate client model created a profound feedback loop that shaped product development. When Émile-Maurice Hermès noticed clients struggling with traditional baggage while traveling by automobile, he conceived the Bolide bag in 1923, the first handbag with a zipper. This innovation came not from market research but from direct observation of evolving client needs. Similarly, when Jean-Louis Dumas (fifth-generation Hermès family member) sat next to Jane Birkin on a flight in 1984 and witnessed her struggle with an inadequate weekend bag, the conversation led directly to the creation of the now-legendary Birkin bag, a design responding to specific, observed needs rather than abstract market positioning.

The human connections forged through these client relationships were inseparable from another defining aspect of traditional luxury: the continuity provided by family stewardship. While modern corporations measure success in quarterly earnings, the great luxury houses operated on a fundamentally different timeline, one where decisions were made with generations rather than fiscal quarters in mind.

This pattern of family stewardship defined the great luxury houses during their formative eras. When Louis Vuitton died in 1892, his son Georges Vuitton assumed leadership, having absorbed the business from the workshop floor up. Georges brought his own innovations while maintaining his father's standards, most notably creating the iconic Monogram canvas in 1896, both a tribute to his father's legacy and a practical solution to the counterfeiting that threatened the business.

The family model created distinctive advantages in an era of increasing industrialization and corporatization. While publicly traded companies faced pressure for quarterly returns and short-term growth, family-owned luxury businesses could maintain longer time horizons, prioritizing quality and reputation over immediate profits. In 1931, when facing declining sales during the Great Depression, Gaston-Louis Vuitton (Georges's son) was presented with several proposals from financial advisors. These included substituting less expensive hardware, reducing the seasoning time for wood from four years to one, and using machine stitching rather than hand-sewing for certain components, changes calculated to reduce production costs by nearly 30%.

His response captured the essence of family stewardship: "Gentlemen, I have been advised that we can save approximately 30% on materials by making certain... adjustments." He then dramatically tore the proposal in half. "My grandfather's name is on every piece we create. I would rather sell one trunk of his quality than ten of something less. If we cannot maintain our standards, we will make fewer pieces, but we will never compromise what the name Vuitton represents."

This focus on legacy rather than quarterly performance allowed family stewards to make decisions that might limit immediate growth but preserved long-term value. Hermès maintained strict production limitations despite growing demand, prioritizing quality and exclusivity over expansion opportunities. When post-World War II prosperity created unprecedented demand for luxury goods, Robert Dumas refused to significantly increase production capacity, famously stating: "We are not in the business of saying yes to everyone."

Family stewardship also created distinctive approaches to talent development. Unlike the modern corporate pattern where executives might move between unrelated industries, luxury houses under family control typically developed leadership from within, often starting future heads in workshop apprenticeships regardless of their eventual role. Jean-Louis Dumas, who would lead Hermès from 1978 to 2006, began his relationship with the company at age five, when his grandfather Émile-Maurice brought him to the workshop before regular hours and placed him on a high stool in the leather cutting room.

This early immersion wasn't childcare but deliberate education, training his eye to recognize excellence before he could articulate it, embedding the rhythms and values of craftsmanship into his consciousness from the earliest age. According to family archives, nearly every Hermès family member who would eventually lead the company completed at least three years working directly in production roles before assuming any management position.

The bonds between houses and their craftspeople often transcended normal employment relationships, reflecting the family-centered model. When master trunk-maker Antoine Gervais celebrated fifty years with Louis Vuitton in 1925, Gaston-Louis Vuitton didn't present the traditional gold watch. He unveiled a custom-designed residence near the workshop in Asnières, built to house the artisan and his family rent-free for life. "Your hands have created trunks that circle the globe," Vuitton announced at the ceremony. "They have shaped not just leather and wood but our reputation itself."

This wasn't simple sentimentality; it reflected the strategic recognition that the company's most valuable assets weren't its materials or even its designs, but the accumulated mastery embodied in its craftsmen. Company records show that multi-generational employment was common in luxury workshops; by the 1950s, approximately 40% of Hermès craftspeople were related to current or former employees, creating an extended family structure that reinforced cultural continuity across generations.

While family ownership provided stability and value continuity, it also created potential vulnerabilities. Succession represented both the greatest strength and challenge of the family model. Well-managed transitions, where the next generation had been properly prepared and gradually integrated into leadership, allowed for remarkable continuity. However, family dynamics, conflicts between siblings or cousins, or a lack of interested or capable heirs could create periods of instability or strategic drift.

The strength of the family model became particularly evident when contrasted with early examples of publicly owned luxury businesses. Houses that maintained family control or tight private ownership typically preserved their distinctive character and quality standards more successfully than those forced to answer to outside shareholders with shorter time horizons. Family-controlled houses like Hermès largely resisted the dilution through excessive licensing, maintaining direct control over all products bearing their name.

Chapter Three

Watching,
Wanting, Wearing

T he early morning light cast a golden hue across Fifth Avenue as she stood there, coffee and croissant in hand, gazing longingly through the window. The world was still waking up, but Audrey Hepburn, or rather, Holly Golightly, had already found her sanctuary. Not in a church or a loved one's embrace, but outside Tiffany & Co., adorned in her little black dress, oversized sunglasses, and multiple strands of pearls. "Nothing very bad could happen to you there," she mused about the jewelry store, taking a delicate bite of her croissant while admiring the sparkling diamonds beyond the glass.

This single scene from 1961's *Breakfast at Tiffany's* cemented in our collective consciousness a profound truth about luxury: what mattered most was how these objects made us *feel*. Safe. Special. Transformed. A single elegant woman, a Manhattan sidewalk, and a jewelry store window created a moment so powerful that the image still evokes wistful longing decades later in those who've never set foot in New York, much less inside Tiffany's hallowed walls.

We were window shoppers all, pressing our noses against the glass, admiring what we couldn't, yet, possess. In that delicious space between desire and fulfillment, luxury brands found their most potent magic. Like Holly, we didn't need to own the diamonds to feel their transformative power. Simply being near them, understanding their codes and significance, momentarily transported us to a world of elegance and possibility. We fell in love with something far more intoxicating than the objects themselves; we fell for the dream they embodied.

This was our first introduction to luxury's most beguiling paradox: the simultaneous accessibility and inaccessibility that would define its evolution. Through film, we could see every detail of Holly's outfit, the Givenchy dress with its elegant simplicity, the pearls luminous against black fabric, the perfect updo, close enough to memorize yet distant enough to remain aspirational. The screen was our window, allowing us a voyeuristic glimpse into a realm that existed beyond our immediate reach.

For centuries, luxury had been the exclusive domain of the aristocracy and old money, experienced firsthand by few and glimpsed from afar by many. But through cinema, luxury became more democratic, not in its ownership, but in its visibility and emotional accessibility. We all could participate in the dream, even if the actual products remained beyond our grasp.

Films like *Breakfast at Tiffany's* created a shared language of luxury that transcended class boundaries. We began to understand the codes, recognize the signifiers, and associate specific brands with particular emotional states. Tiffany's wasn't just a jewelry store; it was a feeling of safety and aspiration. Givenchy wasn't just a designer; it was Audrey's elegant confidence wrapped in fabric.

Cinema provided our most vivid portal into luxury's realm, accomplishing what no advertisement could: showing luxury in motion, woven into the lives of characters we admired and stories that moved us. Before we could afford these goods ourselves, we experienced them vicariously through characters who wore them with effortless grace, treating extraordinary possessions as natural extensions of their extraordinary lives.

When Grace Kelly reached for her Hermès bag to shield her pregnancy from paparazzi photographers in 1956, she transformed a handbag into an icon so powerful that the company renamed it the "Kelly bag" in her honor. This wasn't planned product placement; it was an authentic moment of life imitating art imitating life. In that single gesture, she communicated everything luxury aspired to represent: dignity, elegance, and protection from the vulgar gaze of the masses.

The partnership between Audrey Hepburn and designer Hubert de Givenchy created another template for luxury's integration into cultural storytelling. Their collaboration began when Hepburn, cast in *Sabrina* (1954), sought out the young designer for her wardrobe. Far beyond mere product placement, this moment sparked a genuine creative alliance that would span decades and multiple films. The black dress from *Breakfast at Tiffany's*, the wedding gown from *Funny Face*, these creations transcended their status as movie costumes to become cultural touchstones.

These cinematic moments educated us in luxury's language and codes. We learned that certain objects, a Van Cleef necklace, a Louis Vuitton trunk, a Hermès scarf, carried meaning far beyond their price tags. They functioned as tokens of a particular kind of life, tangible symbols of intangible qualities like taste, discernment, and belonging.

What made cinema such a powerful educator was its duality; it made luxury visible while maintaining its distance. We could see Catherine Deneuve's Yves Saint Laurent wardrobe in *Belle de Jour* (1967) in perfect detail, yet the actual possession of such items remained firmly out of reach for most viewers. This tantalizing combination of visibility and inaccessibility created the perfect conditions for desire to flourish.

When Robert Redford's Gatsby tossed his shirts into the air as Daisy Buchanan wept, saying they were "such beautiful shirts," the scene captured exactly what luxury marketing still strives for today: the recognition that our response to beautiful things is often deeply emotional, even irrational. The power wasn't in the shirts themselves but in what they represented, dreams, longing, the past, possibility.

If movies provided the stage, celebrities were the charismatic players who brought luxury to life before our eyes. These stars bridged worlds: close enough to observe in authentic moments, yet elevated enough to represent aspiration. Through them, luxury transformed from abstract concept to embodied reality, worn and used by individuals we could watch, admire, and eventually hope to emulate.

In early Hollywood, these connections were often organic rather than contractual; stars genuinely patronized certain designers or brands, creating authentic associations. When Marilyn Monroe remarked that she wore "just a few drops of Chanel No. 5" to bed, it wasn't a paid endorsement but a spontaneous comment that created priceless association between the sensual star and the fragrance. The power lay in this perceived authenticity, the idea that these weren't commercial arrangements but genuine preferences.

This dynamic gradually shifted as both Hollywood and the luxury industry professionalized. By the 1980s and 1990s, formal arrangements between celebrities and luxury houses became more common. Giorgio Armani's strategic decision to dress Richard Gere in *American Gigolo* (1980) helped catapult the designer to international stardom, creating a blueprint for the designer-celebrity relationship that would become standard practice.

What made celebrities such effective luxury avatars was their unique position in our cultural imagination; they were simultaneous objects of aspiration and identification. We couldn't be them, but perhaps we could be *like* them in some small way. The luxury items associated with these stars became souvenirs from a world we could see but not touch, tangible connections to an intangible dream.

If classic Hollywood presented one vision of luxury, the 1980s offered a dramatically different interpretation. As Ronald Reagan's America embraced the "greed is good" ethos, television shows like *Dynasty* and *Dallas* presented a new luxury aesthetic to millions of viewers every week, one based not on understated elegance but on conspicuous display.

Dynasty revolutionized the visual language of wealth on screen. With its astounding $35,000 per episode wardrobe budget, the show transformed luxury from whispered suggestion to shouted statement. This was luxury as spectacle, as armor, as unabashed declaration of wealth and ambition. Where previous generations might have considered it gauche to be too obvious about one's spending, *Dynasty* proudly displayed consumption as a virtue.

What made shows like *Dynasty* and *Dallas* so influential was their timing. They arrived as cable television was expanding American viewing options and as a new upper-middle class was emerging with disposable income and aspirations. For these viewers, these shows didn't just entertain; they educated, providing a crash course in the material signifiers of success in Reagan's America.

The power-dressing phenomenon epitomized this shift. The structured suits, statement jewelry, and status handbags showcased on prime-time soaps provided a template for professional women to communicate authority through consumption. The shoulder-padded power suit became both practical workwear and symbolic armor.

This was also the era when logomania first emerged as a defining luxury trend. The 1980s ushered in an era where the brand name itself became the primary vehicle of status communication. Louis Vuitton's monogram canvas, Gucci's interlocking Gs, and Chanel's interlinked Cs moved from discreet signature to prominent display.

As the 1990s gave way to the 2000s, a profound shift occurred in how media presented luxury to audiences. If previous decades had positioned us as viewers gazing at luxury through the glass of our television sets, shows like *Sex and the City* (1998-2004) and later *Gossip Girl* (2007-2012) invited us to become active participants in luxury culture, regardless of our actual purchasing power.

Sex and the City revolutionized luxury's portrayal by elevating brands to explicit characters in the narrative. When Carrie Bradshaw gasped, "Manolo Blahnik Mary Janes! I thought these were an urban shoe myth!" or lamented that she would "literally be the old woman who lived in her shoes," her words transcended mere product description. She was inducting millions of viewers into a shared vocabulary of desire.

The show made certain luxury items, Fendi's Baguette bag, Manolo Blahnik's strappy sandals, nameplate necklaces, instantly recognizable to millions of viewers who might never enter a luxury boutique. "It's not a bag, it's a Baguette," corrected Carrie when mugged at gunpoint, a line that did more for Fendi's brand recognition than countless print advertisements could have achieved.

What made this shift particularly powerful was the focus on entry-level luxury, items that were expensive but not entirely out of reach for middle-class consumers willing to save up. A pair of Manolo Blahniks at $500-700 represented a splurge rather than an impossibility for many viewers. This created a psychological pathway from viewer to consumer that was narrower than in previous eras.

Gossip Girl took this pattern further, targeting a younger demographic and explicitly linking luxury consumption to identity formation. The show became a real-time fashion runway, with items worn in episodes often selling out immediately after airing. What shows like *Gossip Girl* did brilliantly was connect luxury not just with wealth but with personality, suggesting that your choice of luxury items expressed something meaningful about who you were, not just what you could afford.

The infamous "cerulean blue" monologue from *The Devil Wears Prada* (2006), where Miranda Priestly explains exactly how high fashion choices trickle down to mass-market consumption, offered viewers a crash course in fashion's influence system. It acknowledged that while not everyone could afford runway pieces, everyone was participating in the luxury ecosystem, whether they recognized it or not.

While television and film were busy making luxury visible, music, particularly hip-hop, was cementing specific brand names into our collective vocabulary through the power of repetition and rhythmic association.

Hip-hop's relationship with luxury brands began as aspirational storytelling. Early references by artists like Slick Rick, who rapped about Gucci and Mercedes-Benz in the 1980s, positioned luxury goods as symbols of success, evidence of transcending systemic barriers through talent and hustle. These mentions weren't paid endorsements but authentic expressions of aspiration.

As hip-hop achieved global commercial success in the 1990s, luxury name-dropping became more prevalent and specific. When Notorious B.I.G. rapped, "Versace shades watching wall, hit the mall," in his 1994 classic "Juicy," he wasn't just listing expensive brands; he was documenting a journey from poverty to prosperity through specific material markers.

By the 2000s, luxury references in music had evolved from aspirational to declarative, reflecting the growing wealth of successful artists. "Hip-hop functioned as luxury's unofficial ambassador to demographics that traditional marketing often overlooked," explains music industry analyst Marcus Thompson. "It translated the appeal of these brands into cultural language that resonated with audiences who might never read Vogue or watch runway shows."

For luxury brands, this unsolicited promotion presented both opportunity and challenge. The infamous case of Cristal champagne's perceived dismissal of hip-hop consumers led to Jay-Z's public boycott and subsequent promotion of competitor Ace of Spades, a cautionary tale about failing to embrace cultural association, even when it comes from unexpected quarters.

As the new millennium dawned, something profound had happened in our collective relationship with luxury. Through decades of cinematic portrayals, celebrity associations, television narratives, and musical references, luxury had completed a remarkable journey, from distant, rarefied world glimpsed only by the elite to a shared cultural vocabulary accessible to virtually everyone.

We had been educated, whether we realized it or not, in luxury's visual language and emotional promise. We knew that a Birkin bag represented not just exceptional craftsmanship but a certain kind of womanhood. We understood that a Patek Philippe watch communicated not just precise timekeeping but a specific vision of masculine success and inheritance.

"What we witnessed over these decades was nothing less than the democratization of luxury aspiration," explains consumer psychologist Dr. Victoria Chang. "While actual ownership remained restricted by price, the *desire* for luxury, understanding it, coveting it, dreaming of it, became universal. This created consumers who were emotionally primed for luxury long before they could afford it."

This priming had tangible market effects. When these media-educated consumers did achieve sufficient disposable income, they were ready to participate in luxury consumption, armed with brand knowledge and emotional connections built over years of cultural exposure.

Yet, for all this widespread desire, an essential tension remained at luxury's core, the paradox of needing to be visible enough to be desired but exclusive enough to remain special. The media's ability to make luxury visible to millions had intensified rather than resolved this challenge.

As we stood at the dawn of the social media era, this tension was about to be tested like never before. The traditional media gatekeepers, magazine editors, film directors, television producers, had at least provided some control over luxury's representation. But as platforms like Instagram and TikTok emerged, offering direct, unmediated visibility and the potential for truly viral exposure, luxury brands would face unprecedented challenges in balancing accessibility and exclusivity.

Chapter Four

The Dior Warning

T he gray morning light filtering through discount store windows cast a sickly pallor on merchandise that had fallen from grace. Here, in a nondescript retail outlet far from the elegant boulevards of central Paris, a scene of quiet sacrilege unfolded in the winter of 1984. Cotton bathrobes bearing the Christian Dior label drooped limply from plastic hangers, their once-pristine white now dulled to institutional cream. Nearby, a bin overflowed with Dior-branded hand towels marked down to clearance prices, threads visibly pulling loose at the edges.

A customer idly fingered the fabric of a Dior bathrobe, the material thin and scratchy against her skin. For the price of a modest dinner, she could own something bearing one of fashion's most revered signatures. Yet there was nothing reverent about this transaction, nothing that connected this ordinary object to the heritage of the house that had, just a few decades earlier, restored Paris as the unquestioned capital of global fashion.

The scene would have horrified Christian Dior himself, the meticulous couturier whose revolutionary "New Look" had captured the world's imagination in 1947. This was the man who had insisted that "luxury must be comfortable, otherwise it is not luxury," yet the bathrobes bearing his name now embodied neither luxury nor comfort, just mass-produced items stamped with a once-magical name that had been licensed to the point of exhaustion.

Just thirty-seven years earlier, a different scene had unfolded at 30 Avenue Montaigne. There, in an elegant salon decorated in Dior's signature palette of white and gray, fashion editors and society clients had gasped as models glided through the room in cinch-waisted jackets and voluminous skirts that required yards of sumptuous fabric. "It's quite a revolution, dear Christian," Carmel Snow of Harper's Bazaar had declared. "Your dresses have such a new look!" The phrase stuck, becoming shorthand for a post-war renaissance in French couture.

Now, nearly four decades later, those same syllables, D-I-O-R, appeared on products that could be tossed into a shopping cart alongside laundry detergent and breakfast cereal. The name that had once been synonymous with Parisian haute couture now stretched across mass-produced bedspreads and shower curtains, its heritage diluted through hundreds of licensing agreements that spanned continents and categories.

Among those who observed this stark disconnect was Bernard Arnault, a then-obscure 35-year-old real estate developer with an engineer's analytical mind. Where others saw merely a fashion brand in decline, Arnault recognized both a cautionary tale and an opportunity. In the gulf between Dior's illustrious heritage and its diminished present state, he identified the fundamental tension that would come to define luxury's evolution: how the pursuit of broader accessibility can ultimately destroy the very exclusivity that makes a luxury brand desirable in the first place.

When Christian Dior inaugurated his couture house on February 12, 1946, he arrived with a crystalline vision of luxury's post-war incarnation. Backed financially by textile magnate Marcel Boussac, the 41-year-old designer established not merely another fashion label but a sanctuary dedicated to a particular expression of French elegance, one destined to reclaim Paris's supremacy as the global epicenter of style after the bleak occupation years.

The very architecture of 30 Avenue Montaigne embodied this philosophy before a single word was uttered. Transformed into a haven of refinement, its pristine gray and white interiors rejected ostentatious display in favor of whispering sophistication. Each sensory element, from the gentle curve of Louis XVI chairs where clients perched during presentations to the disciplined silence maintained by staff who moved with balletic precision, contributed to an atmosphere of ceremonial significance.

When Dior unveiled his inaugural collection on February 12, 1947, the impact reverberated like a seismic event. His "New Look," distinguished by rounded shoulders, dramatically cinched waists, and voluminous skirts requiring lavish quantities of fabric, represented a radical departure from the austere, utilitarian silhouettes necessitated by wartime rationing. Women accustomed to boxy silhouettes and severe lines suddenly encountered a vision of ultra-feminine luxury that celebrated curves and indulgence.

The craftsmanship underpinning these garments defied ordinary standards. Each dress concealed intricate interior architectures, petticoats, padding, corsetry, creating the structural precision for which Dior became renowned. A single evening creation might demand hundreds of hours from skilled artisans, every stitch, pleat, and embellishment executed with uncompromising precision.

The experience of acquiring a Dior creation constituted a ritual unto itself. Clients, predominantly aristocrats, industrialists' wives, and Hollywood luminaries, were received in the hushed salon and settled onto those elegant chairs. Models presented the collection, each ensemble bearing a unique name and number. Following selection came multiple fittings where the garment was meticulously adjusted to the client's exact measurements. This process might extend over weeks or months, culminating in a perfectly customized creation that embraced its owner like a second skin.

This business approach reflected a philosophy that elevated craftsmanship above commercial conquest. "My dream is to save women
from nature," Dior once declared, articulating his belief in fashion as
a transformative force. His mission transcended mere adornment; he
sought to enhance femininity, to elevate daily existence through exquisite design and meticulous workmanship. In Dior's universe, exclusivity emerged not as a calculated marketing strategy but as the natural
consequence of uncompromising standards.

Yet from inception, Christian Dior operated with a dual vision,
balancing artistic exclusivity with shrewd commercial instinct. This
strategic dimension was largely orchestrated by Jacques Rouët, the
house's General Manager, who recognized early that the Dior name
possessed potential far beyond haute couture's limited sphere. Under
his stewardship, the house established international branches with
remarkable swiftness, launching Christian Dior-New York in 1948 and
Christian Dior London in 1952.

Rouët similarly identified opportunities beyond clothing. In 1948,
the creation of Christian Dior Parfums Ltd. extended the brand into
the lucrative fragrance domain. The introduction of Miss Dior, housed
in its now-iconic bottle with its distinctive houndstooth pattern, allowed women who could never contemplate a Dior gown to possess a
fragment of the dream. This strategy proved commercially brilliant yet
simultaneously planted the seeds that would eventually lead to those
discount store bins of 1984.

When Christian Dior succumbed to a sudden heart attack on October 24, 1957, at just 52 years of age, he left behind not merely a fashion
house but an international institution, one that had redefined luxury
for the modern era. What remained unforeseeable was how the very
mechanisms established to expand his vision globally would eventually threaten to dismantle it entirely.

Christian Dior's untimely departure plunged his maison into existential uncertainty. Jacques Rouët, continuing to guide operations,
initially contemplated closing the house altogether. However, Dior's

substantial economic footprint, then representing a significant portion of French fashion exports, made such closure virtually inconceivable.

The resolution manifested in dual forms: new creative leadership paired with expanded commercial strategy. For the former, the house initially entrusted the 21-year-old Yves Saint Laurent, Dior's assistant, who guided the brand from 1957 to 1960 before departing for military service. His successor, Marc Bohan, would steer Dior's creative direction for an extraordinary 29 years, from 1960 to 1989, providing stability and continuity through an era of dramatic commercial transformation.

This expansion was propelled largely by the licensing strategy pioneered by Rouët, an approach destined to transform not merely Dior but eventually the entire luxury landscape. The rationale appeared sound: licensing the Dior name to third-party manufacturers would generate substantial royalty income with minimal capital investment, effectively underwriting the costly haute couture operation while simultaneously extending the brand's reach to consumers who could never access its highest-tier offerings.

The first licensed Dior creation was neckties, followed rapidly by hosiery, furs, hats, gloves, handbags, jewelry, lingerie, and scarves. These initial categories maintained logical coherence; they complemented fashion, allowing consumers to enhance existing wardrobes with Dior-branded accessories. A middle-income consumer who could never contemplate a Dior couture dress might still acquire a $35 pair of licensed shoes or a $2 box of Dior-branded nylon stockings, gaining entrance to the brand's magical orbit.

This democratization aligned with broader social currents toward less rigid class structures and rising middle-class purchasing power, particularly in America. For countless working women, a Dior scarf or pair of gloves represented an attainable luxury, a personal indulgence connecting them to the glamorous world glimpsed in magazines and films.

Licensing simultaneously addressed a fundamental luxury challenge: achieving scale without sacrificing exclusivity. By stratifying product categories, preserving haute couture's exclusivity while ex-

tending into adjacent categories through licensing, Dior could theo-
retically maintain prestige at the apex while broadening its base. The
high-margin couture operation would continue generating the brand's
mystique and prestige, while licensed products delivered volume sales
and global visibility.

Beginning with high-quality, strategic licensing categories like perfume appeared to validate this approach. Christian Dior Parfums, established in 1948, maintained quality standards that reflected favor-
ably on the parent brand. Miss Dior, Diorissimo, and Eau Sauvage became classics in their own right, respected not merely for the brand they
carried but for their inherent quality and distinctive character.

Under Bohan's nearly three-decade artistic direction, the licensing
strategy not merely continued but accelerated dramatically. What began with accessories gradually expanded into a sprawling empire encompassing hundreds of products manufactured by licensees across
the globe. Ready-to-wear lines emerged with Miss Dior in 1967, followed by Baby Dior children's wear that same year. In 1970, Christian
Dior Monsieur formally entered the menswear arena with offerings
spanning tailored suits to casual attire.

The financial logic proved irresistible. Each licensing agreement
generated royalty income without requiring significant operational investment from Dior itself. This revenue subsidized the increasingly
anachronistic haute couture operation, which maintained prestige but
served an ever-diminishing clientele. Moreover, the global visibility
achieved through licensed products built brand awareness in markets
where Dior maintained no direct presence.

What began as a carefully calibrated strategy, however, gradually
metamorphosed into something far more problematic. As licensing expanded from accessories complementing the New Look silhouette to
diverse products with increasingly tenuous fashion connections, the
delicate balance tipped perilously toward ubiquity.

By the mid-1970s, the Dior signature adorned products its founder
could never have envisioned. A "Christian Dior Home Collection" encompassed ceramic bowls, lucite serving trays, and metal trinket box-

es. The Christian Dior signature graced numerous fine china patterns spanning complete dining services from dinner plates to serving platters.

As licensing proliferated, quality control became increasingly elusive. With hundreds of licensees operating across multiple continents, maintaining consistent brand standards proved virtually impossible. The varying quality of licensed products, from relatively well-executed sunglasses to questionable homewares, eroded the brand's reputation for excellence.

Distribution channels presented equally troubling challenges. As licensed products multiplied, they appeared in retail environments directly contradicting luxury positioning. Dior-branded items emerging in discount outlets, department store clearance sections, and even supermarkets created jarring disconnects between aspirational brand image and everyday shopping experiences.

The French Chamber of Couture's early criticism of Dior's licensing as potentially "degrading" and "cheapening" haute couture's image proved prophetic. What began as an innovative business solution had evolved into an existential threat to the brand's positioning and credibility. The company that once represented Parisian elegance's pinnacle now stood as a cautionary tale about the perils of sacrificing exclusivity for accessibility.

Hermès emerged perhaps as the primary beneficiary of Dior's decline. From its modest origins in 1837 as a harness workshop, the house had maintained unwavering focus on materials and craftsmanship. While Dior licensed its name across hundreds of product categories, Hermès preserved manufacturing in-house, with artisans trained through rigorous apprenticeships. Their iconic bags, the Kelly and Birkin, maintained both quality standards and controlled scarcity.

Chanel, too, benefited from Dior's dilution. Following Coco Chanel's death in 1971, the brand experienced its own period of uncertainty. However, Karl Lagerfeld's 1983 appointment as creative director marked a renaissance beginning. Lagerfeld brilliantly balanced respect for Chanel's heritage codes with contemporary relevance. Crucially, while introducing ready-to-wear that increased Chanel's accessibility, the house maintained strict control over brand image, distribution, and licensing.

By the late 1970s, uncontrolled licensing's consequences had become dire. The company faced significant financial crisis explicitly linked to the "countless licensing agreements" and concurrent counterfeiting problems. This turbulence culminated in the Boussac group filing for bankruptcy, with the Willot Group assuming control, only to face its own bankruptcy shortly thereafter.

The financial contradiction had finally become impossible to ignore. While licensing generated substantial short-term royalty income, the long-term damage to brand equity ultimately undermined the entire business model. Despite ranking among the world's most famous fashion brands, Christian Dior had deteriorated into a distressed asset.

This financial deterioration accelerated alongside a troubling customer exodus. As Dior products infiltrated discount chains and department store clearance racks, the brand's most valuable patrons, those who had historically paid extraordinary premiums for genuine exclusivity and craftsmanship, quietly disappeared. They announced no dramatic farewells; they simply redirected their attention and resources elsewhere, seeking houses still honoring true craftsmanship and exclusivity covenants.

By 1984, the French government sought a buyer for the troubled Boussac Saint-Frères conglomerate that owned Christian Dior. The situation had deteriorated so severely that the government would sell the entire group for the symbolic price of one franc to any investor willing to confront its challenges.

In this context of crisis and devaluation, an unlikely figure emerged with the vision to recognize opportunity where others saw only disaster. Bernard Arnault, a 35-year-old real estate developer who had been successfully operating in the United States, identified untapped potential in the struggling Boussac Saint-Frères group, particularly in its ownership of Christian Dior.

Upon gaining control of Boussac, Arnault moved with characteristic decisiveness. He sold off most of Boussac's industrial assets, retaining only two strategic assets: Christian Dior and the Le Bon Marché department store. This selective approach focused resources exclusively on businesses with luxury potential rather than attempting to save the entire conglomerate.

For Dior specifically, Arnault implemented a comprehensive revitalization strategy centered on regaining control of the brand's image and positioning. This involved the painful but essential process of canceling or not renewing numerous licensing agreements that had diluted the brand. While this initially reduced revenue, it was a necessary sacrifice to rebuild Dior's luxury credentials.

By 1987, just three years after acquisition, the restructured operation generated $112 million in earnings on $1.9 billion in revenue, a remarkable turnaround that validated Arnault's strategic vision. More importantly, it established him as a capable operator in the luxury sector and positioned Christian Dior as the foundation for what would become the world's largest luxury empire.

The Dior acquisition became the template for Arnault's future approach: identifying heritage brands with strong brand equity but operational challenges, implementing swift leadership changes, maintaining brand distinctiveness while integrating into his growing group structure, and exercising remarkable patience in developing these businesses over decades rather than quarters.

The Dior story, from Christian's revolutionary debut to the licensing-driven decline to Arnault's opportunistic rescue, represents luxury's first complete cycle of rise, expansion, dilution, crisis, and revival. This pattern would repeat itself across decades and brands, establishing a template that continues to shape the industry today.

The fundamental tension driving this pattern is luxury's eternal paradox: exclusivity requires not being inclusive, but financial growth demands broader accessibility. This irreconcilable contradiction creates an inevitable progression as luxury brands expand beyond their exclusive foundations, dilute their positioning through increased accessibility, experience crisis when the contradiction becomes unsustainable, and eventually create space for either revival or replacement by newer, more exclusive alternatives.

In the decades following Dior's crisis, this pattern would play out repeatedly across the luxury landscape. Gucci, founded in Florence in 1921 as a leather goods house, would experience its own licensing-driven decline in the 1970s and 1980s, with the brand name appearing on everything from toilet paper to plastic watches. By the early 1990s, family conflicts and excessive democratization had left the brand in crisis. Its subsequent revival under Domenico De Sole and Tom Ford would mirror the Dior recovery.

Burberry would follow a similar trajectory, with its distinctive check pattern becoming ubiquitous through extensive licensing in the 1980s and 1990s. The pattern became so overexposed that it was adopted by "chav" culture in the UK, associating the brand with a demographic far from its traditional positioning. Just as with Dior and Gucci, Burberry's revival would come through new leadership, controlled distribution, creative renewal, and a strategic reduction in pattern visibility.

Throughout luxury's history, certain houses have stood as silent sentinels guarding ancient traditions, like monasteries preserving knowledge through dark ages. While Dior surrendered to licensing's temptations, Hermès artisans continued their patient work, spending 20 hours hand-stitching a single Kelly bag with techniques unchanged for generations. When other brands raced to open hundreds of global outposts in the 1990s, Loro Piana maintained its deliberately small network of boutiques. As familiar names appeared on products of increasingly questionable quality, Brunello Cucinelli quietly constructed a medieval Italian village dedicated to preserving disappearing handwork traditions.

The most profound irony lies in Bernard Arnault's dual role. Having rescued Dior from the consequences of excessive licensing, he would go on to pioneer a more sophisticated form of luxury democratization through LVMH. Rather than uncontrolled licensing, his model relied on directly operated stores, carefully stratified product lines, and strictly controlled brand image. The growing sophistication of luxury man-agement would not eliminate the cycle but merely make its navigation more deliberate.

The Dior story emerges as luxury's foundational parable, a narrative that continues to haunt industry corridors like a ghost that cannot be exorcised. It stands as the first fully documented case study in luxury's medical literature, a patient history detailing the initial symptoms of brand overextension, the progressive deterioration as licensing fever spread unchecked through the corporate body, the crisis when systems began to fail, and finally, the remarkable resurrection under new care.

Chapter Five

The Cult of the "It"

T he first time I walked into a lecture hall at Stanford, I felt the weight of the Céline belt bag against my hip like armor. Beyond a mere handbag, it was a shield crafted of smooth leather and distinctive hardware, carefully selected to protect me as I navigated a world where I felt out of place. At 28, returning to school among teenagers and twenty-somethings from privileged backgrounds, my difference felt palpable. The Céline belt bag, with its architectural silhouette and minimalist hardware, whispered contemporary sophistication without shouting for attention.

The moment I placed it on the lecture hall desk, something shifted in my confidence. The bag, recognizable to those in the know but not flamboyant, signaled that I belonged, that I understood the unwritten codes of this elite environment. My classmates didn't consciously judge me for owning a luxury item; rather, the bag functioned as visual shorthand, a silent ambassador communicating on my behalf.

The extraordinary power of iconic luxury items lies in this protective function, transcending their beauty or craftsmanship. For those of us who have felt like outsiders, whether due to class, culture, or circumstance, these objects serve as bridges between worlds, validating our right to occupy spaces that might otherwise feel unwelcoming.

What I couldn't articulate then, but understand clearly now, is that I was participating in a profound psychological exchange. I was investing in a symbolic shield against the vulnerability of being an outsider, not acquiring a mere consumer good. The iconic items we covet function not as status signals but as psychological armor protecting us in environments where we feel uncertain or exposed.

This function of luxury rarely appears in marketing campaigns or fashion magazines, yet it operates powerfully beneath the surface of consumption. For first-generation wealth, immigrants, and others navigating unfamiliar social terrain, the right luxury item serves as both sword and shield, cutting through potential prejudice while deflecting unwanted scrutiny.

What makes certain luxury items function effectively as social armor while others fail? The answer lies in a delicate balance of recognizability, craftsmanship, heritage, and symbolic resonance.

Effective protective items balance visibility with restraint. Consider the Hermès Birkin, instantly recognizable to the initiated through its distinctive silhouette, hardware, and proportions, yet lacking obvious logos or branding that might appear desperate for validation. This subtle coding allows for what sociologists call "inconspicuous consumption," where status markers remain visible primarily to those who matter while avoiding the appearance of trying too hard.

Exceptional materials and expert craftsmanship form the tangible foundation of the armor's effectiveness. The weight of a Patek Philippe against the wrist, the butter-soft texture of Hermès leather, the precise click of a Chanel turnlock closure, these sensory experiences ground the symbolic in the physical, creating a constant tactile reminder of quality and care.

Successful armor pieces also possess "social liquidity," the ability to function across diverse contexts without requiring reinterpretation. A classic Burberry trench works equally well in Tokyo, New York, or Paris; a Rolex Datejust is recognized as a mark of achievement whether in a boardroom or a creative studio.

Above all, effective armor demands authenticity, both of the object itself and in its relationship to the wearer. Counterfeits fail as protection not because they may be detected as fake, but because the wearer knows they are inauthentic, undermining the psychological confidence the item should provide.

This anatomy of effective armor explains why certain iconic pieces maintain their protective power across decades while others flare briefly before fading. The Hermès Kelly bag, the Cartier Tank watch, the Burberry trench, these items have transcended fashion to become psychological tools, helping generation after generation navigate uncertain social terrain with confidence.

For those who have created their own wealth rather than inheriting it, these luxury goods perform a unique psychological function. They serve as tangible evidence of having crossed an invisible threshold into a world previously beyond reach, beyond mere rewards for success. First-generation wealth carries its own particular anxieties: the fear of being discovered as an impostor, the concern about making social missteps, the worry that despite financial achievement, one might still not truly "belong" among those born into privilege.

The newly wealthy approach luxury differently depending on their path to success. Silicon Valley tech entrepreneurs might lean toward understated luxury that signals intellectual rather than financial capital, the subtle quality of an Hermès Apple Watch band or a perfectly tailored but logo-free Loro Piana sweater. In contrast, entertainment industry successes might embrace more visible luxury as part of their personal brand.

First-generation wealth typically deploys luxury strategically, as a sophisticated tool for managing others' perceptions. A former colleague who rose from a working-class background to become a venture capitalist described his collection of high-end watches as "credibility shortcuts" in business meetings. "When someone notices my Patek, it creates a silent acknowledgment that I belong at the table," he explained.

The psychological comfort these items provide can be profound. Many first-generation wealthy individuals describe moments of insecurity, entering a prestigious restaurant, sitting in a business class lounge, attending an elite school function, where luxury items serve as emotional security blankets.

First-generation wealth also tends to form deeper emotional attachments to luxury goods, viewing them as milestone markers or hard-won trophies rather than ordinary possessions. A self-made finance executive described purchasing her first Cartier watch after closing a major deal: "I look at it every day, and it reminds me how far I've come. It's not about showing off to others; it's a private reminder to myself."

The relationship between first-generation wealth and luxury evolves over time. Initially, many gravitate toward well-known status markers with clear signaling value. As confidence grows and social integration deepens, preferences often shift toward more subtle expressions of luxury, bespoke items, limited editions, or heritage brands known primarily to insiders.

Yet for many who have created their own wealth, luxury items never entirely lose their emotional resonance as markers of transcendence. Even after decades of financial success, these objects continue to serve as bridges between past and present, tangible reminders of journeys that often feel somewhat miraculous even to those who lived them.

This function becomes even more pronounced for immigrants, minorities, and cultural outsiders, for whom luxury serves as a universal passport, a set of symbols recognized across borders that facilitate entry into unfamiliar social contexts. The strategic deployment of luxury as protective equipment becomes particularly apparent when navigating environments where one's accent, appearance, or background might otherwise create barriers.

For immigrants in particular, luxury items often serve as cultural translation tools. When traditional symbols of status from one's homeland, whether educational credentials, family connections, or cultural knowledge, lose currency in a new environment, globally recognized luxury brands provide immediate legibility.

Language barriers intensify luxury's passport function. When verbal communication proves challenging, visual cues take on heightened importance. Unlike regional status markers that require cultural insider knowledge to interpret, global luxury brands function across contexts, providing semantic consistency in environments where other social signals might be misread or overlooked.

Women and minorities in predominantly white or male professional spaces often use luxury strategically to counteract potential marginalization. Female executives in male-dominated industries often describe using high-end professional accessories, from briefcases to watches traditionally marketed to men, to establish authority in contexts where their competence might otherwise be questioned.

Beyond their immediate protective function, these coveted objects often require extraordinary patience to acquire, adding another dimension to their psychological power. "Twenty-two months," the woman next to me whispered at a charity auction in Singapore, her voice a mixture of pride and conspiratorial glee. She was referring to the length of time she had waited for the Hermès Birkin now resting in her lap, the iconic handbag that had transformed from mere accessory into mythological object through the alchemy of controlled scarcity.

This luxury waiting game functions as a modern initiation ritual, a structured trial transforming both the coveted object and its eventual owner. Unlike ordinary consumption, where desire is immediately satisfied through purchase, iconic luxury items often require extended courtship: building relationships with sales associates, demonstrating brand loyalty through other purchases, and simply waiting, sometimes for years, before being granted the opportunity to buy the coveted piece.

The psychological mechanisms at work are profound. Research confirms that effort and delayed gratification significantly enhance per-

ceived value and subsequent satisfaction. The Hermès Kelly bag that
required six appointments and a twenty-month wait becomes more
psychologically valuable than an equally beautiful handbag available
for immediate purchase.

This waiting period serves multiple functions beyond simple supply
management. First, it creates artificial scarcity in a market where true
material scarcity rarely exists. Second, the waiting period serves as a
sorting mechanism, separating the casually interested from the genuinely committed, ensuring coveted items reach those who will value
them most completely.

The language surrounding these waiting periods reveals their rit-
ualistic nature. Luxury customers don't simply buy a Rolex Daytona
or Hermès Birkin; they are "offered the opportunity" to purchase one,
as though receiving special dispensation. Sales associates function as
gatekeepers, evaluating worthiness and determining who moves from
waiting to chosen.

When the coveted item is finally acquired, it carries accumulated
meaning from this extended pursuit. It becomes proof of patience,
evidence of insider status, and validation of worthiness. The object
functions not just as a luxury good but as a trophy commemorating a
successful campaign.

Yet for all their protective power, these coveted symbols can fail
catastrophically when deployed incorrectly, marking one as an outsider
rather than facilitating belonging. Like armor chosen for the wrong
battle or worn improperly, misused luxury items can draw negative
attention, undermining the very social integration they're intended to
facilitate.

The most common form of mis-signaling involves overempha-
sis on obvious status markers, what luxury insiders dismissively call
"logo-mania." When first-generation wealth or cultural outsiders embrace heavily branded items, established elites often interpret this as
evidence of insecurity rather than belonging.

Context-inappropriate luxury creates equally problematic mis-sig-
nals. The Rolex that projects success in a corporate boardroom might

raise eyebrows in a non-profit organization; the Hermès tie that facilitates belonging at a private club might appear ostentatious in a creative startup.

The "old money versus new money" tension creates particularly treacherous signaling territory. Established wealth frequently uses subtle status markers specifically designed to differentiate from nouveau riche display, preferring patina to newness, heritage to fashion, and discretion to visibility.

Cultural variations further complicate appropriate luxury signaling. What registers as tasteful restraint in Western Europe might appear insufficiently respective of status hierarchies in East Asia; conversely, the visible luxury display expected in certain Middle Eastern contexts might appear gauche in Scandinavian environments.

The rise of "stealth wealth" and value-based luxury has created new mis-signaling pitfalls. As sustainability, ethics, and social responsibility gain importance, displaying the wrong kind of luxury, items associated with environmental harm, labor exploitation, or conspicuous waste, can backfire among progressive elites.

The power of iconic luxury items to function as psychological armor reveals truths far deeper than mere materialism or status-seeking. These objects' ability to provide confidence, validation, and protection speaks to fundamentally human needs for belonging, recognition, and security.

The most profound aspect of luxury's protective function lies in its transformative capacity, altering both external perceptions and internal self-concept. The young professional who feels more capable when wearing her grandfather's Patek Philippe, the first-generation college student who stands straighter carrying a subtle luxury briefcase, these individuals aren't merely performing status for others but experiencing genuine psychological transformation.

This transformation borders on the magical, invoking mechanisms reminiscent of traditional talismans or protective amulets. When we attribute protective powers to luxury items, we participate in a form of modern sympathetic magic where objects absorb and project qualities we aspire to embody.

The most poignant aspect of luxury's protective function lies in its limitations. While the right status markers can facilitate acceptance and create favorable first impressions, they cannot substitute for deeper forms of belonging based on shared values, authentic connection, and mutual understanding. The luxury shield may open doors, but passing through them successfully requires more substantial qualities.

Yet this evolution doesn't diminish luxury's emotional significance. For many who have used these objects as tools of transformation, the attachment remains even as its nature changes. The Burberry scarf purchased with months of teenage savings, the first Rolex acquired after a career milestone, these items often transform from active armor into cherished mementos, physical reminders of personal journeys and victories.

What endures across these changes is the profound emotional resonance of objects that bridge the gap between who we are and who we aspire to be, offering tangible evidence of our capacity for transformation. The magic of luxury lies not in the objects themselves but in their ability to connect us to possibilities, to futures we can imagine and eventually inhabit.

Chapter Six

Enter the Wolf of Cashmere

T he Avenue Montaigne atelier of Christian Dior stood uncharac-
teristically quiet on that gray Parisian morning in early 1985. The
grand staircase, once graced by models displaying Dior's revolutionary
"New Look," now echoed with a different kind of footfall, the deliberate, calculated steps of a man more accustomed to construction sites
than couture houses. Bernard Arnault, thirty-six years old and virtually
unknown in fashion circles, moved through the space with precision,
his engineer's eyes absorbing every detail of the legendary maison that
had fallen into disrepair.

Where others saw only decline, Arnault's analytical mind detected
untapped potential. His fingers traced the edge of a worktable where
seamstresses still labored over made-to-order pieces for the house's
dwindling haute couture clientele. The precision of their hand-stitching stood in stark contrast to the cheap, mass-produced items now
bearing the Dior name in department stores worldwide, bathrobes

with already-fraying edges, perfunctory china patterns, and uninspired housewares.

"Show me the licensing agreements," Arnault had requested earlier, his tone matter-of-fact rather than accusatory. Now, seated in what had once been Christian Dior's own office, he methodically worked through a thick stack of contracts. The sheer volume was staggering, hundreds of separate agreements spanning continents and product categories, from the logical extensions like fragrances to the incongruous kitchen linens and quotidian home goods.

What made Arnault's presence here so incongruous was his fundamental difference in approaching the world. Where fashion was emotional, instinctive, and often chaotic, Arnault's engineering mind sought order, efficiency, and measurable outcomes. While the creative spirits of fashion houses typically operated on inspiration and artistic instinct, Arnault brought the cold precision of mathematical certainty.

Yet despite this contrast, or perhaps because of it, Arnault recognized something in Dior that others had overlooked. Beyond the licensing chaos and management troubles, beyond even the beautiful clothes still being produced in small numbers, he perceived the immense latent value in the Dior name itself. He understood that beneath the temporary dilution lay a heritage of tremendous worth, a sleeping beauty of luxury waiting to be awakened by the right strategic approach.

What no one could have anticipated in that moment was that this methodical engineer would not only rescue Dior from its trajectory of decline but would go on to build the world's most powerful luxury empire. The seeds of a vision were germinating, a vision that would simultaneously preserve luxury's heritage while completely transforming its business model.

The journey that brought Bernard Arnault to the corridors of Christian Dior appeared, on its surface, an unlikely one. The son of an industrial family from Roubaix, a city in northern France known more for its factories than its fashion, Arnault had followed a path of cool rationality rather than creative passion. He excelled at mathematics and science, earning admission to the ultra-selective École Polytechnique, France's premier engineering school.

After graduating in 1971, Arnault joined his father's construction company, Ferret-Savinel, where he applied his analytical mind to the concrete realities of building and development. The company specialized in civil and residential construction, about as far from the refined salons of Avenue Montaigne as one could imagine.

It was a fortuitous decision to expand into the United States that would plant the seed of Arnault's future empire. In the late 1970s, he refocused the family business toward real estate development and began investing in Florida, where he achieved considerable success building condominiums. The American business environment, more aggressive, direct, and results-oriented than what prevailed in France, left a profound impression on the young executive.

A pivotal moment in Arnault's evolution came during a taxi ride in New York City. When he mentioned the Rockefeller name to his driver, he was met with blank incomprehension. But when he mentioned Christian Dior, the driver's face immediately lit with recognition. This simple interaction crystallized for Arnault the extraordinary power and global reach of luxury brands, their ability to transcend borders, cultures, and even economic status to create universal recognition and desire.

By 1984, Arnault had achieved considerable success in real estate but remained unknown in luxury circles. When news broke that the French government was seeking a buyer for the bankrupt Boussac Saint-Frères textile conglomerate, most observers focused on its failing industrial operations and substantial debt, reportedly exceeding $100 million. The government's primary concern was preserving jobs, particularly in the textile sector. While others saw a burdensome industrial group in terminal decline, Arnault spotted an extraordinary opportunity hidden within: Christian Dior, the crown jewel among Boussac's holdings.

Together, Arnault and investment banker Antoine Bernheim assembled approximately $80 million, $15 million from Arnault's family resources and the remainder through various investors. This capital enabled him to first acquire control of Financière Agache, which then became the vehicle for acquiring the Boussac group. The strategy was complex but precise, like a mathematical equation designed to isolate the valuable variable, Dior, from a problem cluttered with failing industrial operations.

As he prepared his bid for Boussac, Arnault's mental calculations were precise. The tangible assets, factories, real estate, inventory, were merely components in a larger equation. The true prize was intangible: the Dior name, its heritage, and its latent potential. With the analytical clarity that defined his approach, Arnault recognized that luxury's value resided primarily in perception rather than physical assets.

In the winter of 1984, a brief but momentous exchange unfolded in a government office in Paris. Bernard Arnault, the little-known real estate developer, handed over a symbolic single franc to complete his acquisition of the sprawling, troubled Boussac Saint-Frères conglomerate. The ceremonial coin, worth less than twenty American cents, belied the audacity of the moment. For this token amount, Arnault had secured control of a corporate empire including textile factories, the department store Le Bon Marché, and most significantly, the house of Christian Dior.

The moment carried the quiet drama of a chess master making a decisive move while observers failed to grasp its full implications. Government officials, primarily concerned with preserving French jobs, saw a young businessman willing to take on a failing industrial group. Few recognized that they were witnessing the opening gambit in a strategy that would transform the global luxury landscape.

"I'm focused on the future, not the past," Arnault told anxious employees in his first address. His voice was soft but authoritative, lacking the flamboyance typical of the fashion world but conveying absolute certainty. Those who expected reassuring platitudes were disappointed. Arnault made no promises about maintaining the status quo. Instead, he spoke of transformation, competitiveness, and the difficult path forward.

The transformation that followed was swift and ruthless, earning Arnault nicknames like "The Terminator" and "The Wolf in Cashmere" in French business circles. Within two years, he had divested most of Boussac's non-core assets. The extensive textile operations, the Peaudouce diaper division, and the furniture retailer Conforama were all sold off, generating an estimated $500 million in capital. During this period, Arnault oversaw the elimination of approximately 9,000 jobs across the former Boussac group, prioritizing financial viability over preservation of the existing structure.

From the sprawling Boussac portfolio, Arnault retained only two significant assets: Christian Dior and the prestigious Parisian department store Le Bon Marché. This selective approach revealed his strategic focus on luxury potential rather than industrial operations.

The visual transformation of Christian Dior began almost immediately. In the atelier, where skilled craftspeople continued to produce haute couture pieces, a sense of uncertainty gave way to cautious optimism as Arnault's commitment to the house's heritage became apparent. Resources flowed toward revitalizing the space at 30 Avenue Montaigne, restoring its elegant gray and white color scheme, and recreating the distinctive experience that had once defined the Dior customer journey.

The shock therapy delivered remarkable results. By 1987, just three years after acquisition, the restructured entity, Financière Agache, had returned to profitability, reporting impressive figures: revenues of $1.9 billion generating earnings of $112 million. This financial turnaround, achieved through a combination of strategic divestiture, cost reduction, and focused investment in luxury potential, established Arnault's credibility in the business world.

Arnault's first significant insight at Dior was as clear as it was challenging: the essence that had once defined the house had not disappeared but had been buried under layers of licensing agreements, diffused through thousands of products of varying quality bearing the once-exclusive name. To resurrect that special quality, the ineffable mixture of heritage, craftsmanship, desirability, and exclusivity, would

require not simply improving operations but fundamentally reconceiv-
ing the brand's relationship with its global audience.

The results of his licensing audit were sobering. By the mid-1980s,
the Dior name adorned products that would have horrified its founder.
A "Christian Dior Home Collection" included ceramic bowls, lucite
serving trays, metal trinket boxes, and silver letter openers. The Christian Dior signature appeared on numerous fine china patterns with
names like "Provence Blanc," "Casablanca," and "Millefleurs."

The tangible reality of these licensed products often betrayed their
luxury branding. A Dior bathrobe featured thin cotton rather than
plush terry cloth, with stitching that began unraveling after a few
washes. Dior eyewear, once crafted with jewel-like precision, now
comprised mass-produced frames that differed from non-designer alternatives primarily through the logo on their temples.

"This is not Dior," Arnault reportedly said, holding up a particularly
egregious example of brand dilution, a plastic key chain bearing the CD
logo, mass-produced in Asia and sold in airport gift shops. The object
embodied everything Christian Dior had not stood for: cheapness, dis-
posability, ubiquity.

Arnault's solution was decisive: by 1989, he had set a specific target
to cut the number of Dior licensees and franchised boutiques by half,
reducing them from 280 to fewer than 150 by 1992. This willingness to
sacrifice immediate licensing income in favor of rebuilding long-term
brand equity became a hallmark of his luxury management philosophy.

The strategy created immediate financial pressure. Licensing had
provided reliable revenue with minimal operational investment. Eliminating these income streams meant Dior would have to succeed
through its core operations rather than through the rental of its name.

Complementing the strategic overhaul of licensing was a decisive
change in creative leadership. Marc Bohan had served as Dior's artistic
director for nearly three decades (1960-1989), maintaining the brand's
prestige through changing fashion landscapes. However, in 1989, Arnault orchestrated what contemporary reports described as an "uncer-

emonious ousting," replacing Bohan with Italian designer Gianfranco Ferré.

This appointment was strategically significant, as Ferré was the first non-French designer to lead Dior's creative direction. The choice underscored Arnault's belief that "talent has no nationality" and his focus on securing the best creative force to elevate the brand's fundamental cachet.

"We are not selling clothes," Arnault told his team during this period of transformation. "We are selling dreams." This fundamental insight, that luxury transcends the physical product to encompass fantasy, aspiration, and emotional connection, guided the revival strategy. Every element of the Dior experience underwent scrutiny through this lens, from the architecture of boutiques to the training of sales staff, from advertising imagery to packaging.

By 1990, the early results of this strategic repositioning were becoming visible. The brand had begun its journey away from mass accessibility back toward controlled exclusivity. Products bearing the Dior name were fewer but of higher quality. Distribution had become more selective, with emphasis on the experience in directly controlled boutiques rather than wholesale presence.

What Arnault demonstrated through this focused revival was his intuitive understanding of luxury's essential nature. He recognized that the brand's allure could be reclaimed if the fundamental elements that created it, exceptional quality, creative vision, controlled distribution, and carefully managed scarcity, were restored.

As Arnault was systematically restructuring the Boussac group and beginning the revival of Christian Dior, another significant development was unfolding in the luxury landscape. In 1987, Louis Vuitton (the prestigious leather goods maker) and Moët Hennessy (the esteemed wines and spirits group) merged to create LVMH, forming what was then the world's largest luxury goods company. The merger was intended partly as a defensive move, creating an entity too large to be easily acquired in an era of increasing corporate takeovers.

From his office overlooking the Parisian skyline, Arnault observed this development with strategic interest. With the Dior turnaround progressing, he had begun seeking his next opportunity to expand his luxury holdings.

Yet the appearance of unified strength masked internal discord. The merger had brought together distinctly different corporate cultures and family interests. Tensions simmered between Henry Racamier, the 76-year-old president of Louis Vuitton who had transformed his wife's family business into a global powerhouse, and Alain Chevalier, head of Moët Hennessy. Their divergent visions for the future direction of LVMH created a vulnerability that Arnault was uniquely positioned to exploit.

Sensing opportunity in this discord, Arnault executed a sophisticated takeover strategy. His initial move was subtle but significant: In July 1988, Arnault allied with Guinness plc (which had distribution agreements with Moët Hennessy), forming a holding company that acquired a 24% stake in LVMH for $1.6 billion. This opening gambit provided Arnault with a substantial position without triggering immediate defensive reactions.

Inside LVMH's elegant headquarters on Avenue Hoche, tension mounted as Arnault's intentions became apparent. Board meetings that once focused on brand strategies and market expansions devolved into terse exchanges about corporate governance and voting rights.

When Racamier moved to strengthen his position, Arnault responded by rapidly increasing his stake. He spent an additional $600 million to acquire another 13.5% of LVMH, becoming the single largest shareholder. The financial daring of this move was extraordinary, committing huge sums based on conviction in his strategy rather than certainty of outcome.

The conflict between Arnault and Racamier escalated into what French media dubbed "the handbag war," with both men fighting for control over the direction of the newly formed luxury group. Racamier, despite his advanced age, proved a formidable opponent, using his deep knowledge of Louis Vuitton and his close relationships with board members to resist Arnault's advance.

In January 1989, Arnault made his decisive move, investing another $500 million to secure 43.5% of LVMH's shares and 35% of its voting rights, establishing a blocking minority that prevented any attempt to dismantle the group. He then moved against Racamier, outmaneuvering the Louis Vuitton veteran through a series of boardroom maneuvers that gradually isolated him from his bases of support.

The climax came on January 13, 1989, during a board meeting on Avenue Hoche. Bernard Arnault, just 39 years old, was unanimously elected chairman of LVMH's executive management board. The vote marked the culmination of a brilliantly planned campaign that had unfolded like a chess match, with each move precisely calculated to lead to this final position.

What made Arnault's victory particularly significant was not merely the acquisition itself but what it represented for the future of luxury. By securing control of both Christian Dior and LVMH, he had positioned himself to implement a revolutionary vision for how luxury brands could be structured, managed, and developed globally.

As news of Arnault's triumph spread through Paris, the luxury industry found itself facing a new reality. The traditional model of family-controlled individual houses was giving way to something entirely different, the luxury conglomerate. The independent fiefdoms of individual brands were being assembled into a corporate structure that would leverage their collective strength while preserving their distinct identities.

With control of both Christian Dior and LVMH secured by early 1989, Arnault began articulating and implementing his revolutionary vision for luxury. His approach represented a dramatic departure from how luxury houses had traditionally operated. Where most had functioned as standalone entities, often family-controlled and focused on a specific craft tradition, Arnault envisioned a portfolio of complementary luxury brands operating under a federated structure that balanced brand autonomy with group resources.

"My goal is not to be the biggest, but to be the best," Arnault stated, though his actions suggested he aimed for both. His vision centered on what he termed "star brands," those considered timeless, modern, fast-growing, and highly profitable.

At the heart of Arnault's model was a delicate balance between centralization and autonomy. Financial control, strategic direction, and certain operational functions would be centralized at the group level, creating efficiencies and leverage. However, creative direction and brand identity would remain decentralized, allowing each house to maintain its distinct character and heritage.

"My relationship to luxury goods is really very rational," Arnault once explained. "It is the only area in which it is possible to make luxury profit margins." This statement revealed the underlying commercial pragmatism that would drive his luxury vision, an approach that viewed heritage and creativity not merely as artistic expressions but as strategic assets to be managed for maximum long-term value.

For the revitalization of Dior, Arnault applied this blueprint with meticulous attention. The brand's heritage as a couture house would be preserved and celebrated, serving as the creative wellspring for the entire Dior universe. Simultaneously, new categories would be developed to extend the brand's reach while maintaining quality control.

Arnault understood the crucial role of physical space in luxury positioning. Under his direction, Dior began transforming its boutiques into temples of the brand aesthetic, with architectural elements that echoed 30 Avenue Montaigne's neoclassical elegance. The complete experience was carefully orchestrated: plush carpeting that softened footfalls, subtly perfumed air, precisely calibrated lighting that enhanced product presentation, background music selected to reinforce brand identity without intruding on customer interactions.

Similarly, at Louis Vuitton, Arnault initiated a strategic evolution while respecting the brand's legacy. The house had built its reputation on exceptional travel goods, particularly its distinctive monogrammed trunks and luggage. Under Arnault's guidance, this heritage would be preserved while the brand extended into adjacent categories like hand-bags, small leather goods, ready-to-wear, and accessories.

The early LVMH structure allowed Arnault to begin testing and re-fining this model, establishing the organizational template that would eventually accommodate dozens of prestigious houses across multi-ple luxury categories. By creating a structure that could seamlessly integrate additional acquisitions, Arnault laid the groundwork for the systematic expansion that would follow over the coming decades.

What differentiated Arnault's strategy from mere conglomeration was its focus on brands with authentic heritage and craftsmanship tra-ditions. Unlike typical corporate acquisitions aimed primarily at mar-ket share or cost synergies, Arnault sought houses with genuine luxury credentials and emotional resonance.

The blueprint extended beyond brand portfolio to encompass dis-tribution strategy. Arnault recognized that controlling the customer experience was essential for luxury positioning. Under his direction, LVMH brands would gradually reduce wholesale distribution through department stores and multi-brand boutiques, focusing instead on di-rectly operated stores where the environment, service, and presenta-tion could be precisely managed.

By 1990, with Dior's revival underway and LVMH's structure es-tablished, the outline of Arnault's luxury architecture had crystallized. What remained to be seen was how this blueprint would transform not just the companies under his control but the entire luxury landscape.

As the 1980s drew to a close, a profound irony was taking shape at the heart of Arnault's luxury revolution. The very man who had recognized the dangers of excessive democratization at Dior, who had systemati-cally reversed the brand dilution caused by uncontrolled licensing, was simultaneously laying the groundwork for a more sophisticated form of luxury expansion. This fundamental tension, rescuing Dior from one form of dilution while potentially initiating the next, contained both the genius of Arnault's vision and its inherent contradiction.

What made Arnault's approach revolutionary was not solely the conglomerate structure or the scale of his ambition, but his intuitive understanding of how to manage this tension, at least temporarily. His solution was a sophisticated stratification of each brand's offering. The haute couture and high jewelry would maintain extreme exclusivity through astronomical prices and deliberate scarcity. Ready-to-wear would offer accessible luxury to the affluent but not ultra-wealthy. Accessories, fragrances, and cosmetics would serve as entry points for aspirational consumers.

The strategy extended beyond product to the customer experience itself. Wealthy clients would receive personalized attention, private shopping appointments, and exclusive access to limited editions or special events. The aspirational middle class might purchase accessible items but in standardized retail environments. This experiential stratification enabled brands to maintain the appearance of exclusivity while dramatically expanding their customer base.

As the 1990s dawned, Arnault stood at the threshold of luxury's new era, one that he himself was creating through his bold vision and precise execution. The luxury landscape was increasingly divided between his growing corporate empire and the independent houses that continued to operate according to more traditional models. Brands like Hermès and Chanel remained family-controlled, maintaining stricter limits on growth to preserve exclusivity.

This polarization of approaches created a fascinating dynamic, as luxury's allure began to shift between houses according to their position in the exclusivity-accessibility spectrum. As some brands under Arnault's control gradually became more accessible, consumers seeking true exclusivity would shift their attention to houses that maintained stricter limitations on distribution and growth.

The brilliant paradox of Arnault's vision was that he understood this pattern yet chose to accelerate it nonetheless. He recognized that luxury could be democratized more profitably than ever before through sophisticated brand management, vertical integration, and global scale. The architecture he was creating would fundamentally transform how luxury operated, generating unprecedented profits while gradually altering the very definition of luxury itself.

Bernard Arnault had entered luxury as an outsider but would come to define its future more profoundly than any insider could have imagined. The Wolf in Cashmere was not looking to simply join the luxury establishment; he was rewriting its fundamental rules. The business of luxury would never be the same, and neither would our relationship with the objects of our desire.

Chapter Seven

Status Across Generations

T he Christie's auction room hummed with anticipation, the gentle murmur of well-heeled bidders echoing beneath ornate chandeliers. It was May 2003, and the star lots of the morning session were about to appear: a vintage Rolex Submariner from 1969 and an original Hermès Kelly bag from 1956. Three women from a single family occupied seats in the middle row, each studying the auction catalog with distinctly different expressions.

Eleanor, a poised seventy-two, ran her fingers over the glossy image of the Kelly bag with the practiced touch of someone who had owned its contemporaries. "The stitching on these early models was exquisite," she remarked to her forty-year-old daughter Melissa, whose attention was split between the catalog and her Palm Pilot, where she was checking comparable prices on early online luxury resale sites. Meanwhile, Eleanor's twenty-two-year-old granddaughter Zoe leaned forward in her chair, digital camera at the ready, eager to document what she called her "vintage treasure hunting" for her nascent fashion blog.

"I had a similar Kelly in the sixties," Eleanor reminisced. "It was just a beautiful handbag then, expensive, yes, but something a successful woman could save for. We didn't call them 'investment pieces.'"

Melissa glanced up from her device. "Well, they certainly are now. That Rolex model has nearly tripled in value over the past decade alone." Her tone was analytical, assessing.

"I just love that they have stories," Zoe interjected, eyes bright with enthusiasm. "Imagine where that bag has been, who carried it. That's what makes vintage special, it's authentic in a way new things can't be."

The Christie's specialist took the podium, adjusting his microphone. "Ladies and gentlemen, we're seeing unprecedented interest in these vintage luxury items. What were once simply well-made products are now highly collectible assets. Today's auction reflects the growing recognition of certain luxury pieces as alternative investments with remarkable appreciation potential."

Eleanor raised an eyebrow at this framing. For her generation, luxury had been the culmination of achievement, beautiful objects acquired as rewards for success, meant to be used and enjoyed. For Melissa's generation, these same objects had evolved into strategic acquisitions with both emotional and financial returns. And for Zoe, they represented something else entirely, physical manifestations of stories and authenticity in an increasingly digital world.

As the bidding began, three generations of women watched the same objects through distinctly different lenses, each shaped by the era in which they had first encountered luxury's allure and significance.

History reveals a fascinating pattern in how humans advertise their status, a perpetual dance between overt display and calculated understatement. This is not merely a modern phenomenon but an enduring dynamic that has played out across centuries and cultures. When aristocracy dominated Western society, those secure in their position often embraced subtle signals, small details recognizable only to fellow elites. As new wealth emerged, these newcomers typically adopted more obvious displays to announce their arrival, prompting the established elite to retreat further into understated signals.

This natural cycle dramatically accelerated during the 1980s-2000s, creating the conditions for today's luxury landscape. The 1980s ushered in an era of conspicuous consumption with bold logos and obvious status markers: Versace's baroque patterns, Louis Vuitton's ubiquitous monogram, Gucci's distinctive red and green stripe. The 1990s witnessed a reaction toward minimalism and understatement in certain segments, the rise of Prada's industrial nylon, Jil Sander's severe simplicity, and Helmut Lang's urban restraint. By the early 2000s, logo culture had resurged with renewed vigor, yet in more complex, layered forms.

Each generation encountered status signaling at different historical moments, creating distinct relationships with luxury and its social meaning. Baby Boomers, raised in the relative austerity of the post-war era, often embraced quality and craftsmanship first, with status symbols following as rewards for achievement. When Eleanor purchased her first Gucci loafers in 1975, they represented both quality craftsmanship and tasteful status, visible but not ostentatious. For her, luxury served as confirmation of arrival after years of professional advancement.

Generation X came of age during the conspicuous displays of the 1980s, then witnessed the minimalist reaction of the 1990s. This created a complex relationship with status signals, an appreciation for quality combined with skepticism toward obvious displays. When Melissa bought her first luxury piece, a Prada nylon backpack in 1997, it represented a calculated rejection of her mother's more traditional status markers while still signaling insider knowledge to those who recognized its understated branding. For Gen X, cultural capital often mattered as much as financial capital.

Early Millennials like Zoe encountered luxury during another inflection point. Raised amid both minimalism and the early-2000s logo resurgence, they developed nuanced approaches to status signaling. When Zoe saved for her first designer purchase, a small Louis Vuitton pochette in 2002, she valued it both as a connection to fashion history and as a photogenic object for early social platforms. Her generation learned to read and deploy status signals across multiple contexts, toggling between conspicuous displays for some audiences and subtle signals for others.

The same status symbols carried dramatically different meanings across these generations. Consider the Burberry check pattern: For Eleanor's generation, it represented British heritage and discreet luxury. For Melissa's cohort, it underwent a remarkable transformation, from classic to questionable during the 1990s "chav" associations in the UK, then to ironically fashionable. For Zoe's peers, it metamorphosed yet again through designer Christopher Bailey's reinterpretations, becoming simultaneously heritage and contemporary.

These differences reflected more than mere taste; they revealed fundamentally different relationships with status itself. Eleanor's generation experienced a social context where status derived primarily from career achievement and social position. Melissa's cohort navigated a world where cultural knowledge and insider access increasingly rivaled traditional markers. Zoe's generation emerged into an environment where digital connectivity began creating new status hierarchies based on likes, shares, and online influence.

The period spanning the 1980s through early 2000s represented a golden age of luxury accessibility that is difficult to imagine today. The price points of iconic luxury items during this era created a fundamentally different relationship between consumers and brands, one where aspirational purchases required saving but remained within reach of middle-class professionals.

The statistics tell a striking story. In 1985, a Rolex Submariner Date retailed for approximately $1,325. By 2003, it had reached about $3,900. Today, the same model exceeds $10,000. Adjusted for inflation, the 1985 price would be roughly $3,600 in today's dollars, nearly one-third of the current retail price. This means that what once represented an expensive but achievable purchase for a mid-career professional has transformed into a significant investment requiring substantial disposable income.

Similar patterns appear across iconic luxury categories. A Louis Vuitton Speedy 30 that cost $220 in 1980 rose to roughly $450 by 2000. Today, it exceeds $1,350, a price increase far outpacing inflation. The Hermès Kelly bag that Eleanor referenced witnessing in the 1960s and 1970s for about $800 had reached approximately $5,000 by the early 2000s. Current retail prices start around $12,000, with sought-after versions commanding significantly more on the secondary market.

These weren't merely numbers on price tags; they reflected fundamentally different relationships with luxury goods. Eleanor's generation could purchase significant luxury items through diligent saving and careful planning. A young lawyer in 1985 earning $40,000 annually could acquire that Rolex Submariner by setting aside roughly one month's gross salary. Today's equivalent professional would need to sacrifice nearly three months' income for the same watch.

This price accessibility shaped each generation's perception of luxury's value equation. For Baby Boomers like Eleanor, luxury items represented significant but attainable milestones, rewards for hard work that required commitment but remained within reach. Their value assessment centered on craftsmanship, durability, and long-term enjoyment rather than investment potential.

For Generation X, luxury's value equation began incorporating investment thinking. When Melissa considered luxury purchases in the 1990s and early 2000s, she witnessed the beginning of the "investment piece" narrative. Vintage Rolex watches and certain Hermès bags were already showing appreciation potential, though nothing like today's meteoric rises. Her approach became more strategic, balancing emotional satisfaction with potential future value.

Early Millennials like Zoe encountered luxury during a profound transformation. Coming of age as prices began their steep ascent, they witnessed the emergence of "hype" culture, where limited editions and collaborations created new categories of value. The investment narrative was firmly established, but accessibility was decreasing for traditional luxury icons.

The auction that morning reflected this evolution perfectly. The Rolex Submariner that would have cost $1,500 new in 1985 fetched $9,800 at auction in 2003, already showing impressive appreciation but modest compared to today's vintage watch market where similar models can exceed $25,000. The Kelly bag that would have retailed for approximately $1,200 in the early 1970s sold for $11,000, significant growth but nothing like current auction results where similar vintage Kelly bags regularly command $20,000-$30,000.

As the auctioneer's gavel fell on each lot, Eleanor shook her head slightly at prices she found astonishing for items similar to those she had purchased simply to use and enjoy. Melissa nodded with satisfaction, her predictions about investment potential confirmed. And Zoe captured each winning bid with her camera, documenting what she intuitively recognized as a pivotal moment in luxury's evolving story.

The murmurs in the auction room that morning weren't exclusively in American English. Japanese collectors conferred quietly in one corner, a group of Middle Eastern bidders sat confidently near the front, and several European buyers were scattered throughout the room. The global presence reflected a crucial truth often overlooked in luxury analysis: status signaling is not a universal language but rather a complex dialect with significant regional variations.

During the golden age of the 1980s through early 2000s, these cultural differences were even more pronounced than they are today, shaping how different generations around the world approached luxury consumption. In Japan, the economic boom of the 1980s created a sophisticated luxury market characterized by extraordinary attention to detail and cultural specificity. Japanese consumers became legendary for their meticulous knowledge of product craftsmanship, often surpassing Western customers in their technical understanding of luxury goods.

Meanwhile, the emerging Chinese luxury market of the late 1990s and early 2000s presented a striking contrast. As China opened to Western luxury brands, new consumers typically preferred highly visible logos and recognizable status symbols. A luxury retail executive who opened some of the first Western luxury boutiques in Beijing in the early 2000s noted: "Our Chinese customers wanted unambiguous signals of success, bold logos, recognizable shapes, obvious brand signatures."

In the Middle East, particularly in the Gulf states, luxury consumption during this period often emphasized opulence and exclusivity.

These cultural variations influenced different generations differently, creating unique global-generational intersections. Baby Boomers who traveled for business during the 1980s and 1990s often developed cross-cultural luxury appreciation through direct exposure. Eleanor had visited Tokyo in 1986 on a business trip and recalled being impressed by the department store luxury floors: "The presentation was like a museum, the respect shown to the products was unlike anything I'd seen in New York."

Generation X encountered global luxury contexts primarily through increased media exposure. Fashion magazines of the 1990s regularly featured Tokyo street style, Parisian luxury boutiques, and emerging markets, creating awareness of international variations in status display. Melissa subscribed to international editions of fashion magazines and remembered being fascinated by how differently luxury was presented across markets.

Early Millennials like Zoe were the first generation to experience the beginning of digital global connectivity. Fashion forums and early blogs allowed unprecedented access to international luxury perspectives. "I was on the Purse Forum in college, learning how collectors in Singapore approached Hermès differently than those in Paris," Zoe explained. "It was like having global luxury mentors from my dorm room."

As the auction continued, these cultural variations manifested in distinct bidding patterns. A Japanese collector secured a vintage Cartier Tank watch after careful inspection of its mechanical movement, appreciating its understated elegance and technical precision. A Middle Eastern bidder confidently claimed a rare ostrich Kelly bag in vivid turquoise, valuing its distinctive presence and exceptional materials.

"I remember buying my first proper luxury bag before an important interview," Melissa confided during a break in the auction. "A Ferragamo tote, nothing flashy, but unmistakably quality. It was like wearing armor walking into that law firm. I felt I belonged before I'd said a word." Her comment revealed one of luxury's most powerful yet rarely discussed functions: its role as symbolic armor, providing both psychological protection and strategic advantage in challenging social contexts.

This armor function manifested differently across generations, serving distinct protective needs based on each cohort's social challenges. For Baby Boomers like Eleanor, luxury armor primarily facilitated professional advancement in traditionally male-dominated environments. As one of the first female executives at her financial firm in the 1970s, Eleanor had strategically invested in a wardrobe of Chanel suits and Hermès accessories. "The right pieces conveyed that I understood the unwritten codes," she explained. "They were a shorthand for 'I belong in this room,' particularly important when you're the only woman at the table."

For Generation X faced different social challenges requiring adapted armor. Coming of age during economic instability and corporate downsizing, they navigated environments where traditional career paths were fracturing. Luxury for this generation often served as armor against precarity, providing psychological security amid uncertainty.

For many in Melissa's cohort, luxury armor helped bridge increasingly diverse professional and social worlds. As boundaries between corporate environments, creative industries, and digital spaces began blurring in the 1990s, Gen X developed strategic wardrobes that could move between contexts, perhaps a discreet Cartier watch that worked in both banking meetings and design studios.

Early Millennials pioneered yet another armor application. Entering adulthood during the rise of social media and digital self-presentation, they began deploying luxury items as armor in both physical and virtual contexts. Zoe recalled saving for months to buy a distinctive pair of designer sunglasses for her first industry conference: "I knew they'd be in every photo, signaling I was serious about fashion before I had any real credentials."

The armor function proved particularly significant for those navigating cultural transitions. First-generation wealth across all age groups used luxury strategically to manage perceptions and create belonging. "My father immigrated with nothing, built a business, and bought my mother a classic Cartier watch for their twentieth anniversary," shared a Gen X media executive. "For them, it wasn't about showing off, it was validation that they had secured their place after years of being treated as outsiders."

The psychological research confirmed what these consumers intuitively understood: luxury items can significantly boost confidence and create favorable impression management. Studies showed that wearing luxury brands increased perceptions of competence and status during evaluative situations like job interviews or important presentations.

Yet the armor function carried risks, particularly for those lacking cultural fluency in luxury codes. Choosing overly conspicuous items could backfire, signaling insecurity rather than confidence. Old-money circles might dismiss new-wealth displays as vulgar, while creative industries might view corporate luxury markers as unimaginative.

As the auction concluded, subtle signs of luxury's impending transformation were visible to the attentive observer. The Christie's specialist announced that future auctions would include online bidding capabilities, a seemingly minor operational detail that foreshadowed a seismic shift in luxury accessibility. A young tech entrepreneur several rows ahead had successfully bid on a vintage Patek Philippe while simultaneously checking his BlackBerry. The traditional auction ritual was beginning to incorporate digital elements, hinting at profound changes gathering on the horizon.

The early 2000s represented a pivotal moment when the seeds of today's luxury landscape were being planted, though few recognized their significance at the time. E-commerce pioneers like Net-a-Porter (founded 2000) were challenging luxury's traditional distribution model. The first luxury fan forums were creating communities where enthusiasts shared previously guarded insider knowledge. Early digital catalogs were making product information accessible beyond boutique visitors.

These changes were perceived differently across generations. Eleanor viewed early luxury websites with skepticism, preferring the tactile experience of in-store shopping. "I visited eLuxury.com out of curiosity," she recalled, referencing LVMH's early e-commerce venture launched in 2000, "but couldn't imagine buying something significant without touching it first."

Melissa approached these innovations more pragmatically, appreciating their convenience while maintaining some traditional preferences. She had already embraced auction and resale websites as research tools but still preferred completing significant purchases in person. "I used the early online catalogs to compare prices across boutiques," she explained, "but I wanted to see how a watch worked on my wrist before committing."

Zoe embraced emerging digital luxury platforms with enthusiasm, recognizing their transformative potential. Already active on early fashion forums and blogs, she saw online spaces as legitimate extensions of the luxury experience rather than poor substitutes for physical shopping. "I discovered vintage pieces I'd never have found locally through online research," she noted. "The internet was opening doors, not closing them."

Beyond digital developments, the first signs of luxury's democratization through product strategy were becoming visible. Major luxury houses had expanded their entry-level offerings significantly, small leather goods, cosmetics, eyewear, and fragrance, creating accessible entry points for aspirational consumers. Louis Vuitton's multicolored monogram collection designed by Marc Jacobs in collaboration with Takashi Murakami (launched in 2003) exemplified this approach, offering recognizable luxury at relatively accessible price points.

The initial impact of luxury conglomeration was also becoming apparent. LVMH, formed in 1987, had by 2003 acquired numerous prestigious houses including Dior, Givenchy, Fendi, and most recently (2000) Pucci. Richemont had similarly consolidated fine watchmaking and jewelry brands. This concentration was enabling unprecedented growth through shared resources and expertise, but also standardizing aspects of the luxury experience that had previously been distinctive to each house.

These early developments represented just the leading edge of forces that would dramatically transform luxury in the coming decades. The auction that morning, still conducted primarily in person, still following centuries-old protocols, was already incorporating elements that would soon evolve into sophisticated online bidding platforms, virtual previews, and global livestreams.

As Eleanor, Melissa, and Zoe gathered their catalogs and prepared to leave, they represented three generations unknowingly standing at the twilight of a distinctive era in luxury, a period when craftsmanship, heritage, and exclusivity still largely defined the category, yet when forces of transformation were already gathering momentum.

"Shall we celebrate with lunch at Bergdorf's?" suggested Eleanor, still drawn to traditional luxury rituals.

"Let me check their menu online first," Melissa replied, pulling out her BlackBerry.

"I'll document everything for my blog readers," added Zoe, already thinking about sharing their multigenerational perspective.

Three generations of women walking into a future they would experience in profoundly different ways, their divergent perspectives on luxury continuing to be shaped by those formative early encounters that had established their distinct relationships with quality, status, and value.

Chapter Eight

The Art of Desire

T he photographer called for a brief pause as stylists rushed forward to adjust the model's posture, a barely perceptible shift of her shoulder, a quarter-inch tilt of her chin. The Dior bag she held needed to catch the light just so, revealing the subtle grain of the leather without obscuring the logo. Behind the camera, a creative director conferred with the brand's marketing executive, scrutinizing the composition on a monitor. The setting, a Parisian café meticulously reconstructed in a New York studio, had been crafted down to the antique bistro chairs and precisely weathered tabletop.

The model, a rising actress with 3.2 million Instagram followers, resumed her pose, an effortless elegance that had required four hours of preparation. Her contract specified not just her fee, but the precise terms of how and when she would share images from the shoot with her followers. The Dior executive made notes on her tablet, calculating the expected media impressions against the campaign's seven-figure budget.

This scene, replicated across fashion capitals, executed for count-less brands with military precision, represents the sophisticated machinery behind luxury's seemingly effortless allure. What appears to consumers as a moment of aspirational beauty captured in a magazine spread is, in reality, the culmination of strategic decisions, substantial investments, and meticulous execution. The art of creating desire, of making consumers not just want but yearn for luxury goods, has evolved into a refined science of seduction.

In luxury's golden age, the 1980s through early 2000s, the industry perfected this alchemy of desire, transforming craftsmanship and heritage into dreams worth coveting. Behind the glossy facades of advertisements and boutique windows lay a calculated strategy to engineer longing, one that evolved continuously to maintain its potency while preserving the timeless principles that made luxury so deeply desirable.

The journey from displaying products to engineering dreams began decades earlier, but reached its zenith during luxury's golden age. In the mid-20th century, luxury advertisements presented straightforward propositions. Brands showcased their creations in high-end print publications like Vogue and Harper's Bazaar, focusing on craftsmanship, materials, and design excellence. The approach was product-centric and remarkably direct: here is our exceptional creation, made with the finest materials by skilled artisans.

Consider a typical Hermès advertisement from the 1950s: a beautifully lit leather bag against a minimal background, accompanied by spare text noting the heritage of the maison. The strategy relied on the product's inherent qualities to convey its value, with little attempt to construct elaborate narratives around it. The audience was presumed to be knowledgeable about luxury's codes and capable of recognizing quality without extensive persuasion.

This approach reflected the industry's orientation toward a genuine elite, those with inherited wealth and social standing who constituted the primary market for luxury goods. For these consumers, luxury purchases were an expected part of their lifestyle rather than aspirational acquisitions. Marketing served primarily to inform rather than to seduce.

As luxury brands expanded beyond haute couture into ready-to-wear and accessories, their advertising strategies underwent a subtle transformation. By the 1970s and 1980s, campaigns increasingly incorporated narrative elements and lifestyle associations. Ralph Lauren pioneered this approach in the American market, selling not just clothing but an idealized vision of aristocratic leisure: thoroughbred horses, sprawling estates, and multi-generational family gatherings.

European luxury houses followed suit, though often with more restraint. Louis Vuitton's iconic campaigns featuring Catherine Deneuve traveling with the brand's luggage merged product functionality with celebrity cachet and the romance of luxury travel. The message evolved from "this is what we make" to "this is the life our products enable."

The crucial shift, however, came in the late 1980s and early 1990s, as luxury conglomerates, led by LVMH under Bernard Arnault, recognized that they were selling something far more intangible than craftsmanship or materials. They were selling dreams, identities, and emotional experiences. When Tom Ford revitalized Gucci with provocative, hyper-sexualized campaigns, he demonstrated that luxury marketing could tap into deeper psychological desires than mere product appreciation. His 1990s campaigns didn't just sell clothing and accessories but promised transformation, a metamorphosis into someone more glamorous, more desirable, more powerful.

This shift coincided with, and partly drove, luxury's expanding audience beyond traditional elites to include the professional upper-middle class, the newly wealthy, and aspirational consumers who might save for months to acquire a single iconic item. For these broader audiences, the emotional appeal of luxury, what it signified about one's taste, achievements, and affiliations, often mattered more than technical specifications or heritage details that traditional connoisseurs might prioritize.

The relationship between celebrities and luxury brands has ancient roots, the association of prestigious products with high-status individuals extends back to royal warrants and aristocratic patronage. Yet the modern celebrity endorsement machine represents something fundamentally different: a highly systematized, strategically calculated, and financially quantified approach to leveraging fame for commercial advantage.

In luxury's early decades, relationships between stars and designers often developed organically. Hubert de Givenchy's friendship with Audrey Hepburn created an iconic association that enhanced both their statuses, but it wasn't conceived as a marketing strategy. When Hepburn wore Givenchy in "Breakfast at Tiffany's," the resulting image became cultural shorthand for timeless elegance. Similarly, Grace Kelly's affinity for Hermès led to the naming of the Kelly bag after her impromptu use of it to shield her pregnancy from photographers, a happy accident rather than a planned campaign.

By the late 1980s and throughout the 1990s, however, as luxury expanded its horizons and conglomerates sought growth, these relationships transformed into professional arrangements. What had been informal affiliations evolved into contracts specifying exactly what was expected from both parties. Luxury houses began systematically identifying celebrities whose image aligned with their brand values and target demographics, approaching these relationships with the same strategic planning applied to product development or retail expansion.

Different luxury houses approached celebrity relationships according to their broader business philosophies. LVMH brands, particularly Louis Vuitton and Dior, pioneered aggressive investment in global ambassador networks, signing multi-year deals with top actors, musicians, and athletes across key markets. Chanel maintained a more selective approach, cultivating fewer but deeper relationships with figures who embodied their specific aesthetic, like the enduring partnership with Nicole Kidman. Hermès remained the most conservative, largely avoiding formal ambassador arrangements and letting their products speak for themselves.

The rise of the supermodel in the late 1980s and 1990s further transformed luxury marketing. Figures like Cindy Crawford, Naomi Campbell, Linda Evangelista, and later Kate Moss became powerful catalysts for desire creation. These weren't just models; they were personalities whose glamorous lives became aspirational templates.

Alongside celebrity ambassadors came the growing power of stylists. Once merely backstage assistants, stylists emerged as crucial intermediaries between brands and celebrities, often wielding considerable influence over which designers a star would wear. This "gilded triangle" of brand-celebrity-stylist relationships became increasingly formalized and commercial. A major awards show appearance might involve contractual obligations for specific garments or accessories to be worn, precise positioning on the red carpet to ensure optimal photography, and coordinated media coverage.

Even as these relationships became increasingly commercialized, luxury brands worked diligently to maintain the illusion of organic association rather than paid promotion. Consumers wanted to believe that Nicole Kidman genuinely preferred Chanel or that George Clooney naturally gravitated toward Omega watches, that the relationships reflected authentic affinity rather than contractual obligation.

"I'm sorry, but the Birkin bag has a waiting list."

Few phrases in luxury retail have generated as much desire, and frustration, as this one. The notion that even having the financial means didn't guarantee access to certain luxury items became a powerful marketing tool, elevating these products from mere consumer goods to objects of quest. What consumers often didn't realize was how deliberately this scarcity was engineered.

The psychological principle was simple but profound: humans want what they cannot easily have. By controlling access to their most desirable products, luxury brands could heighten anticipation, create conversations around their exclusivity, and ultimately justify premium pricing.

Hermès perfected this approach with its legendary Birkin and Kelly bags. The house maintained rigorous control over production volumes while establishing a waitlist system that could stretch for years. The official explanation centered on craftsmanship limitations, each bag requiring 18-25 hours of handwork by a single artisan, but industry insiders acknowledged that production could certainly be increased if maximizing sales were the primary objective. Instead, Hermès recognized that controlled scarcity increased not just desire but willingness to pay premium prices, with Birkin bags appreciating 14% annually over the past few decades, outperforming many traditional investments.

The experience of acquiring a Birkin became a status journey unto itself. Stories circulated of wealthy clients being told they couldn't simply walk in and purchase one; they needed to establish a relationship with the house, perhaps buying scarves, jewelry, or ready-to-wear before being offered the opportunity to acquire the coveted bag. Whether officially acknowledged or not, this "earning the right" approach transformed the commercial transaction into something more akin to joining an exclusive club.

Other luxury houses adopted variations of this strategy. Chanel maintained limited production of its iconic flap bags while instituting periodic price increases well beyond inflation rates, a practice that counterintuitively increased demand, as consumers rushed to purchase before the next increase. Louis Vuitton created artificial scarcity through limited-edition collaborations with artists like Takashi Murakami and Stephen Sprouse, generating social media frenzies and secondary market premiums.

The retail environment itself was designed to reinforce this sense of privileged access. Boutiques functioned less as stores and more as private clubs, with doormen, appointment systems, and personalized service creating an atmosphere of exclusivity. Sales associates, increasingly referred to as "client advisors," were trained to manage relationships rather than simply process transactions.

For top clients, the experience of manufactured scarcity could actually transform into curated exclusivity. Private appointments, pre-collection previews, and special access to limited editions created a perception of insider status that was, itself, a form of luxury. A client with a strong relationship with Dior might receive a personal call from their sales associate offering first access to a limited collection before it was announced publicly, an experience that reinforced both the product's exclusivity and the client's valued status.

The language around this manufactured scarcity was carefully crafted. Sales associates were trained to frame availability limitations in terms of craftsmanship, heritage, and exclusivity rather than deliberate supply restriction. "We receive very limited allocations of this style due to the specialized artisanship required" sounded more appealing than "we deliberately produce fewer bags than we could sell to maintain high demand."

The ultimate triumph of this approach was that consumers not only accepted these access limitations but came to value them. The difficulty of obtaining a Birkin or a limited-edition Louis Vuitton collaboration became part of its appeal, a story to share alongside the product itself. Luxury brands had effectively transformed what should have been a friction point, limited availability, into a desirability factor, making the journey to acquisition part of the luxury experience itself.

"We don't do marketing at Louis Vuitton."

This statement, uttered by a senior LVMH executive during an industry conference, drew knowing smiles from the audience. The company had just reported spending hundreds of millions on what most businesses would unmistakably classify as marketing activities: celebrity ambassadors, elaborate campaigns, fashion shows, and digital content. Yet the claim reflected a fascinating paradox in luxury strategy: the deliberate positioning of sophisticated marketing as something else entirely.

This "anti-marketing stance" represented one of luxury's most brilliant strategic inversions. Traditional marketing was positioned as something for mass brands, those who needed to convince consumers of their value. Luxury, by contrast, presented itself as inherently desirable based on intrinsic qualities, with communication serving merely to inform the appreciative connoisseur rather than persuade the uninitiated.

Bernard Arnault articulated this philosophy when he stated, "My approach to advertising is not to convince someone to buy something, but to present the creativity and craftsmanship, the beautiful message and beautiful product." The strategic sleight of hand was remarkable: reframing marketing expenditure as investment in "creativity" and "craftsmanship" rather than commercial persuasion, while pursuing precisely the goal of making consumers desire and purchase the products.

This approach manifested in several ways across the luxury landscape. Press coverage was privileged over advertising, with elaborate fashion shows and events designed primarily to generate editorial content rather than direct consumer views. When Chanel transformed the Grand Palais into extravagant settings for its runway presentations, a supermarket complete with Chanel-branded groceries, a beach with real sand and waves, a cruise ship docked indoors, the resulting media coverage and impressions far exceeded what could be achieved through traditional advertising at comparable cost.

Even paid celebrity relationships were carefully languaged to maintain this illusion. Stars were "friends of the house" or "muses" rather than paid ambassadors. When Natalie Portman appeared in Dior beauty campaigns, the narrative emphasized her authentic appreciation for the brand's values rather than her multi-million-dollar contract.

The positioning extended to retail environments, where sales associates were trained to present themselves not as salespeople but as "brand ambassadors" or "client advisors" offering expertise and guidance rather than pushing transactions. The commercial nature of the interaction was deliberately downplayed in favor of relationship building and education about heritage and craftsmanship.

This anti-marketing stance served several strategic purposes. First, it helped maintain the perception of luxury as something discovered rather than promoted, a distinction crucial for status-conscious consumers who wanted to appear discerning rather than influenced by advertising. Second, it created a useful distance between luxury houses and mass-market tactics, reinforcing the perceived gap between premium and true luxury.

Different luxury houses implemented this philosophy to varying degrees. Hermès represented the purist approach, with minimal traditional advertising and a genuine commitment to letting products and heritage speak for themselves. LVMH brands, particularly under Bernard Arnault's leadership, perhaps executed the most sophisticated version of this strategy, aggressively pursuing commercial growth through marketing while consistently framing these activities in the language of creativity and craftsmanship.

The ultimate success of this strategy was that many consumers genuinely internalized the distinction, perceiving luxury "communications" as fundamentally different from mass-market "advertising," even when the underlying techniques and objectives showed remarkable similarities. Luxury had effectively marketed its marketing as something elevated beyond marketing itself.

Standing before LVMH executives in the early 2000s, Bernard Arnault issued a directive that revealed his prophetic understanding of luxury's digital future: "Luxury must be on the internet, but the internet must become luxurious." The statement captured the fundamental tension luxury brands faced as digital technologies emerged, how to embrace new platforms without sacrificing the exclusivity, control, and high-touch experiences that defined luxury.

Initial reactions to digital channels varied dramatically across the industry. Some houses viewed the internet with open skepticism, seeing it as fundamentally incompatible with luxury values. "Luxury is not clickable," declared a senior Chanel executive in 2009, expressing concerns shared by many traditionalists who believed online experiences could never replicate the sensory richness and personal service of physical boutiques.

Others recognized early opportunities, particularly in communication if not commerce. Brands like Burberry, under Christopher Bailey's creative direction, pioneered livestreamed runway shows and interactive digital campaigns that made luxury more immediately accessible while maintaining brand control.

E-commerce adoption reflected these hesitations. While mainstream retail embraced online shopping in the late 1990s and early
2000s, luxury lagged significantly. Many houses limited their online
offerings to entry-level categories like cosmetics and fragrances, maintaining that high-end leather goods, ready-to-wear, and jewelry required the physical retail experience.

Social media presented perhaps the most profound challenge to
luxury's traditional control of its image and messaging. Platforms
like Facebook (founded 2004) and later Instagram (2010) democratized communication, allowing consumers to share unfiltered opinions
and images of luxury products. The carefully curated brand narratives
crafted through traditional media suddenly faced competition from
user-generated content beyond brand control.

Yet innovative brands began recognizing that digital platforms offered unprecedented opportunities to create desire through new forms
of engagement. In 2009, during Paris Fashion Week, Louis Vuitton
made a pioneering move by inviting select fashion bloggers to their
show, then a controversial decision that signaled recognition of digital
influencers' growing importance alongside traditional fashion media.

By the early 2010s, distinct approaches to digital had emerged across
major luxury groups. LVMH brands generally pursued aggressive digital innovation, particularly in communications if not immediately in
commerce. Richemont, with its heavy focus on watches and jewelry,
moved more cautiously, concerned about appropriate presentation of
high-value items online. Chanel maintained tight control, prioritizing
brand image over commercial opportunity in digital spaces. Hermès
remained the most conservative, viewing digital primarily as an information channel rather than a core component of either marketing or
retail strategy.

These early responses to digital disruption revealed fundamental
tensions in luxury's business philosophy. How could brands simultaneously democratize access through digital channels while maintaining the exclusivity central to luxury appeal? How could they participate

in the conversational nature of social media while preserving their authoritative voice?

The story of Christian Dior, both the man and the maison that bears his name, offers perhaps the most illuminating case study in luxury's transformation. From its revolutionary beginnings to its dilution through licensing and subsequent revival under Bernard Arnault, Dior's journey epitomizes how luxury brands must periodically reinvent themselves while maintaining connection to their foundational heritage.

Christian Dior's 1947 "New Look" collection represented fashion's ultimate disruption, cinched waists and full skirts that rejected wartime austerity and instantly transformed the silhouette of modern femininity. The house quickly established itself as a beacon of Parisian luxury, embodying post-war optimism and renewed French cultural prominence.

After Dior's untimely death in 1957, the house continued under various creative directors, maintaining its reputation for excellence. However, by the 1970s and early 1980s, the company had embraced an aggressive licensing strategy, placing the Dior name on everything from eyewear to bed linens, produced by third parties with variable quality control. While financially lucrative in the short term, this approach eventually diluted the brand's exclusivity and prestige.

This dilution through democratization illustrates a pattern that repeats across the luxury landscape. The very success of a luxury brand creates pressure to expand, to reach more consumers, to generate greater revenue. Yet this expansion, if not carefully managed, inevitably erodes the exclusivity that made the brand desirable in the first place.

Enter Bernard Arnault. In 1984, the young businessman acquired the financially troubled Boussac Saint-Frères group, which owned Christian Dior. While initially interested in the group's other assets, Arnault quickly recognized the untapped potential in the Dior brand, despite its dilution through excessive licensing. He understood that the foundational elements of Dior, its heritage, craftsmanship, and cultural significance, remained intact beneath the surface, ready to be revitalized through strategic intervention.

Arnault's approach to Dior's revival demonstrated his understanding of luxury's essential nature. Rather than simply continuing the existing business model, he implemented a comprehensive strategy to restore the brand's exclusivity and desirability. This included regaining control over licenses, improving product quality, investing in flagship stores that offered immersive brand experiences, and eventually appointing designers like John Galliano who could reinterpret Dior's heritage for contemporary audiences.

The revival of Dior under Arnault's leadership exemplified strategic reinvention through reconnection with brand essence. By rediscovering the brand's fundamental identity while updating its expression for a new era, Arnault demonstrated that luxury's appeal could be restored after dilution.

This pattern, innovation, expansion, dilution, renewal, repeats across the luxury landscape. Brands rise, establishing their unique identity through exceptional products and compelling narratives. Success leads to expansion, often including more accessible product categories and broader distribution. Eventually, this accessibility erodes exclusivity, diminishing the brand's desirability for status-conscious consumers.

As luxury entered the 21st century, this pattern accelerated. Digital platforms, globalization, and changing consumer values compressed the timeframe of luxury's evolution. What might once have taken decades now unfolded in years. The techniques of desire creation, from product-focused advertising to lifestyle marketing to emotional storytelling, evolved ever more rapidly, requiring constant reinvention to maintain their effectiveness.

Yet beneath this acceleration, the fundamental principles remained consistent. Luxury still traded on exclusivity, craftsmanship, heritage, and emotional resonance. The most successful luxury houses were those that understood this transformation and managed it strategically, preserving their core essence while continuously refreshing how they created desire.

As Act I, "The Seduction," draws to a close, we've seen how luxury brands mastered the art of desire creation during the golden age of the 1980s through early 2000s. They evolved from simple product presentation to sophisticated emotional storytelling, transformed celebrity relationships from organic associations to strategic partnerships, engineered scarcity to heighten desirability, maintained the paradoxical stance of anti-marketing, and cautiously began engaging with digital platforms.

Yet even as these brands perfected their techniques for creating desire, the seeds of the next phase were being sown. The very sophistication of their marketing, the expansion of their audience, and the emergence of digital platforms laid the groundwork for what would follow: "The Deal." In this second act, the carefully cultivated desire would be leveraged to dramatically expand accessibility, bringing luxury to broader audiences than ever before, and creating new challenges for maintaining the exclusivity that made luxury special.

The art of desire had become a science, but sciences have their limits. The true test would be whether consumers, having glimpsed behind the curtain to see the mechanics of desire creation, would still feel the enchantment that made luxury transcend mere consumption to become objects of genuine yearning.

ACT II
THE MAGIC PARADOX

We Bought the Dream

They Scaled It Up

"Accessible luxury — these are two words that don't go together."

— **Brunello Cucinelli**

Chapter Nine

Like, Share, Covet

The first time Emma scrolled past a Hermès bag on Instagram, she barely noticed it. The second time, she paused. The Birkin, a cognac-colored 35cm in textured Togo leather, was nestled in the crook of a stranger's arm, photographed from above in perfect morning light, accompanied by a steaming latte in a Limoges porcelain cup and a casually placed Smythson notebook. By the third scroll, she found herself wondering: what kind of life goes with that bag? By the fourth, she was researching prices. By the fifth, her fingertips hovered over the 'Save' button as something shifted inside her, desire had taken root. This journey from casual observer to active coveter took less than a week, a metamorphosis that would have been impossible in the pre-Instagram era when luxury lived primarily in magazines she didn't read and boutiques she didn't dare enter.

Before Instagram launched in October 2010, luxury consumption remained firmly behind the velvet rope. You either belonged to the world where Hermès scarves and Cartier watches were commonplace, or you caught glimpses of it through occasional magazine spreads or celebrity sightings. The divide was clear, the boundaries respected. Then came the revolution that would democratize desire itself.

The psychological impact was immediate and transformative. Social comparison theory, which suggests individuals evaluate themselves by comparing their possessions to those of others, found its perfect laboratory in the endless scroll of Instagram. Where previous generations might have only compared themselves to their immediate social circle, we suddenly had access to an endless stream of aspirational lifestyles. The carefully curated nature of these presentations, always showing the best angles, the perfect lighting, the most enviable moments, created an unprecedented form of upward social comparison that was both more frequent and more intense than anything experienced before.

These weren't merely images; they were portals. Each perfectly composed square offered glimpses into worlds previously accessible only to the wealthy or the well-connected. A Chanel boy bag on a Parisian café table. A wrist draped casually over a steering wheel, adorned with a constellation of Cartier Love bracelets. These weren't advertisements; they were supposedly authentic moments from real lives, lives that suddenly seemed within reach.

The intimacy of the medium made all the difference. Unlike the glossy pages of Vogue that presented luxury as remote fantasy, Instagram served it up in the same digital space where you also saw your cousin's new baby and your college roommate's beach vacation. Luxury was no longer segregated into a separate realm; it intermingled with the everyday, creating a false sense of adjacency. The psychological distance between observer and owner collapsed. If this person, who wasn't a celebrity, who wasn't even anyone you knew, could own this bag, why couldn't you?

The platform's algorithm quickly learned what caught our attention, creating desire pathways with unprecedented efficiency. What made this shift particularly powerful was its subtlety. Unlike traditional advertising, which interrupted content to push products, Instagram wove luxury into the fabric of daily life. It normalized the presence of high-end goods in everyday settings, creating what marketers call "ambient awareness," a constant, low-level consciousness of luxury that permeated our digital existence. The revolution wasn't announced; it simply appeared in your feed, one perfectly filtered image at a time.

Between 2010 and 2015, Instagram fundamentally transformed how luxury appeared in our everyday lives. Where museums and boutiques had presented luxury behind literal glass, untouchable, preserved, distant, Instagram transferred it to the illuminated screens of our devices, constantly visible yet still separated by a digital barrier. The psychological shift was dramatic: from occasional, carefully orchestrated encounters with luxury to daily immersion in its imagery.

The platform didn't only display luxury; it redefined its visual language. Flat lays evolved into an art form, carefully arranged compositions of luxury items that told stories of aspiration. The constant visibility created what psychologists call the "mere exposure effect," our tendency to develop a preference for things simply because they're familiar. As luxury goods populated more and more of our feeds, they transformed from remote status symbols into familiar desires. The extraordinary became everyday, yet somehow retained its allure.

Before social media collapsed our world into a global digital village, luxury brands wielded a powerful tool that had served them for decades: strategic market segmentation. Like master chess players, they presented different facets of their identity to different audiences across geographies and demographics. In Japan, Louis Vuitton's marketing emphasized heritage and craftsmanship. In emerging Chinese markets, the same brand highlighted status and recognition. In old-money European circles, the focus turned to insider knowledge and subtle connoisseurship.

"The beauty of pre-digital luxury marketing," explained former LVMH executive Marie Laurent, "was that we could tell different stories to different audiences. In Paris, we spoke of artisanal traditions dating back centuries. In Shanghai, we showcased celebrities and recognition value. In Moscow, we emphasized conspicuous display. And these audiences rarely saw each other's versions of the brand."

Then came Instagram, Facebook, and eventually TikTok. Suddenly, a campaign created for the Chinese market was instantly visible to old-money Europeans. The sophisticated segmentation strategies that had allowed luxury to grow while maintaining exclusivity became obsolete almost overnight. In their place arose a pressure toward homogenization, creating global messaging that wouldn't alienate any audience, but might not deeply resonate with any of them either.

The Kardashian phenomenon crystallized this dilemma perfectly. When Kim Kardashian displayed her Hermès collection on Instagram, including a Birkin painted by her daughter North West, it simultaneously thrilled aspirational consumers who dreamed of such access while horrifying traditional luxury clients who considered customizing a Birkin sacrilege. There was no way for Hermès to control which audience saw this display or how they would interpret it.

Most luxury houses responded by gravitating toward the lowest common denominator, logo-heavy products that required minimal cultural capital to recognize and appreciate. "What works globally," noted luxury consultant Sophia Chen, "are easily identifiable visual signifiers: the LV monogram, the interlocking Cs, the GG pattern. These require no cultural context or insider knowledge to recognize as valuable." This shift accelerated the trend toward conspicuous consumption, as the most visible, recognizable luxury elements became emphasized across markets.

Yet one luxury house charted a different course. Hermès maintained its selective approach despite social media's democratizing pressure. The brand refused to create easily accessible content, limited its influencer collaborations, and continued to emphasize craftsmanship over recognition.

For us as consumers, this collapse of segmentation created a more transparent but potentially less magical luxury landscape. The curtain had been pulled back, revealing the different faces brands presented in different markets. As social media made all brand activities globally visible, that mystique began to erode.

As Kardashian fame rose, traditional celebrity influence on luxury desire began to wane. The carefully managed, distant glamour of movie stars was gradually overshadowed by something more immediate and seemingly accessible: the influencer in her living room, unboxing a Celine bag while still in pajamas, coffee in hand, dog barking in the background.

By 2016, a new ecosystem had emerged, one where influence was measured not by Hollywood billing but by follower count, engagement rate, and relatability. Names like Chiara Ferragni became powerful forces in luxury consumption, leading their millions of followers to covet and purchase specific items through seemingly authentic recommendations.

"What made influencers so powerful was their perceived proximity," explained consumer psychologist Dr. Rebecca Wilson. "A celebrity on a red carpet in Valentino feels like a different species. But when an influencer shows how she styled a Valentino bag with jeans in her apartment, that feels like it could be you. The psychological distance collapses." This collapse of distance was revolutionary for luxury desire, creating a bridge between aspiration and attainability that traditional marketing had never achieved.

The micro-influencer phenomenon pushed this even further. By 2018, luxury brands weren't just working with mega-influencers boasting millions of followers; they were partnering with niche content creators who had smaller but highly engaged audiences. These micro-influencers, often with 10,000 to 100,000 followers, created the most potent form of luxury desire: the "girl next door with a Birkin" effect.

"I started my account sharing my actual outfits as a junior marketing executive," shared Amanda, who built a following of 75,000. "My first luxury purchase was a Saint Laurent card holder, I saved for months. When I posted about it, the response was incredible. People related to the journey, the saving, the excitement. That's what made it powerful." This narrative of attainability, the idea that luxury could be achieved through determination and smart saving rather than inherent wealth, resonated deeply with us as we saw ourselves in these influencers' stories.

This relatability fundamentally altered how luxury desire operated. When a mega-celebrity carried a Birkin, it confirmed the bag's status but didn't make it feel attainable. When a micro-influencer with a similar job and life circumstances acquired one, it suggested that perhaps with enough saving, strategizing, or luck, we could too. The psychology shifted from "I wish I could have that life" to "I could have that life if I make the right choices."

By 2019, the transformation was complete. Luxury houses that had once exclusively dressed A-list celebrities were actively courting influencers with relatively modest followings. Dior invited digital creators to fashion shows formerly reserved for magazine editors and celebrities. The hierarchy had been inverted, the pedestals dismantled, the living rooms elevated.

As luxury became omnipresent in our digital feeds, a new form of anxiety emerged: FOMO (Fear of Missing Out) specifically related to luxury consumption. Social media created a perpetual highlight reel of others' luxury acquisitions and experiences, triggering complex emotional responses. This wasn't merely envy; it was an acute sense of falling behind in some unspoken competition for status and experience.

"I started feeling like I was falling behind," admitted Lauren, a twenty-eight-year-old consultant. "Everyone in my feed seemed to be buying designer bags, wearing luxury watches, traveling in style. I knew it wasn't real, that people only post their best moments, but knowing that didn't stop the feeling." This cognitive dissonance between rational understanding and emotional response became a defining characteristic of social media's impact on our psychology as consumers.

The pressure operated on multiple levels. First came social comparison, measuring ourselves against peers and finding ourselves wanting. Then arose the anxiety of exclusion, the sense that everyone else was participating in a lifestyle from which we were excluded. Finally, there was the pressure of documentation, the need to have something worthy of sharing in the ongoing performance of digital life.

The psychological toll extended beyond financial stress. The constant exposure to unattainable lifestyles created what researchers termed "luxury fatigue," a state of emotional exhaustion from perpetual wanting. We found ourselves simultaneously drawn to and repelled by luxury content, unable to look away yet increasingly resentful of the desire it created.

"We saw clients taking on debt to maintain appearances on social media," reported a financial advisor. "The pressure wasn't solely to own luxury items, but to document that ownership, to participate in the digital conversation about luxury. It became a cycle: buy, post, get validation, feel pressure to buy more." This cycle represented a new form of consumer behavior, where the social media performance of consumption became as important as the consumption itself.

Yet participation continued because the alternative, opting out, carried its own social penalties. The price of participation might be high, but many of us concluded that the price of abstention was higher. In this environment, luxury consumption became not just about desire but about belonging, a phenomenon that brands recognized and leveraged with increasing sophistication.

By late 2019, subtle shifts were beginning to appear in how the most discerning among us engaged with digital luxury culture. Instagram feeds that had once inspired desire now prompted fatigue. Logo-heavy pieces that had dominated feeds for years were gradually being replaced by more subtle signifiers in certain circles. The sheer ubiquity of certain luxury markers, the Gucci belt, the Louis Vuitton Neverfull, the Cartier Love bracelet, had begun to erode their exclusivity, particularly among those who valued distinction over recognition.

"I started to feel strange about my Gucci Marmont bag," confessed Jennifer, a luxury consumer in her thirties. "When I bought it in 2017, it felt special. By 2019, I was seeing it everywhere, not only on celebrities or wealthy friends, but on college students, in suburban malls, all over my feed. Something that had felt exclusive unexpectedly felt...

common." This sentiment, though not yet widespread, signaled the beginning of a shift that would accelerate in coming years.

The first signs appeared in the rise of "stealth wealth" aesthetics among certain influencers and tastemakers. Brands like The Row, Loro Piana, and Brunello Cucinelli, with their emphasis on quality materials, craftsmanship, and absence of visible logos, began appearing more frequently in sophisticated feeds. These weren't rejections of luxury but evolutions of it, shifts toward forms of distinction that required greater cultural capital to recognize and appreciate.

Simultaneously, a new emphasis on luxury experiences rather than possessions emerged. The most forward-thinking influencers began showcasing unique moments rather than acquisitions, a stay at a remote ryokan in Japan, a meal at an obscure but exceptional restaurant, access to an invitation-only cultural event. These experiences, unlike products, couldn't be mass-produced or easily replicated, offering a new frontier of exclusivity in an increasingly saturated landscape.

Significantly, these shifts weren't rejections of luxury itself but evolutions in how we defined and consumed it. The allure wasn't disappearing; it was migrating, moving toward expressions that hadn't yet been diluted by overexposure, toward forms that maintained exclusivity despite universal visibility. This was luxury's eternal cycle playing out in accelerated form: as certain symbols became democratized through visibility and access, new markers of distinction emerged to take their place.

For most of us, however, this saturation point had not yet been reached. The vast majority still found genuine pleasure and aspiration in the luxury content that populated our feeds. The seeds of transformation were present but dormant, waiting for the conditions that would allow them to flourish.

What none of us could have anticipated was how quickly those conditions would arrive. As 2019 drew to a close, no one predicted the global disruption that would force a collective pause, a moment of reflection on consumption patterns and digital behaviors. The early signs of luxury fatigue and desire for new forms of distinction were subtle indicators of a shift that external circumstances would soon accelerate beyond anyone's expectations.

The story of our relationship with luxury through social media was not ending; it was evolving. The platforms that had democratized desire would continue to shape how we perceived, consumed, and valued luxury. But the nature of that relationship was already beginning to transform in ways that would redefine what luxury meant for a new generation of consumers. The question was not whether the allure would endure, but where it would appear next.

Chapter Ten

The Acquisition Game

T he crystal flutes clinked with a delicate musicality that belied their purpose. It was March 2011, and the air inside LVMH's Paris headquarters on Avenue Montaigne vibrated with the electricity of conquest. Outside, the world still stumbled through the aftershocks of a global financial crisis, but here, champagne flowed as if recession existed only for lesser mortals. Bernard Arnault, his tall frame impeccably tailored in navy Dior, moved through the room with the subtle confidence of a chess grandmaster who had just executed a particularly elegant checkmate.

"To Bulgari," came the toast from Arnault, his voice characteristically soft yet somehow commanding complete silence. "To the marriage of French vision and Italian craftsmanship." Glasses lifted, capturing the light streaming through floor-to-ceiling windows that framed the Eiffel Tower. At €4.3 billion, the acquisition of the storied Italian jewelry house represented one of LVMH's most ambitious moves yet, a bold statement in an uncertain economic landscape. Francesco Trapani, scion of the Bulgari family, stood nearby, his expression a complex mixture of triumph and wistfulness. The family business his grandfather had founded in 1884 was now officially a "Maison" in luxury's most powerful empire.

This scene, echoed with variations across the luxury landscape throughout the 2000s and 2010s, marked a decisive shift in the industry's structure. What had once been a constellation of fiercely independent family businesses was transforming into an intricate chess game of corporate strategy, with billions of euros moving across the board. The players were no longer primarily artisans and merchants but financiers, strategists, and CEOs whose decisions were reshaping luxury's very essence.

Even amid this corporate triumph, discerning observers might have detected the seeds of tension that would eventually blossom into existential questions for luxury. As diamonds glittered on wrists and champagne bubbles rose in flutes, the fundamental forces at play, the conflict between growth and exclusivity, between mass visibility and genuine rarity, between corporate efficiency and artisanal integrity, were initiating the next phase in luxury's eternal cycle.

The financial pressures reshaping luxury during the late 2000s and 2010s operated with the invisible but relentless force of gravity. What consumers coveted as beautifully crafted objects of desire existed simultaneously as assets on balance sheets, entries in portfolio analyses, and subjects of quarterly earnings calls. This dual identity, luxury goods as both cultural artifacts and financial instruments, fueled the unprecedented consolidation sweeping through the industry.

Wall Street and its global counterparts had developed an infatuation with luxury as an investment category. Analysts spoke glowingly of "resilience during downturns," "pricing power," and "expanding global middle class demand," particularly from China. This passionate affair injected unprecedented capital into the sector but exacted a fundamental transformation in return: luxury had to become scalable, predictable, and consistently profitable in ways that traditional artisanal businesses rarely achieved.

The 2008 global financial crisis, rather than dampening this consolidation trend, accelerated it. While luxury sales temporarily contracted in Western markets, the crisis created ideal conditions for cash-rich conglomerates to acquire weakened competitors or family businesses facing succession challenges. Economic uncertainty made the offer of corporate security more appealing to independent houses wrestling with the complexities of global expansion and digital transformation.

The cold mathematics of modern luxury reinforced this consolidation imperative. A stand-alone brand shouldered the burden of its own manufacturing, distribution, marketing, and administration. Within a luxury group, these costs could be shared or optimized across multiple brands. The financial logic was precise: scale created advantages that generated greater scale, while independence increasingly carried inherent structural disadvantages.

This scale imperative created subtle but profound changes in strategic thinking. Heritage luxury brands had traditionally defined themselves by what they wouldn't do, compromises they wouldn't make, materials they wouldn't use, distribution channels they wouldn't enter. The new financial realities gradually shifted the question from "How do we maintain our standards?" to "How do we grow while appearing to maintain our standards?" This rhetorical shift marked a fundamental reorientation of luxury's internal compass from absolute quality to optimized quality-at-scale.

Bernard Arnault navigated the luxury landscape during the 2000s and 2010s with the predatory elegance that had earned him the moniker "wolf in cashmere." Each acquisition revealed itself as part of a grand design comprehensible perhaps only from the strategic heights of his corner office in LVMH's Parisian headquarters. The pattern crystallized increasingly for industry observers: Arnault was methodically constructing not just a portfolio of brands but an ecosystem so comprehensive that it could withstand any market turbulence, capitalize on any consumer trend, and dominate any competitive landscape.

"I don't invest in brands, I invest in magic," Arnault stated during a rare 2012 interview, his engineer's precision with words masking the romanticism of the sentiment. His vision of luxury transcended the commercial to become configurational, a "constellation of stars" where each brand emitted its own distinctive light while contributing to a greater brilliance.

Strolling through Bulgari's Roman headquarters in 2011, shortly after its acquisition, Arnault's gaze lingered on the historical jewelry designs displayed in glass cases. His mind, trained in engineering before business, quickly dissected the strategic significance of the €4.3 billion deal. Bulgari represented not just a storied jewelry house but a missing piece in his luxury constellation, a strong Italian brand with global recognition that would transform LVMH's position in the high jewelry market dominated by Richemont's Cartier.

The acquisition tempo accelerated between 2008 and 2020 as Arnault executed increasingly ambitious moves across the luxury chessboard. The 2011 Bulgari deal was followed by Loro Piana in 2013, Maison Francis Kurkdjian in 2017, and hospitality group Belmond in 2018. Each target reflected not opportunistic deal-making but strategic positioning, addressing specific portfolio gaps or enhancing capabilities in growing segments.

The culmination of this strategic vision manifested in the landmark $16.2 billion acquisition of Tiffany & Co. announced in 2019. This move, LVMH's largest ever, revealed the full maturity of Arnault's acquisition approach. Beyond simply adding another prestigious name to his portfolio, the Tiffany deal addressed multiple strategic imperatives simultaneously: strengthening LVMH's position in fine jewelry, enhancing its presence in the critical American market, and acquiring a genuine cultural icon with global recognition.

Through these calculated moves, Arnault transformed the luxury landscape according to a vision that synthesized creative sensitivity with mathematical precision. As an engineer by training, he visualized luxury not as a collection of beautiful objects but as a complex system where interlocking components created structural advantages impossible for standalone competitors to match.

The brilliance of LVMH's "federation model" lay in its apparent contradiction: maintaining the fiction of independent houses while embedding them within a highly disciplined corporate structure. Each Maison preserved its own creative director, headquarters, ateliers, and distinctive identity. Louis Vuitton remained quintessentially Louis Vuitton, with its own universe of aesthetic codes, materials, and storytelling. A consumer encountering these brands experienced them as distinct creative entities rather than variations on a corporate template.

Yet beneath this carefully maintained independence flowed powerful streams of shared resources, expertise, and strategic direction. LVMH's central functions provided sophisticated support in real estate, enabling brands to secure premium locations in increasingly competitive global marketplaces. Group-level negotiations with suppliers leveraged combined purchasing power while respecting each Maison's specific material requirements.

"What is good for the Maison is good for the group" became an internal mantra that captured this delicate balance. The model created a luxury ecosystem where brands maintained their distinctive identities while drawing nourishment from common soil. LVMH's innovation was recognizing that in luxury, the value resided precisely in the unique identity of each Maison; attempting to homogenize them would destroy the very magic that made them acquisition-worthy.

Arnault articulated this philosophy during a 2015 shareholder meeting: "You can't charge a premium price for giving people what they expect. We give our artists freedom." This statement reflected a sophisticated understanding that luxury thrived on innovation, surprise, and distinctiveness, qualities that required creative autonomy. Yet this autonomy existed within carefully defined boundaries. Creative directors received significant freedom in design and artistic expression but operated within strategic frameworks established at the group level.

On a crisp October morning in 2010, Patrick Thomas, CEO of Hermès, received a phone call that would ignite one of luxury's most dramatic corporate battles. Bernard Arnault was on the line, informing him that LVMH had acquired a 17.1% stake in Hermès. The news struck like lightning across cloudless skies. "If you want to be friendly, you should have started by being friendly," Thomas reportedly replied, his measured tone masking profound shock.

"This is not a financial battle, it is a cultural battle," declared Axel Dumas, a sixth-generation family member who would later become Hermès CEO. Around him, relatives nodded in fierce agreement. For the Hermès family, luxury represented not primarily a business venture but a culture of craftsmanship, a philosophy of uncompromising quality, and a multigenerational commitment to excellence that could never be subordinated to quarterly earnings expectations.

The mechanics of LVMH's stake-building demonstrated both financial sophistication and strategic patience. Rather than purchasing shares directly, Arnault had employed cash-settled equity swaps through various subsidiaries, complex financial instruments enabling accumulation without triggering disclosure requirements. What some observers lauded as brilliant financial engineering, the Hermès family denounced as "an attack" and "the most important fraud in the history of the French stock market."

In response, the family engineered a defensive masterpiece. More than fifty descendants of founder Thierry Hermès, spanning the fifth and sixth generations, united to create an impenetrable structure. They established a holding company that pooled their shares, representing over 50% of the company, with provisions requiring family members to offer their shares first to relatives if they wished to sell.

What made this conflict so emblematic was that it transcended mere financial dispute. It crystallized the fundamental tension at luxury's core. Hermès embodied an approach where production was deliberately constrained to preserve quality and exclusivity. A single artisan crafted each Birkin or Kelly bag from start to finish, investing 18-20 hours of meticulous work. Annual production increases were capped around 6-7% regardless of demand, generating the legendary waiting lists that intensified desire rather than frustrated it.

By 2014, a resolution emerged through the intervention of a court-appointed mediator. LVMH agreed to distribute most of its Hermès shares to its own shareholders and institutional investors, reducing its direct stake to around 8%. For Hermès, the resolution preserved its independence and distinctive approach to luxury, one defined by absolute quality rather than optimal scale.

The battle's conclusion confirmed what many industry insiders already recognized: Hermès was not simply resistant to acquisition but philosophically incompatible with the conglomerate model. Its value derived precisely from its unwavering commitment to craftsmanship, scarcity, and heritage, qualities that would be fundamentally compromised by integration into a growth-oriented corporate structure.

While LVMH's acquisition game dominated luxury headlines, alternative approaches to building luxury businesses flourished during the 2000s and 2010s. These contrasting models represented not merely different corporate strategies but fundamentally divergent philosophies about luxury's essence.

Richemont, under the leadership of Johann Rupert, pursued what might be called a "focused excellence" strategy. While LVMH diversified across multiple luxury categories, Richemont concentrated primarily on "hard luxury," watches and jewelry, where craftsmanship standards were objectively measurable. "We're not in the fashion business; we're in the timeless business," Rupert often remarked.

At the opposite end stood Chanel, defiantly independent and privately owned by the secretive Wertheimer family since 1954. Chanel's approach might be termed "singular perfectionism," concentrating all resources and attention on a single iconic brand. This independence enabled Chanel to pursue distribution strategies that directly contradicted industry trends, maintaining that its core fashion and accessories should be purchased only in physical boutiques.

Emerging as LVMH's most direct competitor, Kering under François-Henri Pinault developed what might be called a "brand reinvention" model. The group specialized in acquiring heritage brands with untapped potential and dramatically reimagining them for contemporary relevance. Under Kering's ownership, Gucci transformed from a troubled traditional house into a boundary-pushing fashion phenomenon through Alessandro Michele's maximalist aesthetic.

These alternative models created a complex competitive ecosystem where no single approach dominated all segments. Each had distinctive strengths and vulnerabilities. The tension between these models ultimately created a more robust luxury landscape, where different visions of excellence could coexist.

As the acquisition game accelerated during the 2010s, subtle changes rippled through luxury's ecosystem, alterations imperceptible to casual observers but increasingly apparent to industry insiders and devoted clients. The corporate imperative for growth, while enhancing shareholder value, silently began extracting a price from the intrinsic qualities that had historically defined true luxury.

Perhaps most significantly, pricing strategies evolved in response to growth pressure. Luxury brands had always increased prices to maintain exclusivity, but the tempo and magnitude of these increases accelerated dramatically after acquisitions. Iconic products that had once been expensive but attainable for upper-middle-class consumers through disciplined saving gradually migrated into territory accessible only to the genuinely wealthy. A Louis Vuitton Speedy bag that cost approximately $700 in 2000 reached over $1,000 by 2010 and approached $1,400 by 2020, increases vastly outpacing inflation or production cost changes.

The craft narratives surrounding luxury production became more elaborate even as production realities grew more complex. Brand communications and store environments increasingly emphasized heritage, handcrafting, and artistic creation. The investment in telling the story of luxury craftsmanship expanded precisely as the absolute nature of that craftsmanship was being subtly redefined.

For established luxury clients with decades of experience, these shifts became gradually perceptible through direct product experience. A loyal Hermès client who had purchased her first Kelly bag in 1985 and her most recent one in 2018 might notice subtle differences, differences slight enough to be dismissed as variation but persistent enough to suggest directional change.

Within luxury groups, these evolutions were understood as necessary adaptations to market realities. "We haven't compromised quality," insisted a brand CEO during an internal strategy meeting in 2015, "we've optimized production for a global market." Yet the cumulative effect of these micro-adjustments across products, categories, and brands was setting the stage for fundamental questions about luxury's value proposition.

As acquisition-driven consolidation advanced, the seeds of luxury's next cyclical phase were being sown, not through dramatic ruptures but through incremental shifts in the balance between absolute quality and optimal scale. The corporate imperative for growth, while creating unprecedented luxury empires, was quietly altering the soul of what was being acquired. The price of empire was being paid not in financial currency but in the subtle dilution of the very allure that had made these acquisitions valuable in the first place.

Chapter Eleven

Luxury Now, Pay Later

The email arrived at 11:47 PM, that twilight hour when rational decision-making surrenders to impulse. "FLASH SALE: Louis Vuitton Neverfull MM now $2,300 (Originally $2,570)." Sarah Chen stared at her phone, the blue light illuminating her face in the darkness of her bedroom. She'd been coveting this bag for three years, saving for it in the back of her mind while student loans and rent claimed priority. She tapped on the listing, her finger suspended over the "Add to Cart" button as she performed the mental calculus she'd rehearsed countless times before. Her marketing salary could technically stretch to cover it, but after rent, loans, and groceries, dropping over two grand on a bag felt like financial recklessness.

Then, a second notification slid onto her screen: "Split into 4 payments of $575 with Klarna. Pay later, slay now!" The words throbbed like a heartbeat against the white background. Suddenly, the impossible transformed into the plausible. Four payments of $575? That was barely more than an extravagant grocery bill, a digestible sum that could vanish into the rhythm of monthly expenses. The transformation was instantaneous and alchemical, from an intimidating lump sum to a sequence of manageable installments.

Sarah's breathing quickened as she navigated through the purchase flow. The familiar Louis Vuitton monogram pattern seemed to dance across her screen, already hers in her imagination. She visualized herself carrying it to the office, the rich leather patina developing character, the subtle nods of recognition from those who understood its significance. For $575 down, less than a weekend getaway, she could join that exclusive circle now, not in some distant future when all her financial obligations might align perfectly.

The checkout page opened like a portal to an elevated existence. The soft tap of her credit card information being auto-filled, the momentary hesitation as she weighed the implications, and then the decisive tap on "Complete Purchase." The screen flashed, whirled, and displayed a confirmation number. Her heart raced as adrenaline coursed through her veins, the physical manifestation of the dopamine surge that accompanies acquisition. By 12:03 AM, Sarah had both a confirmation email and a shipping notification. In less than twenty minutes, she had crossed an invisible threshold, entering the ranks of luxury owners without waiting for the traditional prerequisites of accumulated savings or inherited wealth.

The sensation was electric, a blend of exhilaration, anxiety, and disbelief. This wasn't how her mother had purchased her first designer bag in the 1990s. That had been a methodical process of dedicated saving, perhaps six months of setting money aside, a pilgrimage to the boutique, and a ceremonial full-price transaction. There had been no split payments, no midnight impulse buys, no ability to possess before fully paying. There had been only patient dedication, mounting anticipation, and ultimately, the well-earned reward.

The financial landscape that enabled Sarah's midnight purchase emerged with remarkable speed. Buy Now, Pay Later platforms, Klarna, Affirm, Afterpay, materialized seemingly overnight like retail fairy godmothers, transforming the intimidating price tags of luxury goods into approachable installments with a digital wave of the wand. This wasn't a subtle evolution in market dynamics; it was a revolutionary reimagining of how we access and acquire items that once required months or years of disciplined saving.

BNPL services eliminated the waiting period entirely. Take the item home first, pay later in installments, often with zero interest or fees if payments are made on schedule. The psychological impact was profound. A $2,300 handbag viewed as a single transaction triggered immediate sticker shock and frequently led to purchase abandonment. The same handbag presented as four payments of $575 bypassed those mental barriers, transforming what seemed unattainable into something within reach. This wasn't merely clever marketing; it represented a fundamental recalibration of how we perceive and process financial decisions.

The luxury sector, initially reluctant to embrace these platforms, gradually acknowledged their potential as conversion rates soared. By 2023, Klarna had formed partnerships with high-end retailers including Neiman Marcus and Bergdorf Goodman, while maintaining relationships with true luxury brands like Versace. Affirm boasted connections with Jimmy Choo, Gucci, and Oscar de la Renta. The integration appeared seamless, a simple additional payment option at checkout that subtly revolutionized the calculus of luxury acquisition.

What astonished luxury retailers most wasn't simply the increased sales volume but the demographics of this new wave of customers. Contrary to expectations that BNPL users would primarily be financially stretched young consumers, data revealed that over a third of users earned more than $100,000 annually. These affluent customers weren't using installment plans out of necessity but for sophisticated cash flow management, to preserve credit card limits for other purposes, or to optimize rewards programs. What began as a tool for democratizing luxury had evolved into a multifaceted financial instrument appealing across income brackets.

The rise of BNPL coincided with, and arguably accelerated, a shift in how we think about luxury acquisition. The traditional luxury journey had been one of patience, dedication, and delayed gratification. You saved diligently, perhaps for years, before making a significant purchase. The anticipation was part of the experience, the waiting a form of initiation that enhanced the eventual reward. BNPL compressed this timeframe dramatically, removing the waiting period while preserving the reward. The psychological weight of the purchase was distributed across time, but the gratification remained immediate.

This shift was perhaps most dramatic for younger luxury consumers. For Gen Z and Millennials who came of age during economic uncertainty, who watched parents struggle through recessions, who graduated into challenging job markets with significant student debt, traditional paths to luxury ownership often seemed impossibly distant. BNPL services created a bypass, a mechanism for experiencing luxury without waiting for financial circumstances that might never materialize.

By 2024, the global BNPL market had swelled to nearly $500 billion, with projections suggesting it could reach $825 billion by 2029. What had begun as a niche financial innovation had become a dominant force reshaping not just how we pay, but our fundamental relationship with desire, acquisition, and ownership.

While BNPL platforms were transforming the primary luxury market, another revolution was unfolding on parallel tracks. The luxury resale market, once the domain of dusty consignment shops and risky eBay transactions, was undergoing a spectacular metamorphosis. Digital platforms like The RealReal, Vestiaire Collective, and Fashionphile had transformed the "secondhand" market into the more appealingly termed "pre-loved" or "vintage" category, removing the stigma while creating new pathways to luxury ownership.

A Chanel flap bag that might retail for $9,000 new could be found in excellent condition for $4,500 on these authenticated platforms. Hermès Birkins that were practically unobtainable through official channels due to artificially limited supply and relationship requirements suddenly became accessible, still breathtakingly expensive, but purchasable without having to develop a relationship with a sales associate or spend thousands on scarves and homeware first. These platforms didn't just offer discounted luxury; they democratized access to items that had been kept deliberately scarce.

The psychological transformation was profound. What had once been whispered about as "used goods" became celebrated as "vintage treasures" or "investment pieces." The narrative shifted from depreciation to appreciation, from compromise to sophistication. Social media influencers showcased their "vintage finds" alongside new purchases, sometimes highlighting the superior quality of older pieces compared to current production.

The resale market's explosive growth reflected these psychological appeals. From a niche market worth approximately $5 billion in 2010, luxury resale exploded to a $25-30 billion industry by 2020, with projections suggesting it could reach $50 billion by 2025. This wasn't simply a matter of economic necessity driving consumers to more affordable options; it represented a fundamental shift in how luxury was perceived, acquired, and valued.

For luxury brands, this secondary market represented both opportunity and threat. On one hand, strong resale values enhanced a brand's reputation for quality and timelessness. On the other, brands had no direct control over pricing, presentation, or authenticity in these channels. Some houses responded by launching their own certified pre-owned programs, attempting to recapture control of their products' second lives.

What remained undeniable was that resale, like BNPL, had transformed luxury from something you aspired to and eventually achieved into something you could access now, through alternative channels. The democratizing effect was powerful. The same forces that had once kept luxury exclusive, limited production, controlled distribution, premium pricing, were being circumvented through digital innovation.

The financial innovations enabling wider luxury access did more than change how we paid; they fundamentally altered how we think about luxury, value, and desire itself. Payment fragmentation, breaking a forbidding total into manageable chunks, performed a kind of psychological alchemy, transforming the impossible into the attainable without changing the actual price. The mind's natural tendency to focus on immediate costs rather than total expenditure made $575 four times seem entirely different from $2,300 once, even though the mathematical reality remained identical.

This cognitive sleight-of-hand built on well-established psychological principles. Behavioral economists had long observed what they termed "present bias," our tendency to dramatically discount future costs and benefits compared to immediate ones. When faced with four payments of $575, our brains registered primarily the first payment due immediately, with the subsequent payments fading into a hazy future.

Social media magnified these psychological dynamics exponentially. Instagram and TikTok created what researchers termed "social proof loops," where visibility of others making similar purchases validated individual decisions. Witnessing friends or influencers showcasing luxury items, often without disclosure of how they were financed, created both desire and a false sense of normalcy around these purchases.

"I remember when I got my first notification that my payment for my Prada bag was due," recalled Jessica Lin, a twenty-six-year-old graphic designer. "I was at dinner with friends, having just spent $95 on cocktails and appetizers without thinking twice. The $387.50 installment suddenly seemed ridiculous to stress about in comparison. What I didn't calculate was how those payments would keep coming, every two weeks, long after the initial excitement had faded."

What made BNPL particularly effective was its ability to restart this emotional cycle before the previous one concluded. By the time remorse might materialize around the third or fourth payment, many consumers were already contemplating or completing their next purchase, creating overlapping waves of acquisition excitement that masked the less pleasant phases of the consumption cycle.

This fragmentation affected not just financial decision-making but our relationship with delayed gratification and the luxury journey itself. Traditionally, luxury purchases represented milestones, achievements marked by careful saving, thoughtful selection, and eventual reward. The waiting period wasn't merely a financial necessity but a psychological space where anticipation built, research deepened, and the eventual acquisition gained meaning beyond the object itself. BNPL collapsed this timeframe, delivering the reward before the effort, fundamentally transforming the psychological experience of luxury consumption.

As financial innovation transformed the acquisition process, a parallel narrative emerged to justify luxury expenditures: the investment thesis. "It's not an indulgence; it's an investment" became the ultimate rationalization, recasting what might otherwise appear as frivolous spending into prudent financial planning. This framing wasn't entirely novel, certain watches and jewelry had long been considered stores of value, but it expanded dramatically as resale platforms provided transparent data on secondary market valuations and price trends.

The Hermès Birkin bag emerged as the quintessential example of this phenomenon, its status as an "investment piece" cemented by eye-catching auction results and seemingly relentless appreciation. A Matte Himalaya Niloticus Crocodile Birkin 35 with 18k White Gold & Diamond Hardware commanded an astounding $300,322 at a 2018 Hong Kong auction, shattering previous records and generating headlines worldwide. Even standard Birkins showed impressive returns: models purchased for $2,000 in 1984 were fetching $13,200 in 2020, a 166% return when adjusted for inflation.

According to Knight Frank's Luxury Investment Index, luxury handbags were the top-performing collectible investment in 2019 with a 13% annual return, outperforming art (5%), stamps (6%), and even fine wine. During turbulent economic times following the pandemic, while traditional investments fluctuated wildly, certain luxury categories showed remarkable resilience.

The investment narrative dramatically transformed how consumers approached luxury purchases. Rather than asking simply, "Can I afford this?" or "Do I love this?" potential buyers began considering questions like "Will this hold its value?" and "What's the potential appreciation?" Shopping evolved into a form of portfolio management, with considerations of brand heritage, limited availability, and historical performance influencing purchasing decisions that had once been primarily emotional.

Social media elevated this investment narrative into performative status display. Users shared screenshots of price histories alongside unboxing videos, highlighting potential appreciation rather than merely aesthetic appeal. "Just added this Chanel Classic Flap to my investment portfolio " became a common caption, the financial framing providing social validation for what might otherwise be perceived as materialism or extravagance.

The investment frame offered particularly compelling justification for purchases facilitated by BNPL services. If a bag was projected to appreciate by 10% annually, using Klarna or Affirm to finance it could be reimagined as a shrewd financial move rather than impulsive consumption. "I'm investing $500 down on an asset that will gain 15% value by the time I make the final payment" sounds more responsible than "I'm charging a bag I can't truly afford."

What remained largely unaddressed in this narrative was the highly selective nature of luxury appreciation. While Birkins, certain Chanel models, and limited-edition pieces indeed showed impressive returns, the vast majority of luxury purchases declined in value the moment they left the boutique. Mass-produced items, seasonal designs, and heavily logo-emblazoned pieces rarely retained value, let alone appreciated. The investment narrative was valid for a narrow subset of the luxury market but was applied much more broadly as rationalization for general luxury consumption.

The financial democratization of luxury didn't impact all consumers equally. Distinct generational attitudes toward debt, ownership, and status created dramatically different responses to BNPL and resale platforms. These weren't merely variations in preference; they reflected profound differences in financial circumstances, formative experiences, and value systems that shaped each generation's luxury journey.

Baby Boomers, who matured during post-war prosperity, typically maintained traditional perspectives on luxury acquisition: save first, purchase outright, own completely. They regarded BNPL services with skepticism, often preferring credit cards for substantial purchases despite potentially higher interest rates.

"I paid cash for my first Gucci bag in 1985," recalled Patricia Morrison, now 68. "I'd saved for eighteen months, and walking into that boutique knowing I could pay in full was a moment of genuine accomplishment. I doubt I would have experienced the same satisfaction if I'd walked out still owing three-quarters of the price."

Gen Z displayed the most dramatic divergence from traditional luxury pathways. Having grown up during radical digital transformation and economic uncertainty, they approached luxury with distinct perspectives on ownership, investment, and status. Their comfort with BNPL was notably higher than older generations, with projected adoption rates reaching 47.4% by 2025.

"For my generation, credit cards feel predatory," explained Alex Kim, a twenty-two-year-old fashion student. "BNPL is transparent, four payments, no hidden interest if you pay on time. When I buy a designer piece for my portfolio shoots, I'm investing in my career. The payments are just part of the process."

Perhaps most significantly, younger generations showed greater comfort with fluid ownership models. Where Baby Boomers and even Gen X often viewed luxury items as lifetime acquisitions to be eventually passed down, Millennials and Gen Z frequently participated in circular consumption patterns, buying pre-owned, enjoying items temporarily, then reselling to fund the next purchase. This approach transformed luxury consumption from a rare, significant life event into an ongoing cycle of acquisition and divestment, facilitated by resale platforms and financing options.

As financial tools like BNPL and resale platforms dramatically expanded access to luxury goods, a subtle but profound shift began to occur, not the death of luxury, as some predicted, but a migration of its essential allure. This quality, the ineffable essence that transforms expensive items into objects of desire beyond their material value, didn't disappear as access broadened. Instead, it began flowing toward new expressions of exclusivity, creating a perpetual cycle of desire, access, dilution, and rediscovery that had characterized luxury throughout its history.

The earliest indicators of this acceleration appeared gradually yet unmistakably. As logo-heavy designs from major houses became increasingly accessible through BNPL platforms, discerning luxury consumers gravitated toward more understated pieces. The psychological reward of luxury ownership had traditionally stemmed partly from recognition, the knowing acknowledgment from those "in the know." As recognition became too widespread, the status value diminished, driving a search for new, less conspicuous signifiers.

"Three years ago, everyone at brunch had a Louis Vuitton Neverfull or a Gucci Marmont," observed Emma Richards, a thirty-two-year-old lifestyle blogger. "Now, the women who were carrying those bags are showing up with Loewe, Bottega Veneta, or The Row, brands with minimal or no visible logos. The people who know, know. And those who don't, don't. That's the whole point."

The wealth signifiers themselves were evolving. As designer logos became accessible through installment payments and resale platforms, status increasingly attached to experiences rather than objects, access to exclusive events, limited-edition collaborations, or personalized services. The allure migrated from simply owning luxury to experiencing it in ways that couldn't be fragmented into installment payments or purchased secondhand.

For luxury brands, this transformation created complex strategic challenges. The financial democratization that fueled short-term growth simultaneously accelerated the dilution cycle that threatened long-term desirability. Maintaining exclusivity while embracing tools that fundamentally expanded access required increasingly sophisticated market segmentation.

Sarah Chen experienced this evolution firsthand. Six months after her midnight Neverfull purchase, as she completed the final Klarna payment, she realized her relationship with the bag had transformed. The initial exhilaration had faded, replaced by comfortable familiarity. But her social media feed now showcased fresh objects of desire, limited-edition collaborations, vintage pieces from the 1990s, emerging designers with smaller production runs. The allure hadn't vanished from her Louis Vuitton; it had simply migrated to the next horizon of desirability, one requiring its own financial strategy and acquisition journey.

This perpetual migration wasn't a failure of the concept but its essential nature, an endless cycle of desire, acquisition, normalization, and renewed desire that has defined luxury consumption throughout history. Financial democratization didn't disrupt this cycle but accelerated it, compressing timeframes and broadening participation while preserving the fundamental human drives that keep the cycle turning: the desire for beauty, for status, for something extraordinary that exists just beyond our current grasp.

Chapter Twelve

Entry-Level Empire

T he autumn light cascaded through the windows of LVMH's Parisian headquarters, casting a golden glow across the burnished mahogany conference table where twelve executives sat, dressed in identical navy suits with subtle variations that only the initiated could detect: a hand-rolled edge on a pocket square, the barely-there Berluti patina on a shoe, the whisper of a Loro Piana cashmere blend in a jacket. On the wall-mounted screen, a PowerPoint slide displayed what appeared, at first glance, to be a straightforward financial projection. Yet the numbers represented nothing less than the complete reimagining of luxury's potential.

"Gentlemen," began the head of strategy, a man who had ascended at LVMH after completing his MBA at INSEAD, "what you're examining is the projected revenue for a single Dior lipstick launch compared to an entire seasonal ready-to-wear collection." His manicured finger tapped on the screen where two bar graphs stood side by side, one modestly tall, representing the clothing line that would grace fashion magazines and runways; the other soaring to three times the height, representing a simple tube of pigmented wax encased in navy blue packaging.

Someone emitted a low whistle. Bernard Arnault, seated at the head of the table, permitted himself the faintest smile, not of surprise, for he had understood this particular mathematics for decades, but of satisfaction at seeing his vision so elegantly quantified. The strategy head continued, "The lipstick requires minimal development cost, can be produced at scale, and will retail for forty-two euros. Our analysis indicates we can distribute three million units globally in the first year alone."

A second set of graphs appeared, comparing the anticipated profit margins. The ready-to-wear collection, with its hand-finished details and limited production runs, would operate at perhaps 30% margin. The lipstick line, despite its luxury positioning, would yield nearly 85% once at scale. Fashion was art; cosmetics were alchemy, transforming basic ingredients into pure profit through the magic of desire.

Another executive, this one from customer analytics, took control of the presentation. "We've mapped the customer journey," she explained, advancing to a new slide that displayed a pyramid. At the foundation sat fragrance and cosmetics, then small leather goods and accessories, followed by ready-to-wear, then handbags, and finally high jewelry and couture at the summit. "Our data confirms that 68% of customers who begin with beauty products progress to a leather goods purchase within three years. One-third of those eventually become ready-to-wear clients."

The room fell silent as the executives contemplated the implications. They weren't merely selling cosmetics or wallets or sunglasses; they were architecting an ascension path, a deliberately crafted staircase of desire that would guide consumers upward through the luxury hierarchy. The entry products weren't simply profitable in themselves; they were the front doors to the temple, the first taste of a luxury journey that might span decades and, ideally, generations.

Arnault cleared his throat. "The challenge," he said, his voice quiet but commanding absolute attention, "is balance." He rose and approached the screen, indicating the pyramid. "We must ensure that the experience at each tier feels authentically luxurious, while maintaining clear differentiation between levels." His finger moved to the pyramid's foundation. "Those entering here must feel they possess something genuine, something exceptional, but they must also, eventually, desire what lies above."

What Arnault articulated wasn't merely a pricing strategy but a psychological architecture, one designed to satisfy immediate desire while simultaneously cultivating new aspirations. It relied on a delicate calibration that would become the defining challenge of modern luxury: how to be simultaneously accessible and exclusive, both democratic and aristocratic, both global behemoth and intimate artisan.

The elegant simplicity of a Christian Dior lipstick in its navy case, just thirty grams of product sealed in a metal tube, disguised the strategic complexity behind its existence. In LVMH's expansive portfolio, these small indulgences represented not minor additions but deliberate entry points calculated to perform psychological and financial functions far beyond their physical dimensions. The creation of these gateways to luxury embodied one of the most consequential business transformations of the early 2000s, fundamentally altering the relationship between aspiration and acquisition.

Fragrance emerged as perhaps the ideal entry category. A bottle of J'adore Dior, retailing for $80, delivered a multisensory luxury experience at an attainable price point. The purchase offered genuine luxury pleasure: the substantial weight of the cut-glass bottle with its distinctive golden neck, the lingering notes of jasmine and bergamot that evoked Mediterranean gardens, the recognizable silhouette on the bathroom shelf that signaled discernment. The olfactory connection created an intimate bond with the brand that transcended the visual.

Small leather goods performed similar gateway functions through different mechanisms. A Louis Vuitton card holder, while representing a significant investment at $250-350, provided an authentic piece of the brand's heritage materials and craftsmanship at roughly one-tenth the price of a handbag. The sensory aspects were equally compelling:

the distinctive aroma of treated canvas or leather, the perfect alignment of the monogram pattern, the butter-smooth glide of a zipper.

Sunglasses presented a particularly visible entry option. When Luxottica secured licenses to produce eyewear for virtually every major fashion house in the late 1990s and early 2000s, they established a category that combined practical utility with prominent brand signaling. A pair of Gucci or Chanel sunglasses transformed an everyday accessory into a brand statement visible from across the street, offering high brand exposure for a relatively moderate investment of $300-500.

These entry categories shared essential characteristics that made them ideal gateways to luxury brands. They required no sizing, eliminating a major barrier to online or impulse purchasing. They delivered high tactile or sensory pleasure, providing genuine luxury experiences despite their accessibility. They featured clear brand identification, offering the status benefits of luxury ownership. And crucially, they could be manufactured at substantial scale without compromising their fundamental luxury character, at least in theory.

The financial mathematics proved irresistible. L'Oréal's luxury division, which produced cosmetics and fragrances for brands including Yves Saint Laurent, Armani, and Ralph Lauren under license, reported operating margins exceeding 20% in the early 2000s on revenues of several billion euros. LVMH's Selective Retailing segment, which included Sephora, grew to contribute nearly 30% of total group revenue. These entry categories weren't merely supporting players but increasingly the financial foundations of luxury conglomerates.

Behind these accessible products lay sophisticated marketing architectures. Promotional materials intentionally juxtaposed entry items alongside more exclusive offerings, establishing visual connections between a €50 lipstick and a €5,000 handbag. Store displays positioned small leather goods near their more expensive relatives, encouraging aspirational comparisons. Advertising campaigns featured recognizable house codes, Dior's cannage pattern, Vuitton's monogram, Gucci's red and green stripe, across all price points, crafting a unified brand identity that encompassed everything from the moderately accessible to the wildly exclusive.

The true strategic brilliance resided in the "ladder of ascension" these products established. Beauty purchases often led to small accessories, which led to larger investments, with each step reinforcing brand loyalty while elevating the consumer. "The lifetime value of a customer who begins with fragrance and eventually progresses to ready-to-wear exceeds €250,000 on average," reported one luxury marketing executive in 2008. "The entry purchase is merely the beginning of a relationship we hope will span decades."

This relationship evolved through carefully orchestrated touch-points. A fragrance purchase might include a small sample of face cream, with an invitation to visit a beauty counter for a complimentary consultation. A card holder purchase would arrive in packaging nearly identical to that of a handbag ten times its price, with the same attention to presentation and ritual. These experiences didn't merely sell products; they inducted consumers into brand communities and cultivated their fluency in the codes and rituals of luxury consumption.

The scene unfolded countless times daily across luxury capitals: a young woman, perhaps still in graduate school or early in her career, tentatively approached the Christian Dior beauty counter at Saks Fifth Avenue or Galeries Lafayette. The marble-topped counter gleamed under precisely positioned lighting, creating an island of calculated elegance within the bustle of the main floor. Here, at this liminal space between mainstream retail and exclusive luxury, she would experience her first taste of a storied French fashion house for approximately $42.

The beauty advisor, extensively trained in both product knowledge and customer psychology, would greet her with warm formality, establishing a tone that distinguished this interaction from the casual familiarity of mass-market cosmetics. The conversation might begin with skin concerns or color preferences, but inevitably incorporated references to "Monsieur Dior's vision" or "the house's heritage," cultural capital delivered alongside beauty advice. The lipstick would emerge from a drawer rather than sitting in open displays, presented with reverence typically reserved for precious objects rather than everyday cosmetics.

"The theater of luxury retail commences at these entry points," explained a former LVMH training director. "Whether it's a beauty counter or a small leather goods display, we choreograph every element to convey a concentrated essence of the luxury experience. We're not simply selling products; we're crafting the first chapter of a narrative we hope the customer will want to continue." The experience was meticulously designed to feel like an initiation, accessible yet elevated, welcoming while maintaining exclusivity.

This retail architecture evolved significantly during the early 2000s, as luxury brands recognized the strategic importance of these gateway categories. Where beauty counters had once been licensed afterthoughts, they became carefully controlled brand embassies. Dior, Chanel, and other houses invested in branded fixtures that created distinctive environments within department stores, employing materials and design elements that echoed their flagship boutiques.

Within monobrand stores, small leather goods and accessories moved from back corners to prominent positions near entrances. At Louis Vuitton's global flagship on the Champs-Élysées, renovated in 2005, visitors first encountered a carefully curated selection of wallets, card cases, and small accessories displayed on illuminated vitrines of the same quality used for high jewelry. The message was clear: these might be the most accessible products, but they received the same reverential presentation as their more expensive counterparts.

Staff training emphasized the critical importance of these entry experiences. "You may be presenting a €50 lipstick today," read one Dior beauty training manual from 2008, "but you are representing a house that creates €50,000 couture gowns. Every interaction should embody that heritage." Beauty advisors received education not only in product formulations but in brand history, enabling them to share anecdotes about Christian Dior's superstitions or the significance of the New Look, cultural context that elevated a simple transaction into a luxury experience.

The brilliance of this architecture lay in its capacity to create authentic luxury moments at accessible price points. A customer purchasing her first Chanel lipstick would experience the distinctive black packaging, the interlocking CC logo, the subtle gardenia scent referencing Coco Chanel's favorite flower, and the satisfying click of the cap closing, sensory signatures that delivered genuine pleasure while cultivating desire for deeper brand immersion. The entry product might be relatively accessible, but the experience surrounding it incorporated elements from the house's most exclusive offerings.

Behind the gleaming counters and within the perfectly weighted packaging, a more nuanced reality existed. The expansion of luxury into accessible categories necessitated careful determinations about where quality could be maintained and where compromises were essential to achieve scale and margin objectives. These decisions, largely invisible to consumers but vital to brand integrity, embodied the central challenge of democratized luxury: delivering authentic brand experiences at previously unimaginable volumes.

The material composition of entry products revealed strategic decisions about quality allocation. A €42 Dior lipstick contained pigments from the same Italian suppliers that created custom colors for couture collections, preserving consistent color quality across price tiers. However, the packaging, while visually identical to that used for more expensive products, utilized standard-grade rather than premium metals, with machine rather than hand finishing. This selective approach to quality maintained the experiential elements most perceptible to consumers while finding efficiencies in less immediately apparent aspects.

Small leather goods demonstrated comparable calibrations. Where a premium Louis Vuitton bag featured eight stitches per inch secured with beeswax-treated thread, an entry-level card holder might employ six stitches per inch and standard thread, a minor compromise in durability that remained imperceptible to all but the most discerning observers. The canvas or leather exterior retained identical specifications to those used in premier products, preserving the tactile experience and visual presentation, while interior materials might be simplified.

Production methods evolved significantly to accommodate increased volumes. Traditional luxury production involved individual artisans completing entire pieces from start to finish. As entry categories expanded, houses adopted partial assembly line approaches where specialists performed specific tasks, one cutting materials, another stitching, a third applying edge treatments, increasing efficiency while maintaining human involvement at each stage. This allowed scaled production without the complete mechanization that would undermine luxury positioning.

The geographic distribution of production revealed another dimension of calculated compromise. While heritage houses maintained French or Italian production for their premier offerings, entry categories increasingly shifted to carefully controlled facilities in lower-cost regions. Louis Vuitton expanded production from traditional French workshops to sites in Spain and the United States. "Made in France" remained the rule for iconic handbags, while small accessories might feature more ambiguous "Made in EU" labeling, technically accurate but lacking the cachet of specific French provenance.

Consumer perception research guided these decisions. A 2008 study commissioned by a major luxury group found that certain quality markers disproportionately influenced perception: weight suggested quality more reliably than stitching detail; hardware finish impacted perception more than interior materials; packaging presentation outweighed product durability in initial quality assessment. These insights allowed strategic allocation of resources to elements that most effectively communicated luxury values.

The expansion of entry-level luxury did not unfold uniformly across houses. Different brands, guided by varying philosophies, ownership structures, and market positions, developed distinctive approaches to the democratization challenge. These strategic divergences revealed not merely different business models but fundamentally different conceptions of luxury itself.

LVMH, under Bernard Arnault's direction, embraced perhaps the most sophisticated approach to tiered accessibility. Rather than democratizing individual brands completely, the conglomerate maintained a portfolio spanning various exclusivity levels. Brands like Louis Vuitton and Dior created internal hierarchies with clear entry points, while still preserving genuinely exclusive categories at their highest tiers.

Richemont, with its stronger focus on hard luxury (watches and jewelry), developed a category-based approach to democratization. The group preserved strict exclusivity in its jewelry maisons like Cartier and Van Cleef & Arpels, where production constraints and material costs naturally limited accessibility. Meanwhile, it explored more approachable entry points in categories like writing instruments (Montblanc), leather goods (Dunhill), and ready-to-wear (Chloé), allowing different product categories to serve distinct market segments.

Hermès distinguished itself through deliberate resistance to conventional democratization. While offering entry categories like enamel bracelets and scarves, the house maintained artificially limited production volumes even for these accessible items, creating genuine scarcity rather than merely perceived exclusivity. "We don't want to be number one, we want to be unique," CEO Patrick Thomas declared in 2009, articulating a philosophy that prioritized distinctiveness over scale.

Chanel developed an alternative approach, using aggressive price increases rather than quality stratification as its primary mechanism for managing exclusivity. Between 2010 and 2020, the house implemented price hikes substantially exceeding inflation across all categories, with its Classic Flap bag rising from approximately $2,850 to over $7,000 during this period. These dramatic increases preserved financial exclusivity even as production volumes expanded, effectively pricing entry-level consumers out of core categories while maintaining quality consistency.

Independent luxury houses like Brunello Cucinelli and Loro Piana largely eschewed the entry-level strategy, maintaining consistently premium price points across limited product ranges and emphasizing material excellence over brand recognition. "We are not interested in rapid growth or becoming a fashion brand," Cucinelli remarked in a

2015 interview. "Our commitment is to exceptional craftsmanship at appropriate prices."

Behind the artful staging of entry-level luxury lay an economic reality that transformed luxury from elite indulgence to global powerhouse. The financial performance of these accessible categories didn't merely enhance luxury groups' bottom lines; it fundamentally reconfigured their business models and fueled extraordinary expansion.

The numbers revealed a compelling story. By 2015, LVMH's Selective Retailing division, which included beauty retailer Sephora, generated €11.2 billion in revenue, nearly one-third of the group's total. Perfumes and Cosmetics contributed another €4.5 billion, while Fashion and Leather Goods (which encompassed significant entry-category sales through small leather goods) accounted for €12.4 billion. Collectively, categories containing substantial entry-level products represented over 70% of total revenue for the world's largest luxury group.

Profit margins in entry categories defied conventional wisdom about the relationship between exclusivity and profitability. A 2017 analysis by a leading consulting firm found that beauty products delivered operating margins of 20-25% for luxury houses, comparable to or exceeding those of their more exclusive offerings. Small leather goods yielded margins of 65-70%, higher than many premium handbags due to efficient material utilization and streamlined construction.

This financial engine enabled large luxury groups to sustain activities that would otherwise be economically unfeasible. Haute couture, the handcrafted, made-to-measure clothing created by houses like Dior and Chanel, typically operated at a loss, with gowns requiring hundreds of hours of skilled labor commanding prices that still couldn't cover their true production costs. These prestigious but unprofitable operations thrived because fragrance and cosmetics bearing the same brand names generated sufficient profits to subsidize them.

The rise of the entry-level empire represented a grand bargain in luxury's evolution, a social and economic contract between brands and consumers that redefined both parties' expectations and experiences. The brands presented what appeared to be authentic participation in luxury at attainable price points; consumers accepted a more commercialized, visible form of luxury than previous generations had experienced. This implicit agreement underpinned two decades of remarkable growth, but by the late 2010s, subtle indicators suggested it might be approaching its natural limits.

The concrete benefits for consumers were substantial. For a few hundred dollars, or even less in beauty categories, one could possess an authentic piece of a heritage luxury house, complete with the signature packaging, retail ceremony, and brand narrative that had once been reserved for the genuinely affluent. The psychological satisfaction of this access, the pride of ownership, the status acknowledgment, the personal pleasure of engaging with quality materials, provided real value, regardless of whether the purchase represented an entry point or a destination in itself.

Brands benefited even more profoundly. They attained unprecedented scale, evolving from niche artisanal enterprises into global corporations with billion-dollar valuations. They established direct relationships with millions of consumers rather than thousands, building vast repositories of customer data and communication channels. They secured financial stability through diversified revenue streams that balanced seasonal fashion with consistent beauty sales, volatile regional performance with global reach, high-risk innovation with reliable heritage products.

Yet this arrangement contained inherent contradictions that became more evident over time. The most fundamental tension resided in luxury's definitional connection to exclusivity. As more consumers carried Louis Vuitton bags, wore Gucci belts, or displayed Chanel cosmetics on their vanities, the distinctive signal value of these items inevitably diminished. A 2019 consumer study found that 37% of long-term luxury customers reported "decreased satisfaction with brand visibility" compared to when they first engaged with premium houses, suggesting the democratization diluted the very exclusivity that made luxury desirable initially.

Quality concerns represented another emerging challenge. As production volumes expanded dramatically, from thousands to millions of units, maintaining consistent standards became increasingly difficult. Online luxury forums by the late 2010s contained growing threads about perceived quality changes, with longstanding customers comparing contemporary purchases unfavorably to items acquired years earlier.

The ubiquity of entry-level luxury created additional complications. As logo-bearing products proliferated across social media and public spaces, their distinctive impact diminished. The Burberry check, once a marker of British heritage and quality, became so widely displayed that the brand itself retreated from its use in the early 2010s, fearing overexposure. Louis Vuitton's monogram, Gucci's green-red-green stripe, and other visual signatures faced similar challenges, becoming so common that they risked shifting from aspirational to ordinary in consumer perception.

By 2019, subtle shifts in strategy suggested luxury groups recognized these emerging challenges. Several major houses implemented significant price increases across entry categories, effectively reducing accessibility while maintaining revenue growth. Others reimagined their entry products with less prominent logos and more subtle designs, responding to growing consumer preference for understated luxury. Some brands reduced wholesale distribution in favor of directly operated retail, sacrificing volume for greater control over the purchase experience.

More fundamentally, the maturation of entry-level luxury coincided with evolving consumer values that complicated its future. Younger luxury consumers increasingly questioned the environmental and social implications of consumption, challenging the traditional luxury narrative of continuous acquisition. The emergence of the secondary market through platforms like The RealReal and Vestiaire Collective created alternative paths to luxury ownership that bypassed official entry categories entirely.

The entry-level empire that had engineered unprecedented growth for luxury between 2000 and 2020 thus approached a critical juncture. Its financial success was undeniable, transforming luxury from niche to mass-affluent and creating some of the world's most valuable companies in the process. Yet its foundational premises, that luxury could be simultaneously exclusive and accessible, that quality could be maintained at massive scale, that visual recognition created sustainable desire, faced growing skepticism from both insiders and consumers.

The grand bargain had delivered extraordinary benefits to both brands and consumers, but nothing in luxury remained unchanged. Just as licensing had evolved into more sophisticated entry strategies, these gateway approaches would inevitably transform again in response to shifting desires and expectations. The cyclical nature of luxury ensured that as one form of access reached its natural boundaries, new expressions of exclusivity, quality, and aspiration would emerge to capture luxury's migrating allure. The entry-level empire had fundamentally transformed luxury's landscape, but the narrative was still unfolding.

Chapter Thirteen

The First Cracks

Victoria Harrington paused before her custom-built closet in her Upper East Side apartment, sliding open the smoked glass doors that concealed a collection worth more than many Manhattan homes. It was late 2009, and the headlines that morning had announced another major bank teetering on collapse. Outside her window, the stark November sky seemed to reflect the economic mood, gray, unyielding, and infinitely uncertain. She pulled out a richly textured caramel-colored cashmere sweater, running her fingers over the barely perceptible Loro Piana label stitched discreetly inside. No exterior branding, no visible logo. Nothing but exquisite material and craftsmanship that spoke in whispers rather than shouts.

"When did we become so loud?" she murmured to herself, eyes drifting to the next section where her mid-2000s acquisitions hung like vibrant, logo-laden advertisements. A Gucci jacket with interlocking Gs marching across the leather trim. A Louis Vuitton Murakami multicolor bag with the monogram printed in candy-bright hues against white leather. A Fendi baguette so covered in double-Fs that the leather base was barely visible. Each piece represented thousands of dollars and a cultural moment that suddenly felt... inappropriate.

Victoria slid her hand across the row of handbags, stopping at a vintage Hermès Kelly from 1993, simple, structured, and elegantly logo-free. She'd bought it during what fashion insiders had once called the "minimalist revolution," when Tom Ford was reinventing Gucci with sleek silhouettes and Jil Sander was creating clothes so understated they almost whispered. Back then, in the aftermath of the 1980s excess and logo explosion, discretion had become the hallmark of true luxury.

She remembered visiting the newly renovated Gucci boutique on Madison Avenue in 1994, gasping at the transformation from the over-branded chaos of the previous decade to Ford's vision of restrained sexiness. The logos had shrunk, nearly disappeared. The designs communicated wealth through materials and cut, not through repeated brand symbols. When had that changed? When had they collectively decided that discretion was no longer the ultimate luxury? And why did it suddenly feel like the tide was turning once more?

Victoria wasn't alone in her reassessment. At dinner parties across the city, she'd noticed a subtle shift. The ostentatious displays, the Vuitton Neverfull totes stuffed with Prada shopping bags, the Gucci belts with prominent buckles, had begun disappearing from the arms and waists of her social circle. Longtime luxury clients like herself were speaking in hushed tones about "vulgarity" and "overexposure," coded language for the discomfort they felt as their beloved brands became increasingly accessible to the aspiring middle class. The financial crisis had transformed obvious displays of wealth from aspirational to almost dangerous, signals of being disconnected from the reality of a suffering world.

She thought back to something her mother had told her about the 1970s energy crisis and its impact on the Cadillac-driving class. "Luxury never disappears," her mother had said, sliding into her significantly smaller Mercedes. "It just learns to hide when necessary." Victoria sensed that luxury was indeed learning to hide again, retreating from logo-emblazoned statements back to subtle signals legible only to those in the know.

By early 2010, the ripples of the financial crisis had transformed into waves that radically altered luxury's landscape. Major fashion houses, once buoyed by years of conspicuous consumption, found themselves rapidly recalibrating their aesthetic approach. At Yves Saint Laurent, Stefano Pilati sent models down the runway in palettes of navy, black, and gray, somber colors for somber times. At Prada, nylon backpacks that had once prominently featured triangular logo plaques were replaced by versions with the emblem reduced to near invisibility. After a decade of expansion and logo proliferation, luxury was undergoing what fashion critics termed "aesthetic austerity measures."

"I'm seeing clients gravitating toward pieces that communicate their quality through materials and craftsmanship, not through obvious branding," explained Marguerite Chen, a personal shopper at Bergdorf Goodman since 1997. "It's exactly what happened after the 1987 market crash. My clients don't want to be perceived as oblivious to the economic suffering around them. Discretion becomes a form of respect."

Chen had watched this cycle play out before. The economic booms of the 1980s had ushered in an era of logo extravaganza, with Gucci, Fendi, and Louis Vuitton emblazoning their signatures across everything from handbags to socks. That excess had given way to the minimalist 1990s, when the "stealth wealth" aesthetic of designers like Helmut Lang and Jil Sander defined luxury as the absence of obvious branding. But as the economy recovered and then soared through the early 2000s, the logos returned, bigger and bolder than ever, culminating in the chromatic explosion of collaborations like Louis Vuitton's partnership with artist Takashi Murakami.

Now, history was repeating itself. The Wall Street Journal reported that sales of logo-heavy products had dropped by nearly 30% in luxury department stores, while "investment pieces," those classically styled items free from obvious branding, were proving more resilient. The psychological dynamics were clear: flaunting wealth during a recession wasn't just tacky; it suggested a dangerous disconnection from reality.

But the logo paradox ran deeper than mere economic cycles. As luxury brands had expanded their reach through more accessible product categories, keychains, small leather goods, entry-level handbags, they had necessarily increased the visibility of their logos. After all, if the primary value of a $300 cardholder was its association with a prestigious brand, that association needed to be immediately visible. The democratization strategy had relied on logos as ambassadors. Now, those same logos were becoming liabilities for the very client base that could still afford major purchases despite the recession.

For the most discerning consumers, luxury was retreating into a more nuanced language, one that required cultural and aesthetic literacy to decode. While the aspirational middle class might recognize a prominent GG logo, fewer could identify Bottega Veneta's signature intrecciato woven leather technique or distinguish handmade Loro Piana cashmere from standard versions. This sophisticated visual vocabulary allowed the truly wealthy to signal to peers without broadcasting to everyone else.

The 2010 launch of Kanye West's collaboration with Louis Vuitton, a collection of high-top sneakers priced at over $1,000, should have been a celebration of luxury's successful marriage with urban streetwear. Instead, it inadvertently illuminated a growing fault line. As fashion editors crowded around displays in the brand's Soho boutique, Victoria Harrington walked in, glanced at the sneakers, and walked right back out.

"The craftsmanship was impeccable," she later told her friend over lunch at La Grenouille. "But I didn't come to Louis Vuitton for sneakers. I came for the leather goods that my mother and grandmother carried. When did luxury houses decide to become... cool?" She whispered the last word as if it were slightly profane.

Victoria's reaction epitomized a widening disconnect between traditional luxury consumers and the urban-influenced direction major houses had embraced. Throughout the 2000s, luxury brands had increasingly incorporated elements of streetwear and hip-hop aesthetics, chunky sneakers, oversized silhouettes, bold logos, and graphic prints.

What began as cautious appropriation had evolved into full-throated embrace, with Gucci collaborating with graffiti artist GucciGhost, Louis Vuitton partnering with Supreme, and nearly every major house appointing creative directors who privileged urban relevance over traditional codes.

The origins of this shift traced back to the 1980s, when Harlem couturier Dapper Dan (Daniel Day) began creating unauthorized custom garments for hip-hop artists using luxury logos. Working from his boutique on 125th Street, Dapper Dan transformed monogrammed fabrics from Gucci, Louis Vuitton, and Fendi into dramatic, oversized jackets and tracksuits for clients like LL Cool J, Salt-N-Pepa, and Eric B. & Rakim. Rather than embracing this cultural reinterpretation, luxury houses initially responded with lawsuits that shut down his operation in 1992.

"They didn't understand how aspirational these brands were for us," explained hip-hop journalist Kevin Powell. "In neighborhoods where opportunities were limited, a Louis Vuitton logo represented possibilities, a visual shorthand for success. What Dap did was recontextualize these symbols, making them speak our language."

By the late 2000s, the tables had turned completely. The very aesthetic that luxury houses had once rejected through legal action had become their design north star. Gucci, under Alessandro Michele's direction, even released a jacket in 2017 that was a direct homage to one of Dapper Dan's 1980s creations, later establishing an official partnership with the designer. The irony was palpable: what was once considered counterfeit had become canonical.

For younger consumers and new luxury adopters, this embrace of streetwear codes felt natural and exciting. For traditional clients, it created profound alienation. They had invested in these brands precisely for their connection to European heritage, craftsmanship traditions, and understated elegance. The new urban aesthetic, with its emphasis on visible logos and streetwear silhouettes, contradicted the very values that had drawn them to luxury in the first place.

"I walked into Gucci last week and couldn't find a single bag that wasn't smothered in logos or some kind of embellishment," lamented Catherine Astor, a 60-year-old Boston socialite. "Everything was so... cacophonous. Where were the beautifully made, simple leather bags that I've carried for decades?"

The disconnect wasn't merely aesthetic; it reflected deeper class tensions. Traditional luxury clients, often from old-money backgrounds or established professional classes, had been taught to signal status through subtlety and insider knowledge. Their approach to luxury was encoded in phrases like "quality over quantity" and "investment dressing." The nouveau riche and aspirational consumers, by contrast, often preferred more legible status symbols that communicated success immediately and visibly. As luxury brands increasingly catered to the latter group's preferences, the former felt increasingly alienated.

While luxury brands had successfully cultivated the Chinese market over the previous decade, by 2012 something unexpected was happening. The very consumers who had enthusiastically embraced Western luxury were developing a more nuanced and critical perspective, particularly regarding the urban, logo-heavy aesthetic that dominated many collections. This shift was especially pronounced among sophisticated clients who had moved beyond initial status-seeking to a more refined appreciation of craftsmanship and cultural context.

"Early Chinese luxury adopters wanted recognizable Western status symbols," explained Angelica Cheung, then-editor of Vogue China. "But as the market matured, consumers began asking deeper questions: Does this design respect our aesthetic traditions? Does this brand understand our cultural values? Is this an authentic expression or merely opportunistic exploitation?"

Similar recalibrations were occurring across Asia. In Tokyo, where luxury consumption had always been more focused on quality and craftsmanship than obvious branding, consumers increasingly favored Japanese brands like Yohji Yamamoto and Comme des Garçons, whose intellectual approach to design transcended the logo-centricity dominating Western luxury. In Seoul, young affluent consumers pioneered a distinctive style mixing Western luxury with emerging Korean designers, creating hybrid expressions that better reflected their cultural context.

This growing dissatisfaction with Western luxury's urban turn and cultural tone-deafness created space for regional alternatives to emerge. In China, brands like Shanghai Tang and Shang Xia offered luxury products deeply rooted in Chinese aesthetics and craftsmanship traditions. The latter, initially backed by Hermès, presented a vision of contemporary Chinese luxury that respected traditional techniques while avoiding pastiche or stereotype.

"What we're witnessing isn't rejection of luxury itself," observed Vanessa Friedman in a 2013 Financial Times column. "It's a sophisticated reassessment of what constitutes genuine luxury in specific cultural contexts. The era of one-size-fits-all global luxury is ending, replaced by something more nuanced and locally relevant."

High-profile missteps plagued luxury houses attempting to engage with diverse cultural contexts. Dior's "Sauvage" campaign featuring Johnny Depp amid Native American imagery provoked fierce criticism for cultural appropriation. Louis Vuitton's "Spirit of Travel" advertisements set in India drew condemnation for depicting the country through a colonial lens of exotic fantasy. Dolce & Gabbana's catastrophic Chinese marketing campaign featuring a model struggling to eat Italian food with chopsticks sparked nationwide boycotts and a humiliating public apology from the designers.

These high-profile stumbles revealed a deeper authenticity crisis within luxury. Brands that had built their identities on specific European cultural narratives, French savoir-faire, Italian craftsmanship, British heritage, were struggling to meaningfully engage with other cultural contexts. The surface-level adoption of cultural references without deeper understanding or respect increasingly rang hollow to consumers, particularly those from the cultures being referenced.

"Authenticity isn't about borrowing aesthetic elements," explained cultural critic Suhel Seth. "It's about genuine engagement with the values, practices, and contexts that give those elements meaning. You can't simply apply a South Asian print to a Western silhouette and call it 'authentic Indian luxury.' That's cultural extraction, not cultural respect."

As consumers became more globally connected and culturally aware, their ability to discern authentic engagement from superficial approximation sharpened. Chinese consumers could instantly identify inaccurate uses of traditional motifs. Middle Eastern clients could distinguish between genuine understanding of modest fashion requirements and token concessions. Indian luxury shoppers could recognize when their rich textile heritage was reduced to exotic decoration rather than honored for its sophisticated techniques and symbolic meanings.

This growing cultural literacy coincided with a broader reevaluation of what constituted "authentic luxury." For decades, luxury had defined authenticity primarily through brand heritage, stories of European craftspeople and founders, often romanticized and carefully curated. But as luxury democratized and globalized, consumers began questioning these narratives, particularly when they contradicted visible realities. How authentic was a "Made in France" label when production had clearly shifted to other regions? How genuine was a commitment to craftsmanship when products showed obvious signs of cost-cutting?

In this context, cultural authenticity emerged as a powerful new form of luxury currency. Brands that demonstrated genuine understanding of and respect for diverse cultural contexts gained significant advantage. Hermès' investment in Chinese luxury house Shang Xia, with its focus on authentic Chinese craftsmanship, represented one successful approach. The brand employed Chinese designers and artisans, drew on legitimate Chinese aesthetic traditions, and created products that expressed Chinese luxury values rather than imposing Western luxury codes on Chinese motifs.

"What consumers are increasingly seeking isn't just quality or status, it's meaning," noted anthropologist Grant McCracken. "Luxury brands succeeded historically because they provided products dense with cultural meaning. As that meaning has been diluted through mass production and superficial cultural borrowing, consumers are seeking alternatives that offer deeper, more authentic connections to their own cultural contexts."

In her elegant Paris apartment near the Parc Monceau, Charlotte Dellal carefully wrapped her collection of logo-adorned luxury accessories in acid-free tissue, placing them in storage boxes destined for the back of her closet. The British shoe designer, known for her vintage aesthetic and irreverent style, had once embraced the logo-laden offerings from major luxury houses. Now she was consciously curating a different kind of wardrobe, one defined by understated quality, artisanal craftsmanship, and subtle sophistication.

"I found myself increasingly drawn to pieces that whisper rather than shout," she explained, smoothing the collar of a perfectly tailored cream jacket from The Row, the luxury label founded by Mary-Kate and Ashley Olsen in 2006. "There's something powerful about wearing clothes where only those who truly understand quality can recognize the inherent value."

Charlotte represented a growing cohort of "luxury migrants," sophisticated consumers actively seeking alternatives to mainstream luxury's logo-centric, urban-influenced aesthetic. These first migrants weren't abandoning luxury itself but rather redefining what constituted true luxury in their eyes. Their migration wasn't just reactive; it was a deliberate quest for a different kind of exclusivity, one based on knowledge, authenticity, and subtlety rather than obvious status markers.

This quieter luxury movement gathered momentum in the early 2010s, with several key brands emerging as destinations for disaffected traditional luxury consumers. The Row offered meticulously crafted minimalist garments with emphasis on exceptional materials and perfect proportions. Brunello Cucinelli created a vision of luxury centered on Italian craft traditions and humanistic values. Bottega Veneta, while part of the Kering conglomerate, distinguished itself through its "when your own initials are enough" philosophy, eschewing visible logos in favor of its signature intrecciato weaving technique that only those "in the know" would recognize.

"What these brands share is a focus on the intimate, tactile experience of luxury rather than its social signaling function," noted fashion historian Valerie Steele. "They privilege the relationship between the wearer and the garment, how it feels against the skin, how it moves with the body, how it ages over time, over how it communicates status to observers."

The financial profiles of these luxury migrants revealed interesting patterns. They weren't necessarily reducing their luxury spending but redirecting it toward different expressions. Many were high-net-worth individuals with established wealth rather than aspirational middle-class consumers reaching for status symbols. Their migration represented a significant potential threat to mainstream luxury brands, as these consumers often had the highest disposable income and strongest influence on taste within their social circles.

"What we're witnessing isn't just a fashion trend but a value realignment," observed cultural analyst Alicia Kennedy. "These consumers are questioning the fundamental proposition of democratized luxury. If everyone can have it, what makes it special? If branding becomes more important than craftsmanship, what justifies the premium price? If cultural references are used without depth or respect, what makes luxury culturally meaningful?"

Victoria Harrington paused on Madison Avenue, shopping bags from The Row and Loro Piana in hand, and gazed at the Louis Vuitton window display she'd once eagerly anticipated each season. The latest collection featured bold logos splashed across streetwear-influenced silhouettes, designs that would have once seemed unthinkable from the storied French house. She felt a strange mix of nostalgia and alienation, like returning to a beloved childhood home only to find it transformed beyond recognition.

"The quality remains undeniable," she mused, "but the soul has changed." With that acknowledgment came an unexpected feeling of liberation. The enchantment she'd once found in these established luxury temples hadn't vanished into thin air; it had simply relocated to new expressions that better aligned with her evolving values.

Victoria wasn't alone in this realization. By 2014, the fissures that had appeared in luxury's gleaming facade in the aftermath of the financial crisis had widened into discernible cracks. The early symptoms, discomfort with logo proliferation, alienation from urban aesthetics, hunger for cultural authenticity, migration toward quieter luxury expressions, were coalescing into a more profound reassessment of luxury's very meaning. Traditional clients like Victoria were actively questioning not just the aesthetic direction of their once-beloved brands but the entire value proposition of democratized luxury.

These questions extended beyond surface-level preferences to the fundamental tension at the heart of luxury's transformation: can something be both exclusive and accessible? The democratization strategy had succeeded brilliantly in expanding luxury's reach, bringing unprecedented profits and global recognition. Yet that very success had inevitably diluted the exclusivity that formed luxury's core appeal. As logos became ubiquitous, as flagship stores opened in secondary and tertiary markets, as entry-level products proliferated, something essential seemed to be slipping away, that ineffable quality that made luxury feel genuinely special.

Industry insiders were beginning to acknowledge this tension. "We've reached a saturation point," admitted one LVMH executive who requested anonymity. "There's growing awareness that we can't continue expanding accessibility without consequences for our most valuable client relationships. The question is whether we can maintain growth without compromising the fundamental exclusivity that defines luxury."

For consumers, the widening cracks manifested in increasingly selective engagement with luxury brands. Rather than wholesale abandonment, they practiced strategic consumption, embracing certain brands or specific product categories while rejecting others, creating personalized luxury landscapes that reflected their individual values and aesthetics. The era of unquestioning luxury loyalty was ending, re-

placed by a more discerning, critically engaged approach to consumption.

Fashion's perpetual rhythm, from the logo-heavy excess of the 1980s
to 1990s minimalism, back to logo prominence in the 2000s, and now
this post-recession retreat, suggested that luxury wasn't dying but
rather shedding its skin. The allure was transforming, not vanishing,
seeking new vessels that could restore the exclusivity, craftsmanship,
and cultural resonance that had always been luxury's true covenant
with its most devoted adherents.

As Victoria continued her walk up Madison Avenue, she passed a
discreet boutique she'd never noticed before. Inside, a Japanese artisan
was carefully demonstrating traditional paper-making techniques to
an enthralled client. The items for sale, exquisitely crafted homewares
and accessories, bore no visible logos, yet their exceptional quality was
immediately apparent to the educated eye. Victoria entered, drawn by
an authentic expression of craftsmanship that rekindled the feeling
she'd first experienced decades ago, when luxury still felt genuinely
magical and deeply personal. Perhaps the cracks weren't endings but
beginnings, the necessary fissures through which new forms of luxury
could emerge.

Chapter Fourteen

Behind the "Made In" Label

I n a bright, perfumed Parisian boutique near Place Vendôme, a sales associate presents a gleaming calfskin handbag to an enraptured client. The bag rests on a velvet tray like a crown jewel, its gold hardware catching the light. "This," the associate explains in hushed tones, "is made entirely by hand in our French atelier by artisans who train for years before touching a single piece." She points to a discreet stamp: "Made in France." The client runs her fingers over the perfect stitching and buttery leather, all tactile promises justifying the €4,500 price tag.

Yet this object of desire harbors a secret. Its journey began thousands of miles away and passed through at least four countries before earning its "Made in France" designation. The first chapter unfolded in a vast factory in Guangzhou, China, where workers cast and polished hardware components. These metal elements traveled to Bucharest, Romania, to await integration with leather components.

Meanwhile, hides from Italian tanneries made their way to Cluj, Romania, where machines cut them into pattern pieces under the supervision of workers earning €400 monthly. The factory floor bore little resemblance to the artisan workshop described to clients; instead of master craftsmen creating each piece from start to finish, it featured production lines where workers performed segmented tasks.

Once assembled, these semi-finished bags journeyed to Portugal for interior linings and quality checks. Only in the final stage did bags reach France, where artisans added the most visible elements: logos, brand-identifying patterns, and final hardware. French craftspeople performed meticulous quality control, completing the "last substantial transformation" that legally permitted the coveted "Made in France" designation.

This manufacturing odyssey, spanning continents and involving workers with dramatically different skills and compensation, remains invisible to the client sliding her credit card across the marble counter. The production reality contradicts both the sales narrative and marketing imagery of ateliers filled with silver-haired craftsmen using heritage tools. Such workshops do exist within most luxury houses but represent an increasingly small fraction of total production.

The disconnect between this handbag's actual journey and its origin story represents the central paradox of modern luxury manufacturing: how to reconcile the craft-centered narrative justifying premium prices with the volume demands of a global business. This tension, between myth and manufacturing, between heritage and scale, lies at the heart of luxury's evolution during the 2010s.

In luxury marketing, birthplace is destiny. The phrases "Made in France," "Made in Italy," and "Swiss Made" function as talismans conjuring generations of craftsmanship and quality assurance. These geographical designations wield such power that brands build entire narratives around specific workshops. When customers pay thousands for a luxury item, they're partially purchasing the mystique of a specific geography imbued with craftsmanship heritage.

By 2010, however, this geographical narrative faced an existential challenge. The democratization of luxury created unprecedented demand that traditional manufacturing centers couldn't satisfy. A

Parisian workshop once producing hundreds of bags annually now needed to output thousands. This impossibility forced executives to confront a strategic dilemma: expand manufacturing while preserving the illusion that nothing had changed.

The expansion first targeted nearby countries with lower labor costs. Southern and Eastern European countries, Spain, Portugal, Romania, Bulgaria, evolved into vital production hubs throughout the 2010s. The economics proved irresistible: a skilled Romanian leather worker earned approximately one-tenth the salary of their Parisian counterpart. By 2015, substantial production for nearly all major luxury houses had migrated to these regions, though this shift remained absent from brand communications.

The legal framework facilitating this geographic sleight-of-hand lies in the concept of "last substantial transformation." Under EU regulations, if the final significant manufacturing step occurs in France or Italy, the resulting product can legally carry the coveted "Made in France" or "Made in Italy" designation, regardless of where earlier production occurred. This principle transformed manufacturing strategies, with brands ensuring the final, legally significant step happened in traditional luxury centers.

In practice, this created elaborate production choreographies: components manufactured in China, leather cut and partially assembled in Romania, linings added in Portugal, final assembly in France, resulting in a "Made in France" bag. While technically legal, this approach created a growing disconnect between origin stories presented to consumers and the complex reality of global manufacturing networks. A 2018 investigation found over 2,000 facilities across Eastern Europe producing for luxury brands, employing more than 345,000 workers rarely appearing in brand narratives.

Even more discreetly, Asia, particularly China, emerged as a significant production source for luxury goods. China's manufacturing expertise flourished dramatically, with some facilities capable of producing items virtually indistinguishable from European-made counterparts. Brands navigated this territory cautiously, mindful of consumer prejudice against Chinese manufacturing. Prada stood among the most transparent, acknowledging in 2011 that approximately 20% of its production occurred in China, a revelation other brands carefully avoided despite similar manufacturing decisions.

The challenge for luxury executives lay in navigating this tension, expanding manufacturing capacity while safeguarding the origin mystique justifying premium pricing. Some brands invested in technology-enhanced "showcase" workshops in traditional centers, creating Potemkin villages of craftsmanship where visitors could witness "traditional" production while most items were produced elsewhere. Others maintained strict control over final assembly to ensure legal compliance with "Made in" requirements.

By the late 2010s, however, this balancing act grew increasingly precarious. Digital transparency, investigative journalism, and social media made production realities harder to obscure. Consumers began questioning the authenticity of origin claims, particularly as quality discrepancies became evident in some mass-produced luxury goods.

As geographic origins came under scrutiny, material quality underwent its own quiet revolution. The diminutive flap of a classic Chanel bag makes a distinctive sound when opened, a crisp yet subdued click as the interior clasp releases. For decades, that sound represented an acoustic signature of quality, the result of 24-karat gold-plated hardware. Around 2008, something changed. Chanel quietly substituted genuine gold-plated hardware with gold-toned metal alloys. To the casual observer, the difference was imperceptible. To authentication experts and devoted collectors, it signaled a pivotal shift in luxury's relationship with materials, and with quality itself.

This shift wasn't announced in brand communications. It was discovered through side-by-side comparisons of vintage and contemporary items, with newer pieces showing different weight, wear patterns, and tarnish resistance. Internally, the decision was driven by financial mathematics: gold prices had skyrocketed, and eliminating gold plating saved approximately €40 per bag. Multiplied across hundreds of thousands of bags annually, this adjustment represented millions in cost reductions without a corresponding price decrease.

Similar material evolutions occurred across the luxury landscape throughout the 2010s. Traditional vegetable tanning of leather, requiring months to create supple, patina-developing material, was steadily supplanted by chrome tanning methods completing in days. The finished leather appeared similar initially but aged differently, lacking the rich character development of traditionally tanned hides. Laboratory analysis revealed increased rigidity, diminished breathability, and synthetic coatings designed to mask natural variations.

This emphasis on photographability, how materials present in digital imagery rather than how they feel or age, transformed material selection across the industry. Heritage leather types requiring specialized techniques gave way to more standardized alternatives that photographed better, even if they lacked the tactile richness or aging potential of traditional materials.

The strategic calculus driving these material substitutions reflected cold precision. Executives methodically evaluated which changes would be perceptible to average consumers versus which would only be noticeable to experts or over extended time periods. Material decisions balanced immediate appearance against long-term performance, prioritizing the former in an era of rapid consumption where many luxury purchases were made for immediate social impact rather than longevity. As one former LVMH executive candidly revealed, "We stopped selling heirlooms and started manufacturing aspirational accessories designed for a three-to-five-year lifecycle."

These material changes were inextricably bound to manufacturing scale. Traditional materials often couldn't be sourced in sufficient quantities or required techniques incompatible with industrial processes. Exotic skins became increasingly difficult to source ethically and at scale, leading to the development of "embossed" leathers mimicking their appearance. Hand-woven fabrics were supplanted by machine-loomed versions with similar appearances but different textures and durability.

In each case, these substitutions were recast as improvements when acknowledged at all. Chrome-tanned leather was presented as more consistent and durable. Metal alloys were celebrated as tarnish-resistant. Through meticulous language engineering, material compromises driven primarily by cost and scale considerations underwent alchemical transformation into consumer benefits, preserving the narrative of uncompromising quality even as material reality diverged from this fiction.

As materials evolved behind the scenes, luxury brands crafted sophisticated marketing narratives to maintain the craftsmanship mystique. A Dior marketing campaign from 2015 opens with a weathered hand guiding leather through a sewing machine, the camera lingering on the artisan's fingers, evidence of decades dedicated to the craft. "Every Dior bag passes through the hands of our artisans, whose expertise represents generations of savoir-faire." The scene shifts to a silver-haired craftsman meticulously hand-painting edges and applying hardware. The message is unmistakable: Dior bags are made by hand, by masters of traditional craftsmanship.

Meanwhile, in a factory outside Cluj, Romania, a different reality unfolds. Rows of workstations where young women operate specialized machines. Each performs a single, repetitive task before passing the item to the next station. The production environment resembles automotive assembly more than artisanal workshop. Workers receive training in specific operations rather than comprehensive craftsmanship; many execute their specialized tasks with precision but would be unable to construct an entire bag from raw materials.

This chasm between craftsmanship narrative and manufacturing reality represents one of luxury's most carefully orchestrated illusions during the 2010s. While brand communications exalted artisanal heritage, the realities of mass production steadily colonized luxury manufacturing. Automation infiltrated gradually, beginning with component preparation before conquering assembly processes once considered sacrosanct. Computer-controlled cutting machines sliced through leather with micron precision, eliminating waste while introducing perfect uniformity that paradoxically obliterated authenticity.

To bridge this widening gulf, brands constructed an elaborate linguistic architecture. "Hand-finished" emerged as the favored euphemism, encompassing products primarily fabricated by machines but momentarily touched by human hands for final embellishments. "Artisanal oversight" described quality inspections performed by experienced workers examining machine output. This semantic sleight-of-hand enabled brands to perpetuate craft narratives while achieving industrial scale.

The reality of luxury craftsmanship by the late 2010s varied dramatically across products and brands. Hermès maintained higher levels of genuine handcraft, with artisans completing approximately 80% of Birkin bag construction manually, though even this heritage-focused house had introduced significant mechanization compared to previous decades. Louis Vuitton canvas goods involved roughly 20% handwork, primarily in finishing touches. Investigations into Dior's manufacturing revealed some products contained less than 5% human labor input, despite marketing emphasizing artisanal heritage.

Behind these craftsmanship narratives and material evolution lies a coldly rational financial calculus. In a wood-paneled boardroom high above Paris, luxury conglomerate executives gather around a presentation displaying a single, compelling number: 60%. "This," the CFO explains, "is our minimum acceptable gross margin for leather goods. Anything less and we cannot sustain our marketing investments or deliver the shareholder returns expected from a luxury leader." While creative directors focus on runway innovations, this financial imperative silently shapes every manufacturing decision, from material selection to production location to quality control standards.

The financial architecture supporting luxury manufacturing reveals a fundamental calculation that executives rarely acknowledge publicly: quality degradation becomes profitable when brand strength exceeds consumer discrimination. By the 2010s, most major luxury houses had cultivated brand equity strong enough to withstand subtle quality compromises, allowing strategic trade-offs that optimized profit while maintaining sufficient quality to satisfy all but the most discerning customers.

The economics of manufacturing location told a similar story. Moving production from France to Romania reduced labor costs by 75%. When Romanian wages increased following EU minimum wage adjustments, brands began exploring Albanian and eventually Asian alternatives. This perpetual search for lower costs created what one industry analyst termed "the race to the bottom in pursuit of the top."

Perhaps most revealing was the Italian manufacturing investigation that stunned the luxury world in 2019. A Dior supplier in Italy was found producing bags for €53 each that retailed for €2,600, a markup exceeding 4,800%. When confronted with these findings, LVMH's CFO issued a carefully worded statement: "We had no idea about the situation as it happened with the supplier of a supplier," highlighting the plausible deniability created by complex subcontracting arrangements.

By the late 2010s, luxury houses had mastered what one brand strategist described as "the minimum viable luxury, the least amount of quality necessary to maintain the perception of excellence." This insight drove increasingly aggressive cost optimization, betting that brand power could compensate for tangible quality degradation. Market results largely confirmed this calculation; despite documented quality declines, luxury sales continued climbing, driven by marketing narratives and social validation rather than intrinsic excellence.

As luxury houses navigated these tensions, an unexpected mirror emerged to reflect their transformations. On a marble table in a Guangzhou workshop, two black leather bags rest side by side. To the untrained eye, they appear identical: same distinctive shape, comparable hardware, matching stitching patterns. One carries a €2,800 price tag from a Parisian boutique; the other was produced at a fraction of that cost without brand authorization. This is the reality of luxury counterfeiting circa 2018: not the obvious knockoffs of previous decades, but sophisticated replicas challenging distinctions between authentic and fake.

The counterfeit industry underwent a significant transformation during the 2010s, evolving from obvious knockoffs to increasingly sophisticated replicas that could deceive even knowledgeable consumers. This evolution paralleled, and partly resulted from, luxury's own manufacturing changes. As authentic production moved to regions like Eastern Europe and Asia, skilled workers and production knowledge spread beyond brand-controlled facilities. By 2019, the global counterfeit market had swelled to over \$2.2 trillion annually, with luxury fashion goods representing a significant percentage.

What made these high-end counterfeits particularly threatening was their quality revolution. While previous generations of fakes were easily identified through substandard materials and construction, the new wave utilized genuine leather (sometimes from the same tanneries supplying authentic brands), comparable hardware, and production techniques mirroring authorized manufacturing. Authentication experts increasingly focused on minute details to distinguish real from replica as obvious quality differences disappeared.

This convergence of authentic and counterfeit quality created an uncomfortable dynamic for luxury executives. The most sophisticated counterfeits inadvertently exposed the industrialization of authentic luxury production; if unauthorized producers could replicate luxury quality using standard manufacturing techniques and widely available materials, what remained of luxury's claims to exceptional craftsmanship and unique production methods?

Perhaps most concerning was the counterfeiting of quality itself. As some authentic luxury products experienced quality compromises driven by cost optimization, certain premium counterfeits paradoxically maintained higher quality standards in specific aspects. Some replica producers advertised their use of full-grain leather while authentic versions had shifted to corrected or split leather; others highlighted hand-stitching in areas where authentic products had moved to machine stitching.

What remained undeniable was the counterfeit market's function as a mirror reflecting luxury's own transformations. As authentic luxury

increasingly prioritized brand over craftsmanship and scale over exclusivity, counterfeiters adapted, creating products that mimicked the
visible but copied the compromised.

As the 2010s drew to a close, the technologies that luxury brands
embraced to combat counterfeiting threatened to expose the carefully
maintained opacity of their supply chains. The CEO of a major luxury
house studies a blockchain prototype that promises to trace every component from raw material to finished good. The executive's expression
reveals the industry's fundamental quandary: the same technology offering protection against counterfeiting would inevitably expose the
complex realities of luxury production. "If we adopt this, we can no
longer say a bag is simply 'Made in Italy.' Consumers will see it was
assembled there, but with components from Romania, hardware from
China, and thread from Turkey."

By the late 2010s, a convergence of forces began challenging luxury's carefully maintained manufacturing opacity. Blockchain initiatives
like LVMH's Aura platform, initially embraced as authentication tools,
inadvertently created infrastructure for radical transparency. Similar
challenges emerged from resale platforms developing sophisticated
quality assessment protocols that highlighted disparities between vintage and contemporary pieces.

Consumer attitudes evolved rapidly, particularly among younger
demographics. Gen Z purchasers, influenced by social media transparency and ethical considerations, increasingly questioned traditional
luxury propositions. A 2019 study found 68% of luxury consumers under 30 prioritized authenticity over prestige, with many actively seeking smaller brands offering genuine craftsmanship over established
names with questionable practices.

Social media platforms accelerated transparency pressures. Instagram's evolution from curated perfection toward "authenticity" created spaces where manufacturing revelations could quickly reach millions. YouTube "authentication guides" inadvertently exposed quality
inconsistencies in authentic products.

Strategic responses varied among luxury houses. Some, like Hermès, doubled down on vertical integration and authentic craftsmanship, accepting lower growth to maintain integrity. Chanel responded with aggressive price increases, positioning itself firmly in the ultra-luxury segment while investing in French manufacturing facilities. Others explored technological solutions, using automation to achieve consistency while reducing reliance on problematic labor practices.

The most forward-thinking executives recognized that transparency would inevitably transform luxury's proposition. Rather than maintaining increasingly tenuous claims about production methods or geographical origins, they began reimagining luxury's value as combining exceptional design, brand heritage, and authenticated quality rather than mythologized craftsmanship. This pivot represented a significant evolution from luxury's traditional narrative but offered a potentially sustainable path forward in an age of inevitable transparency.

As the 2010s drew to a close, luxury manufacturing stood at this crossroads: continue investing in maintaining manufacturing mythology despite increasing difficulty, or embrace a new paradigm of verified quality and transparent production. The choice facing luxury conglomerates was fundamental: evolve toward genuine transparency and sustainable quality, or risk catastrophic brand erosion when inevitable exposures occurred. The resolution of this dilemma would determine whether luxury could maintain its cultural and commercial dominance in an age of radical transparency.

Chapter Fifteen

The Instagram Identity

Diana's fingers hover over the tray of fine jewelry, selecting each piece with surgical precision. A Cartier Love bracelet slides onto her wrist with a satisfying clink, joining two more in graduated gold tones. Next comes the Van Cleef & Arpels Alhambra bracelet, its four-leaf clover motifs catching the afternoon light. She layers diamond tennis bracelets in descending order before positioning her new acquisition, a rose gold Rolex Datejust, as the crown jewel of her wrist stack.

Behind her, chaos reigns. Shopping bags from Dior, Chanel, and Louis Vuitton form mountainous piles on her unmade bed. Three colors of the same Bottega Veneta Cassette bag spill from their dust bags, price tags still attached. The floor resembles a minefield of Christian Louboutin shoeboxes. None of this disorder will be visible in the final image, just a perfectly composed wrist adorned with $60,000 worth of jewelry, casually resting on marble.

Diana adjusts the ring light, checking her phone screen. Not quite right. She nudges the Diptyque candle, angles her Chanel No. 5 bottle so the logo faces the camera, and scatters rose petals across the marble. In the background, her television plays "The Real Housewives of Beverly Hills," where Kyle Richards showcases her hermetically sealed cabinets for Birkin bags.

"Perfect," she whispers, clicking the shutter. Sixty-three shots later, she selects the best one, applies the Valencia filter, and crafts her caption: "Sunday self-care vibes #LuxuryLifestyle #CartierLove #VanCleef #RolexGirl #SelfMadeWoman."

Her thumb hesitates over "Share." The algorithm has been brutal lately. Last week's Chanel unboxing barely broke 900 likes, despite costing nearly two months' salary. Would this post keep her ahead? Would followers notice that two bracelets were borrowed from her sister? Would the Affirm payment notification for the Rolex arrive while she was still basking in validation?

None of that matters now. Diana presses "Share" and watches the first like appear, followed by a cascade of heart emojis and "Goals!" comments. The dopamine rush is immediate, powerful, and shamefully fleeting. By evening, she'll already be planning next week's post, perhaps the Dior Saddle bag her credit card can't accommodate but her Instagram persona can't survive without. She no longer recalls the quiet thrill felt five years earlier, alone in her apartment, unboxing her first luxury purchase, a simple Louis Vuitton wallet she'd saved six months to buy. That wallet now sits forgotten in a drawer, its purpose served, its magic transferred to the screen, its joy transmuted into metrics.

When Instagram launched in October 2010, it was a simple square-format photo-sharing app. No one could have predicted how dramatically it would reshape our relationship with luxury. What began as a digital photo album swiftly morphed into the world's most influential stage for identity construction, with designer goods serving as its primary building blocks. The platform arrived at a pivotal moment, just as social media spilled beyond teenagers' bedrooms into adult life, as smartphones democratized photography, and as the post-recession economy left many hungering for aspirational escapes.

As discussed in earlier chapters, Instagram's algorithm learned what caught our attention, creating desire pathways with unprecedented efficiency. But the platform didn't merely amplify existing luxury desire; it fundamentally transformed what luxury meant for personal identity.

Chiara Ferragni emerged as one of luxury's first digital pioneers. Starting with her blog "The Blonde Salad" in 2009, Ferragni transitioned to Instagram where her formula proved deceptively simple: blend high-end pieces with accessible fashion, creating an aesthetic both aspirational and attainable. By 2014, she was collaborating with Dior and Louis Vuitton, her transformation from Italian law student to global ambassador proving that digital identity could be constructed post by post, brand by brand.

As these digital personas proliferated, traditional boundaries between editorial and personal content dissolved. "The Instagram aesthetic" became shorthand for a particular luxury presentation, crisp, controlled, aspirational but with a calculated veneer of authenticity. Brands initially resisted, then cautiously embraced, and finally aggressively courted this new influencer breed. By 2015, Danielle Bernstein (@weworewhat) was earning six figures annually showcasing designer products. These digital tastemakers manufactured authority through engagement metrics.

The parallel rise of reality television accelerated this transformation. "Keeping Up with the Kardashians," which debuted in 2007, evolved alongside Instagram, with the family's televised consumption patterns establishing templates that viewers eagerly replicated online. What began as occasional indulgence morphed into lifestyle expectation. By the mid-2010s, the televised tour of luxury closets had become a reality TV fixture, elevating collection rather than curation as the new aspiration.

For a generation raised on these dual influences, branded accumulation became intrinsically linked to identity. A 2018 study found that 72% of Millennials made purchasing decisions based on Instagram posts, not for the products themselves, but for their potential as identity markers in digital narratives. The value of a designer item increasingly resided in its photogenic qualities, its capacity to elevate one's digital persona above the algorithmic noise. By 2020, Instagram had reached a billion monthly users, with luxury tags among its most engaged categories.

Between 2013 and 2017, a visual shorthand for wealth crystallized that transcended cultural and geographic boundaries. The formerly diverse expressions of affluence converged into a universal language, instantly decipherable across continents. At its epicenter was the "rich girl stack," a precise arrangement of bracelets cascading down the wrist, typically anchored by at least one Cartier Love bracelet ($6,900), one Van Cleef & Arpels Alhambra design ($4,600), and assorted diamond tennis bracelets. This wrist stack evolved into a semiotic system as codified as any royal insignia, immediately broadcasting both wealth and fluency in the grammar of conspicuous display.

The Hermès Birkin underwent a similar metamorphosis. Once the embodiment of French craftsmanship, each bag requiring 18 to 24 hours of handwork by a single artisan, it transformed into the ultimate Instagram trophy. With over 5.6 million Instagram posts dedicated to it by 2020, the Birkin evolved from a waiting list curiosity to an investment asset appreciating 500% in value over 35 years, outperforming both the S&P 500 and gold. In this transformation, something fundamental shifted. The appreciation for minute details, the saddle stitching, the carefully turned edges, the subtle tonal variations of different leathers, became subordinate to the bag's recognizability on a small smartphone screen.

Reality television propelled this standardization. Shows like "The Real Housewives" franchise established behavioral templates for consumption, each season escalating expectations. What began as occasional indulgence transmuted into lifestyle requirement, with cast members' worth increasingly gauged by closet dimensions and collection breadth.

This standardization permeated beyond products to environments. The luxury closet tour emerged as a fixture of both reality television and social media, with strikingly consistent aesthetics across different personalities and platforms. The visual lexicon became unmistakable: pristine white cabinetry with glass doors, central island display cases, specialized handbag shelving, and invariably a vintage Louis Vuitton trunk as decorative accent. These spaces weren't conceived for practical storage but for documentation, elaborately designed stages for the performance of abundance.

The irony of this standardization grew increasingly glaring: the desperate pursuit of individuality through identical status markers. As fashion theorist Valerie Steele observed in a 2019 interview: "When everyone carries the same bag, in the same size, in the same color, with the same charm dangling from it, it no longer functions as a distinction marker. It becomes uniform rather than unique." Yet the platform's architecture actively encouraged this conformity. Instagram's algorithm favored recognizable signifiers, the distinctive GG pattern of Gucci, the quilted leather of Chanel, the crimson soles of Louboutin, creating a self-reinforcing cycle where the most identifiable luxury items garnered the most engagement.

Even language crystallized into formulaic patterns around luxury display. Captions evolved into exercises in rehearsed nonchalance: "Little something for myself," "Just a casual Tuesday," "This old thing." These phrases, endlessly echoed across thousands of posts, coalesced into their own peculiar dialect, simultaneously acknowledging yet disavowing the conspicuous nature of the consumption being showcased.

By 2015, a new form of anxiety had infiltrated the cultural lexicon: FOMO, Fear of Missing Out. While not exclusive to luxury consumption, it found its most potent expression there. Each scroll revealed another unattainable handbag, another rarefied event, another flawlessly curated existence. What had once been intermittent exposure to wealth transformed into constant, inescapable, and algorithmically targeted bombardment.

The acceleration of trend cycles reached dizzying velocities. Whereas fashion seasons once progressed at a dignified annual rhythm, Instagram compressed them into weekly micro-trends. The Bottega Veneta Pouch bag catapulted from obscurity to ubiquitous must-have status

in mere weeks during 2019. By the time average consumers had saved
enough to acquire it, the next It-bag had already claimed the spotlight.

Financial innovation materialized to accommodate this manufactured urgency. Buy Now, Pay Later services like Afterpay and Klarna,
originally conceived for modest purchases, began witnessing substantial adoption for luxury acquisitions. A 2020 study revealed that 42%
of luxury purchases by consumers under 30 involved some variation
of payment splitting. Instagram's shopping integration, introduced in
2018, rendered impulse luxury purchases virtually frictionless: see it,
covet it, divide it into four manageable payments, possess it.

The psychological toll manifested in myriad ways. Clinical studies
documented alarming increases in anxiety, depression, and compul-
sive shopping behaviors among heavy Instagram users. The platform's
infinite scroll engineered a dopamine-driven loop where users sought
temporary relief from FOMO through consumption, only to immediately confront new objects of desire. A 2019 survey uncovered that 27%
of Millennials confessed to accumulating debt specifically to maintain
appearances with peers on social media.

For younger users, particularly Gen Z, FOMO evolved into something
more complex: FOLO (Fear of Living Offline). The pressure to document
every experience with appropriate luxury props became overwhelm-
ing. A simple coffee outing required designer sunglasses, a branded bag,
and carefully chosen accessories. Life events were planned around their
Instagram potential rather than personal enjoyment.

Rental services emerged as both solution and symptom. Rent the
Runway reported that 35% of their luxury rentals were explicitly for
"content creation purposes" by 2020. Users would rent high-end pieces
for weekend photo shoots, creating the illusion of ownership without
the long-term investment. Professional stylists began offering "Instagram styling" services, helping clients create the appearance of endless
wardrobe options while working within limited budgets.

The experience degradation tracked alongside Instagram's rise. As
the platform made luxury goods visible to millions who previously had
no exposure to such items, brands faced a complex challenge: meet-

ing exploding demand while maintaining the exclusivity perception that justified premium pricing. Most opted to increase volume while decreasing service intensity, a strategy that delivered short-term revenue growth at the expense of long-term experience equity. By 2018, weekend lines outside Louis Vuitton, Gucci, and Chanel boutiques in major cities became standard, with waiting times regularly exceeding two hours.

The unboxing ritual emerged as an attempted recreation of the lost ceremonial aspects of luxury acquisition. What brands no longer consistently provided in-store, consumers recreated at home for digital audiences. The typical luxury unboxing video, which accumulated billions of views across platforms by 2020, followed a precise format: slow removal of the shopping bag, careful extraction of the box, gradual untying of the ribbon, reverent lifting of the lid, and finally, the climactic reveal of the item nestled in tissue paper.

As one luxury consultant observed in a 2019 industry report: "Brands want the revenue that comes with mass appeal but the prestige that comes with exclusivity. These goals are fundamentally incompatible beyond a certain scale threshold."

By late 2019, the transformation was complete: the reverent temple of luxury had become a bustling marketplace, with both the virtues (accessibility, energy, community) and flaws (crowds, reduced service, transactional relationships) such evolution entailed. The experience degradation created a curious contradiction: luxury goods had never been more visible yet had never felt less special to acquire.

On a rainy Sunday in 2019, lifestyle influencer Amelia unpacked her latest haul for her 870,000 followers. "Welcome to another unboxing, guys!" she exclaimed, gesturing toward a mountain of shopping bags from Gucci, Prada, Loewe, and Fendi. What followed wasn't the reverential unveiling of luxury treasures that characterized earlier unboxing videos, but a rapid-fire procession of acquisitions, a Gucci Marmont bag examined for fifteen seconds before being tossed aside for a Prada nylon backpack, which received an equally cursory appraisal before Amelia moved on to Loewe sunglasses. Eight minutes and fourteen luxury items later, she concluded with a breathless promise: "Don't forget to subscribe for next week's haul. It's going to be even bigger!"

This evolution from curation to collection, from appreciation to accumulation, defined luxury consumption between 2017 and 2020. Content creation demands had outpaced any reasonable capacity for appreciation. The early luxury YouTubers of 2012-2015 might spend an entire twenty-minute video discussing the craftsmanship, history, and personal significance of a single handbag. By 2019, the "luxury haul" format had become standard, with multiple items acquired and displayed in rapid succession, none receiving more than cursory attention.

Reality TV reinforced this collection mentality. Shows regularly featured castle-sized closets filled with unused items, their tags still attached. Netflix's "Selling Sunset" merged this closet fetishization with real estate, showcasing luxury homes where custom closet systems were major selling features, designed not for functional storage but for optimal content creation.

The decreasing attention span for individual items reflected broader digital consumption patterns. Instagram's feed had evolved from chronological to algorithmic by 2016, prioritizing engagement over continuity. Stories introduced in 2016 and limited to 15 seconds further accelerated this compression. By 2020, the average Instagram user spent just just 1.7 seconds on any individual post before scrolling to the next. Luxury content adapted to this acceleration: more items, less detail, faster turnover.

This shift created a paradoxical devaluation. Luxury items, once treasured for their craftsmanship and longevity, became nearly disposable in digital context, props acquired for content creation rather than objects of genuine desire. The industry term "one and done" emerged to describe pieces purchased specifically for social media documentation, worn or used once, then relegated to closet corners or resale sites. The secondhand luxury market expanded 12% annually between 2016 and 2020, fueled partly by this content-driven cycle of acquisition and disposal.

Language shifted accordingly. The reverential tones of early luxury content, "I saved for this piece for years," "This represents a significant milestone," gave way to casual acquisition markers: "Added another to the collection," "This week's haul," "Can't remember if I had this in black already." This linguistic evolution reflected the normalization of luxury acquisition and the decreased emotional investment in individual pieces.

Behind these changes lurked a fundamental question: what happens to objects traditionally valued for their permanence when they become subject to the temporary nature of digital content? The luxury industry had built its identity on forever pieces, items passed down through generations, accumulating stories and patina. Instagram's content requirements inverted this relationship, demanding constant novelty and creating a throwaway luxury mentality at odds with the industry's historical promises.

When global lockdowns began in March 2020, luxury consumption faced a decisive moment. The traditional drivers, store visits, social occasions, travel, vanished overnight. Yet rather than decreasing, luxury spending accelerated dramatically. Adobe Analytics reported that online luxury purchases increased 31% during the first pandemic months, while overall retail spending contracted. This surge reflected a perfect storm: increased screen time, emotional coping mechanisms, and the redirection of travel budgets toward tangible goods.

For many, social media became the primary window to the outside world during isolation. Average daily Instagram usage increased from 30 minutes pre-pandemic to nearly an hour by May 2020. This intensified exposure to luxury content created new pressure points. The contrast between pandemic anxiety and curated luxury feeds generated cognitive dissonance, a surreal juxtaposition of global catastrophe and continued consumption.

The luxury unboxing ritual took on particular significance during this period. With traditional retail experiences suspended, the ceremonial aspects of acquisition transferred entirely to the digital realm. Influencers adapted quickly, creating "lockdown luxury" content that acknowledged the strangeness of the moment while maintaining consumption narratives. "I know it seems frivolous to be unboxing a Chanel bag during a pandemic," became a common disclaimer, usually followed by "But we all need some escapism right now."

Financial factors accelerated the trend. Government stimulus payments, decreased spending on commuting and entertainment, and historically low interest rates created unexpected liquidity for many middle-class consumers. Luxury brands responded with expanded online presences, virtual consultations, and home delivery services. By summer 2020, many luxury houses had recovered their initial pandemic losses, driven by what McKinsey termed "revenge shopping," the release of pent-up consumer demand after periods of restriction.

Yet this acceleration contained contradictions. The very intensity of pandemic luxury consumption began generating its first significant backlash. As unemployment reached historic highs and economic uncertainty spread, the tone-deaf nature of conspicuous consumption became increasingly apparent. Comment sections under luxury haul videos filled with critical reactions questioning the appropriateness of such display during widespread suffering.

This critical discourse coincided with early signals of a shift in aesthetic preferences. The "Succession effect" began emerging in design circles, referring to the HBO show's portrayal of extreme wealth through understated, logo-less luxury. The show's costume designer had meticulously crafted a "quiet luxury" aesthetic where the wealthiest characters wore expensive yet unbranded pieces in neutral tones, the antithesis of Instagram's logo-heavy visual language. Google searches for "minimal luxury" and "understated wealth" increased 134% between March and December 2020.

Prominent influencers began noticing these shifts. Early adopters like Lydia Elise Millen began incorporating more subdued pieces into their content, moving away from logo-heavy items toward craftsmanship-focused brands like Loro Piana and Brunello Cucinelli. YouTube videos titled "Quality Over Quantity" and "Building a Capsule Luxury

Collection" gained traction, suggesting a nascent correction to the accumulation mindset.

For an increasing minority, the pandemic's global perspective shift prompted deeper questions about luxury's fundamental purpose. When isolation stripped away the social validation aspect of consumption, the intrinsic value proposition faced greater scrutiny. What was the point of status symbols without an audience? What was luxury's role in a world facing existential challenges?

As 2020 drew to a close, subtle shifts began appearing at luxury's edges. Style consultant Katherine Chen posted a video that diverged from her usual content. Rather than showcasing new acquisitions, she methodically emptied her closet, separating items into keep, sell, and donate piles. Her Gucci Marmont bags, once proudly displayed in every color, now struck her as "obvious." The stacked logo bracelet collection that had been her signature looked "busy" and "trying too hard." Instead, she lovingly handled a camel cashmere coat from The Row, explaining its quality construction and timeless design. "I'm keeping the pieces that would look as relevant in photos from twenty years ago as they do today," she explained to her surprised followers. "Everything else has to go."

This moment reflected an emerging pattern. The first significant countermovement to conspicuous consumption was taking shape, not as rejection of luxury itself, but as a redefinition of what constituted luxury. Online luxury communities began noting quality concerns across democratized brands. Forums dedicated to Chanel, Louis Vuitton, and other houses filled with comparative posts examining vintage pieces against contemporary counterparts, often finding the older items superior in materials and construction.

The pandemic's forced digital acceleration intensified screen fatigue, driving desire for physical, tactile experiences. Subtle, texture-focused luxury began gaining traction: cashmere from Loro Piana and Brunello Cucinelli, handcrafted leather goods from Hermès and Moynat, The Row's minimalist designs. These brands emphasized craftsmanship over logos, quality over quantity. Their appreciation required physical interaction; a photo couldn't capture the hand-feel of double-faced cashmere or the perfect balance of a knife-edge welt.

Cultural commentary began questioning the sustainability of conspicuous consumption. Articles analyzing the psychological costs of maintaining digital personas proliferated across publications from The Atlantic to The New York Times. A 2020 piece in Harper's Bazaar titled "The End of the Influencer Era?" sparked widespread discussion about authenticity fatigue in digital spaces.

Despite these early signals, mainstream luxury consumption continued unabated through 2020. The contradiction between growing critical awareness and continued participation reflected luxury's deeply embedded role in contemporary identity construction. This tension would define luxury's immediate future: the peak of democratization containing the seeds of its eventual transformation. The allure hadn't disappeared; it was subtly migrating, seeking new expressions that would eventually redefine luxury altogether.

The Instagram identity had simultaneously expanded luxury's reach and diluted its essence. What would emerge from this contradiction remained to be seen, but the whispered questions were growing louder: When everything is luxury, is anything truly luxurious? When identity becomes performance, where does the authentic self reside? And perhaps most urgently: When the algorithm demands constant acquisition, how much is ever enough?

Chapter Sixteen

Pandemic Paradox

The gleaming glass doors of Louis Vuitton's Avenue Montaigne boutique slid open, activated by the security guard who recognized Camille from behind his mask. Inside, the typically bustling showroom stood eerily quiet. The scent of leather and subtle perfume hung undisturbed in the still air. A single associate waited at attention beside a carefully arranged display featuring the season's newest Capucines bag, its burgundy calfskin glowing under precisely positioned spotlights.

"Madame Dubois, welcome," the associate greeted her, voice slightly muffled behind a logo-embossed mask. "We've prepared the items you expressed interest in yesterday. Would you prefer champagne or still water while you browse?"

Camille had been a Vuitton client for years, but this was different. The store had been closed to the public for weeks during Paris's second lockdown in November 2020. This "by-appointment-only" experience, once the exclusive privilege of the boutique's highest spenders, had transformed into the standard offering for anyone fortunate enough to secure a coveted time slot. Born from necessity to comply with capacity restrictions, this format had revealed unexpected advantages that luxury executives were quietly celebrating.

In the back office, Regional Director Thomas Leclerc swiped through the day's metrics on his tablet. Only twelve clients would cross the threshold today, a mere shadow of pre-pandemic traffic, yet projected sales would surpass a typical pre-COVID Thursday by nearly 40 percent. Meanwhile, across Paris, twenty-eight client advisors conducted virtual appointments from their apartments, sending personalized selections via WhatsApp to clients who had once emphatically insisted they would "never buy luxury online."

"It's counterintuitive," Leclerc explained later to LVMH executives on a global Zoom call, "but this crisis has revealed we can sell more while exhibiting less." The maisons had stumbled upon a revolutionary operational model that created artificial scarcity through limited physical access while simultaneously expanding reach through digital channels, the holy grail of luxury strategy.

This tableau, repeating at Louis Vuitton boutiques from Madison Avenue to Ginza, embodied luxury's pandemic paradox. The façade of exclusivity remained, strengthened, even, by appointment-only policies and restricted physical access. Yet behind this velvet rope, heritage houses were feverishly democratizing their offerings through WhatsApp sales, virtual appointments, social media campaigns, and strategic partnerships with buy-now-pay-later services. The global health crisis hadn't curtailed luxury's ambitions; it had catapulted them forward at breathtaking speed.

"I don't personally see a scenario where it goes back the way that it was," declared The RealReal CFO Matt Gustke in the summer of 2020, his voice carrying the confident certainty of someone witnessing a permanent shift. He wasn't discussing lockdowns or mask mandates, but the astonishing resilience of luxury consumption amidst global catastrophe. While COVID-19 had decimated most retail categories, leaving shuttered storefronts and bankrupt chains in its wake, luxury was experiencing not merely survival but an unexpected renaissance.

The apocalyptic predictions had seemed perfectly rational during the crisis's early phase. In April 2020, Bain & Company forecast a 25-30% plunge in global luxury sales for the first quarter, with three possible scenarios projecting full-year contractions ranging from a concerning 15% to a catastrophic 35%. Industry titans braced for financial carnage, ruthlessly slashing marketing budgets, indefinitely postponing fashion shows, and halting planned store expansions across continents.

But a fascinating phenomenon materialized as weeks of isolation stretched into months of confinement. For the fortunate professional class who maintained financial stability while working from home offices, the health crisis generated twin surpluses: unprecedented savings and abundant psychological need. With restaurants darkened, borders closed, and entertainment venues shuttered, discretionary income that would have funded experiences suddenly had nowhere to flow, except toward the tactile comfort and status affirmation of luxury goods that could be delivered directly to doorsteps.

Rolls-Royce CEO Torsten Müller-Otvös articulated the psychological undercurrent many luxury executives privately acknowledged: mortality awareness was fueling indulgence on an unprecedented scale. "Quite a lot of people witnessed people in their community dying from Covid, that makes them think life can be short, and you'd better live now than postpone it to a later date," he explained in a Financial Times interview. "That has helped Rolls-Royce." The luxurious coffin-makers of centuries past would have recognized this phenomenon immediately; death proximity has always loosened purse strings.

This "YOLO economy," you only live once, manifested in purchasing behavior that defied economic gravity. By December 2020, socially-distanced lines snaked outside Hermès boutiques in Guangzhou and Paris not for vaccines but for Birkin bags with five-figure price tags. The French saddle-maker-turned-luxury-icon would report a staggering

€6.39 billion in 2020 sales, falling a negligible 6% below its pre-pandemic 2019 figures despite months of padlocked boutiques.

Affluent consumers, deprived of their traditional status-signaling venues (the exclusive restaurant reservation, the first-class airplane cabin, the five-star resort cabana), redirected their status expression into photographable luxury acquisitions perfect for Instagram display. Simultaneously, middle-class professionals, confined to the increasingly claustrophobic familiarity of their homes, rationalized luxury splurges as psychological medicine against isolation anxiety, a pandemic-era evolution of the famous "lipstick effect" that historically drives beauty sales during economic downturns. The handbag had become the new lipstick.

By early 2021, the narrative had undergone a complete metamorphosis. Louis Vuitton, Dior, and BMW published triumphant sales reports showcasing figures that eclipsed not only 2020's crisis-affected results but remarkably outperformed pre-pandemic 2019 benchmarks. The luxury sector hadn't simply recovered; it had undergone an astonishing acceleration, as though the global calamity had functioned as a nitrous oxide injection into its engine.

Most striking of all, this unprecedented resurgence unfolded against a backdrop of historic economic devastation. While millions confronted unemployment, eviction threats, and financial catastrophe, luxury conglomerates celebrated record-breaking profits that would have seemed obscene to acknowledge publicly. The health crisis hadn't redistributed wealth, quite the opposite, but it had dramatically expanded luxury acquisition channels, widening the chasm between those who could comfortably afford these status symbols and those stretching to acquire them through credit arrangements, installment plans, and precarious financial juggling.

The sector's extraordinary resilience during global catastrophe illuminated a profound transformation in luxury's fundamental nature, from heritage-focused craftsmanship to emotion-driven consumption. When confronted with mortality's shadow, consumers didn't retreat to practical necessities as conventional wisdom might predict; instead, many plunged deeper into luxury's promise of emotional fortification against an increasingly chaotic world.

"We accomplished three years of digital transformation in three months."

This declaration, echoing through elegant boardrooms across the luxury landscape in mid-2020, carried particular irony in a realm where stubborn resistance to e-commerce had been elevated to a core brand principle. For decades, prestigious houses had insisted that their creations couldn't possibly be appreciated through a screen. The boutique "experience" was essential, we were told. The relationship with a personal sales associate was irreplaceable. The tactile interaction with products was fundamental. Then COVID-19 padlocked boutiques worldwide, and these same luxury stewards experienced a collective epiphany: digital commerce wasn't merely adequate; it was extraordinarily effective.

The transformation unfolded with both breathtaking scope and velocity. Pre-pandemic, online sales accounted for roughly 11% of global personal luxury goods purchases. By 2022, that figure had nearly doubled to 20%. What would have taken years under normal circumstances occurred in a matter of months, catalyzed by necessity rather than choice.

The digital shift arrived in waves. The first, reactive phase focused on survival: rapidly scaling existing e-commerce capabilities, training in-store associates to become remote client advisors, and establishing virtual appointment systems. Burberry, which had invested in digital infrastructure earlier than most competitors, redirected almost 60% of its marketing budget to Instagram alone, abandoning traditional channels in favor of where consumer attention now exclusively resided.

By late 2020, luxury houses had entered a third phase: strategic digital reimagination. Rather than simply replicating physical experiences online, they began designing digital-native experiences that would have been inconceivable before the pandemic. Gucci launched an experimental virtual hangout called Gucci Garden on gaming platform Roblox, where digital avatars could browse and purchase digital Gucci items. When a virtual Gucci bag in this space sold for over $4,000 worth of Robux currency, more than the physical bag's retail price, industry observers recognized a profound shift in how luxury value could be created and captured.

Meanwhile, client advisors who once prided themselves on white-glove in-store service metamorphosed into digital content creators almost overnight. Mandarin-speaking sales associates at Harrods livestreamed product demonstrations to Chinese clients. Personal shoppers at Neiman Marcus curated digital look books sent via WhatsApp. The pandemic had forced a reckoning with a truth the industry had been reluctant to acknowledge: for a generation raised on social media, the digital experience wasn't a poor substitute for physical retail; it was often preferred.

The statistics illuminated this transformation with undeniable clarity. Mobile shopping app installations increased 20% year-over-year in 2020. Luxury consumer engagement on social platforms spiked between 30-45% during lockdown periods. Conversion rates from social media to purchase in luxury categories nearly doubled. The once-distinct worlds of social media browsing and serious luxury shopping had fully merged, creating a seamless pathway from inspiration to acquisition.

The ultimate irony emerged as this digital acceleration coincided with a period of record price increases across luxury categories. As physical access contracted, digital access expanded, and prices rose, creating a peculiar dynamic where luxury goods became simultaneously more visible, more available, and more expensive. The democratization of desire progressed unchecked, while the democratization of ownership became increasingly stratified by financial means.

The explosive growth of BNPL services during the pandemic, up to 200% by some measures, represented another paradox in luxury's democratization journey. The sector historically built on exclusive access had embraced financial tools explicitly designed to broaden access. Major luxury retailers including Oscar de la Renta, Gucci, Neiman Marcus, and Bergdorf Goodman established partnerships with Affirm,

Afterpay, and Klarna, integrating these payment options directly into their checkout processes.

"Today, you have to give lots of flexibility to shoppers, and this is one of the expectations," explained Carl Cunow, co-founder of luxury swimwear brand Onia, which offered Klarna at checkout. The sentiment echoed across the industry as luxury executives, once fiercely protective of their price integrity, recognized that in the pandemic economy, payment flexibility had become non-negotiable.

For brands, the appeal was multifaceted and compelling. BNPL services charged merchants higher fees than traditional payment processors, typically 4-6% per transaction versus 1-3% for credit cards, but the data justified the expense. Consumers using BNPL options spent more per transaction and purchased more frequently. The psychological effect of breaking a large purchase into smaller amounts reduced cart abandonment and encouraged upselling.

Luxury brands cleverly positioned these services not as tools for the financially constrained but as modern, digital-first payment options offering "flexibility." This semantic distinction preserved the aspirational positioning of their brands while expanding accessibility to younger consumers who might otherwise defer purchases. The strategy worked: though BNPL services initially targeted budget-conscious shoppers, by 2024 approximately 25% of consumers earning over $100,000 annually were using BNPL by choice rather than necessity.

The BNPL phenomenon revealed much about how luxury consumption had evolved. Classical luxury theory held that exclusivity through high prices was fundamental to luxury's appeal, the financial barrier created the desire. Yet here were the most prestigious brands in the world actively helping consumers circumvent these barriers through installment plans.

Behind closed doors, luxury executives acknowledged the strategy's long-term risks. "We're effectively training consumers to focus on the installment amount, not the total price," confided one LVMH director at an industry conference. "That gives us pricing power now, but it might create problems when we need to increase prices further." This concern proved prescient when price increases throughout 2021 and 2022 pushed entry-level luxury products beyond what even four-payment installment plans could comfortably disguise.

For consumers, especially during pandemic isolation, BNPL services transformed aspirational purchases into seemingly rational decisions. Bored at home, scrolling through Instagram, seeing influencers showcase luxury items, the psychological distance between desire and purchase had shrunk precisely when traditional spending outlets remained closed. BNPL options reduced this distance further, making each individual payment feel manageable even as the aggregate debt mounted.

"I honestly can't tell which is which anymore," admitted Sarah Davis, founder of luxury resale company Fashionphile, examining two identical-looking Chanel flap bags placed by side. "And that should terrify the luxury industry."

The rise of "super-fakes," counterfeit luxury goods of such high quality they were virtually indistinguishable from authentic items, had accelerated dramatically during the pandemic. These weren't the obvious Canal Street knockoffs with crooked logos and shoddy materials; these sophisticated replicas used premium leathers, accurate hardware weights, proper stitching counts, and sometimes even incorporated authentication chips that redirected to official brand websites when scanned.

The pandemic created what industry analysts called a "perfect storm" for counterfeit growth. As luxury houses outsourced manufacturing to reduce costs and maintain profit margins, they inadvertently loosened control over their supply chains. Factories in the same regions producing authentic luxury goods began applying their technical knowledge to unauthorized production. Meanwhile, pandemic-related factory shutdowns in early 2020 created product shortages, opening space for counterfeiters to fill the void.

The most dramatic development wasn't just the flood of fakes but their astounding quality improvements. In some cases, authentication experts admitted privately that certain counterfeits exhibited better craftsmanship than authentic pieces, particularly for brands that had quietly reduced quality standards while raising prices during the pandemic. When one viral social media post showed stitching inconsistencies in a $9,000 authentic Chanel bag alongside the perfect stitching of its $600 counterfeit counterpart, it crystallized growing consumer skepticism about luxury's price-to-quality proposition.

Social media platforms became central to this distribution ecosystem. Instagram, Facebook, and particularly TikTok emerged as hotspots for counterfeit luxury goods, with "dupe influencers" gathering millions of followers by comparing authentic items with their near-identical counterfeits. What luxury brands once relied upon, the difficulty in finding convincing fakes, had been solved by social algorithms connecting interested consumers directly to sellers.

For luxury brands, the proliferation of super-fakes during the pandemic represented more than lost sales; it threatened the fundamental value proposition of luxury. If a $600 counterfeit could deliver comparable (or occasionally superior) materials, craftsmanship, and aesthetic impact to a $6,000 authentic item, what exactly were consumers paying for? The traditional answer, heritage, craftsmanship, and exclusivity, rang increasingly hollow in a market flooded with convincing alternatives.

"In May, our orders increased by 119 percent and in June they increased further to 144 percent, compared to the year prior," revealed Fanny Moizant, president and co-founder of luxury resale platform Vestiaire Collective, describing the unexpected pandemic boom in secondhand luxury.

While luxury brands were still adapting to lockdowns in spring 2020, the resale market was already experiencing an unprecedented surge. Fashionphile, specializing in pre-owned designer handbags and accessories, reported its highest non-promotional sales day in company history on April 15, 2020, a pattern that would repeat throughout the pandemic as consumers confined to their homes reconsidered both their spending and their relationship with luxury.

The pandemic accelerated a transformation already underway in luxury consumption. Economic uncertainty prompted value-conscious purchasing, while extended time at home led many to reconsider their possessions. "COVID-19 has made a lot of people reconsider their values," Moizant explained. "Sustainability has never felt like a more urgent issue. Many consumers are now questioning how they can enjoy fashion trends in a more responsible way."

This reconsideration manifested in both buying and selling behaviors. ThredUp's 2020 Resale Report found that 50% of people were cleaning out their closets more frequently during the pandemic, creating a surge in supply for resale platforms. Simultaneously, with brick-and-mortar retail largely inaccessible, shoppers spent 2.2 million hours browsing ThredUp in May 2020 alone, a 31% increase post-COVID.

For luxury brands, the explosive growth of resale during the pandemic represented both opportunity and threat. On one hand, a robust secondhand market could enhance the perception of luxury goods as investments, justifying higher initial prices. On the other, every secondary sale potentially displaced a new purchase at full retail. Most concerning was the price transparency created by these platforms, which revealed the growing gap between primary and secondary market values for certain brands.

Some forward-thinking luxury houses began engaging directly with the resale ecosystem. Burberry partnered with TheRealReal, while Alexander McQueen collaborated with Vestiaire Collective. Gucci launched "Vault," an experimental platform combining vintage Gucci items with new collaborations. These initiatives acknowledged the unstoppable momentum of resale while attempting to maintain brand control over the secondary ecosystem.

The demographics driving this trend were revealing. Millennials and Gen Z, already more sustainability-conscious than older generations, dominated resale platform growth during the pandemic. These younger consumers viewed secondhand luxury not as a compromise but as a savvy, environmentally responsible choice that allowed access to heritage brands at more attainable prices. For them, the stigma once associated with "used" goods had completely disappeared.

By late 2021, research indicated that the secondhand luxury market was growing four times faster than the primary market and was projected to double in value over the following five years. This trajectory suggested a fundamental shift in how consumers related to luxury: from a model based on linear consumption (buy new, own forever) to a circular ecosystem of temporary ownership and continuous circulation.

As 2021 progressed, luxury houses found themselves in an unprecedented position. Despite, or perhaps because of, the global pandemic, their financial results had never been stronger. LVMH reported record revenue of €64.2 billion for 2021, a 44% increase over 2020 and, more tellingly, a 20% increase over pre-pandemic 2019. Hermès performed even more impressively, with 2021 sales 33% higher than 2019 levels. Across the luxury sector, profits soared as pent-up demand, emotional purchasing, and digital acceleration combined to override economic uncertainty.

Yet beneath these stellar financial results, contradictions multiplied. The very dynamics fueling luxury's pandemic resilience, digital democratization, payment plan accessibility, secondhand circulation, and even high-quality counterfeits, were simultaneously eroding the exclusivity that traditionally defined luxury. The sector had reached what strategists would later identify as "peak democratization," the point where accessibility and ubiquity began actively undermining the perception of specialness essential to luxury's appeal.

Bernard Arnault, addressing LVMH shareholders in early 2022, showed uncharacteristic concern amid record profits: "We must be vigilant that the extraordinary demand we are experiencing does not lead to ordinary experiences for our clients." This statement acknowledged the central paradox: the more people who owned Louis Vuitton, Dior, or Tiffany products, the less special each item became, regardless of price or quality.

The clearest manifestation of this breaking point came through un-precedented price increases. Chanel implemented four price adjust-ments in 18 months, with its Classic Flap bag increasing from $5,800 in November 2019 to $8,800 by November 2021, a 52% jump with no cor-responding improvement in materials or craftsmanship. Louis Vuitton, Hermès, Gucci, and other major houses followed similar trajectories, with average increases of 25-40% across core products.

These aggressive price adjustments represented desperate attempts to restore exclusivity through financial barriers after years of delib-erate accessibility expansion. Yet they occurred precisely when quali-ty concerns were mounting, fueled by viral social media comparisons between current products and their superior vintage counterparts or between authentic items and their increasingly excellent counterfeits.

For aspirational consumers who had entered the luxury ecosystem through strategically priced entry products, these increases created a stark choice: financial overextension through BNPL services, retreating to the secondhand market, or abandoning certain brands altogether. The democratization that had fueled luxury's expansion began show-ing its limits.

Meanwhile, sophisticated consumers, particularly in China and among younger Western demographics, began shifting their prefer-ences toward less logo-driven, more understated luxury or exploring emerging designers offering quality without heritage premiums. The early signs of what would later be termed the "quiet luxury" movement emerged not as a fashion trend but as a direct response to the perceived dilution of traditional luxury signifiers.

The pandemic had not created these contradictions; it had accelerat-ed and intensified them to their breaking point. Luxury's decades-long flirtation with democratization, from expanded distribution to digital accessibility, from aspirational pricing to payment plans, had culmi-nated in a moment of maximum exposure. The sector's extraordinary financial success during a global crisis masked deeper questions about sustainability, quality, authenticity, and the very definition of luxury in a world where its traditional signifiers had been thoroughly democratized.

As luxury houses celebrated their pandemic resilience and plotted further expansion, the seeds of the next phase in luxury's cyclical evolution had already been planted. The questions that emerged would shape the sector's future: Could luxury maintain premium pricing while continuously expanding access? Would consumers continue accepting price increases without corresponding quality improvements? Could heritage luxury houses compete with both high-quality counterfeits and emerging designers offering comparable quality without the heritage premium?

The answers to these questions would not arrive immediately, but the trajectory was clear. Luxury had reached its democratization zenith during the pandemic, the point where accessibility had been maximized without yet triggering widespread consumer disillusionment. What would follow, as night follows day in luxury's eternal cycle, was the inevitable contraction, reassessment, and evolution that occurs when exclusivity has been sacrificed too completely at the altar of growth.

ACT III
THE MAGIC MIGRATES

We Sought New Wonder

They Chased New Wealth

"True luxury is meaningful, it's authentic. It's the opposite of a logo."

— Phoebe Philo

Chapter Seventeen

Sticker Shock

L isa Park stood frozen before the glass counter in Chanel's Madison Avenue boutique, her reflection fragmented across the pristine surface as though her identity had shattered upon hearing the price. Spring light illuminated the quilted leather Classic Flap bag resting on black velvet. The lambskin gleamed with an almost liquid sheen, familiar yet suddenly foreign.

She'd begun her Chanel journey in 2015, purchasing her first flap to celebrate her promotion, a $4,900 investment that felt momentous but manageable. Three years later, she'd added another at $6,700, wincing at the increase but rationalizing it as inflation. Her most recent acquisition in 2022 had commanded $8,800, prompting a week of spreadsheet calculations before she convinced herself it still represented value.

"I'm sorry, could you repeat that?" Lisa asked, forcing a polite smile.

"The Medium Classic Flap is now $10,800," the associate repeated, her practiced tone betraying the faintest note of apology beneath cultivated confidence. "It's still an excellent investment piece. Would you like to try it on?"

Lisa's mind raced through calculations that suddenly seemed grotesque. $10,800. More than her monthly mortgage payment. Three months of her daughter's college tuition. A family trip to Japan. All for what had essentially remained the same arrangement of leather and metal for decades, unchanged design, identical materials, comparable craftsmanship.

What struck Lisa wasn't simply the number, though crossing the five-figure threshold sent an electric shock through her. It was the vast chasm between this staggering price and any value she could rationally attribute to the item. She'd built a career as a marketing executive meticulously analyzing price-to-value relationships. Her entire professional identity centered on this precise calculation, and this equation simply refused to compute.

"I appreciate you showing me," Lisa said, gathering her camel-colored Max Mara coat, a six-year-old investment piece that had actually become more beautiful with age. "I think I'll need to think about it."

Outside on Madison Avenue, spring sunshine warming her face, Lisa felt something unexpected: profound relief washing over her like cool water. The spell that had held her captive for nearly a decade had shattered completely. This latest increase had snapped the fraying thread connecting desire to rationality with an almost audible *ping*.

She wasn't alone in this awakening. That evening, curled on her sofa with a glass of wine and her laptop, a quick search revealed thousands of similar reactions cascading across social media platforms.

"Just walked out of Chanel empty-handed. $10,800 for the SAME bag that was $4,900 in 2015? Make it make sense. I'm a marketing director and I CANNOT justify this to myself anymore," wrote an Instagram user whose profile showed a carefully curated feed of previous luxury unboxings.

A Reddit thread titled "The Day I Stopped Buying Luxury" had accumulated over three thousand comments in just forty-eight hours. The conversation had that rare quality of genuine viral momentum, the unmistakable signature of a collective nerve being struck.

"They've lost their minds," wrote a PurseForum moderator who identified herself as a twenty-year Chanel client. "I'm not angry anymore, I'm just... done. There comes a point where even the most devoted customer has to acknowledge when they're being taken advantage of."

The most revealing insights came from industry insiders speaking from behind carefully constructed anonymous accounts.

"I've worked in luxury retail executive positions for fifteen years," wrote one commenter whose profile hinted at director-level experience at a major European luxury house, "and what we're witnessing now is completely unprecedented. This isn't remotely about normal price adjustments for inflation or craftsmanship costs. It's a calculated, board-approved strategic repositioning that deliberately severs the aspirational middle-class customer base who ironically built these brands into the global powerhouses they are today."

As she closed her laptop, Lisa realized her relationship with certain brands wasn't ending so much as entering an entirely new phase, one where blind devotion had been replaced by clear-eyed assessment, where the intoxicating alchemy of desire had given way to the cold sobriety of mathematics.

The disenchantment wasn't descending upon Lisa alone. Across the global luxury landscape, from Hong Kong to London to Manhattan, millions of consumers were experiencing the same painful awakening simultaneously, a collective realization cascading through the moneyed middle class like a virus of awareness.

The meteoric rise of luxury prices isn't subjective perception but cold, mathematical fact. The Chanel Medium Classic Flap that paralyzed Lisa with its $10,800 price tag began its commercial journey in the mid-1980s at approximately $1,000, reaching $4,900 by 2015 and $8,800 in 2022, before finally breaching the $10,000 threshold in 2024.

While inflation would have transformed that 1980s $1,000 investment into approximately $2,800 in today's currency, the actual $10,800 price tag represents a staggering 260% premium above what standard inflation metrics would justify, nearly four times higher than natural price appreciation.

This pattern repeats across iconic products. Louis Vuitton's canvas Speedy 30, introduced in 1979 at $150, now commands $1,550, a 933% increase for coated cotton canvas. The Cartier Love bracelet rose from $250 in 1969 to $7,350, a 2,840% increase for an unchanged design.

"What we're witnessing bears little resemblance to standard price appreciation patterns," explains economist Dr. Marian Chen, who specializes in luxury markets. "This represents a deliberate strategic repositioning that weaponizes brand heritage and artificial scarcity to command exceptional premiums. When a manufactured product increases 260% above inflation while production scales exponentially, we've transcended normal business dynamics entirely."

Perhaps most revealing is the acceleration curve. From 1980 to 2010, luxury prices maintained modest 2-3% annual increases beyond inflation. Between 2010 and 2019, as Instagram fueled unprecedented desire, increases doubled to 5-6% above inflation. But the post-pandemic period obliterated all precedents, with flagship items experiencing 15-20% upward adjustments in single years.

Chanel implemented three separate price hikes in 2021 alone, in January, July, and November, followed by two additional adjustments in 2022, creating a dizzying five price changes in an 18-month period for identical products. Louis Vuitton raised prices by 18% in 2022 and another 13% in 2023, before implementing a 2024 pricing freeze that analysts attributed not to conscience but to internal metrics suggesting they had reached an absolute ceiling of consumer tolerance.

Between 2019 and 2024, luxury goods prices increased 54% while cumulative inflation registered just 19%, luxury inflation outpaced general economic conditions by nearly triple. During this same period, U.S. median household income grew by only 15%, expanding the gap between earnings and luxury accessibility by 39 percentage points.

In practical terms, a signature designer handbag that represented 80 hours of median-wage labor in 1990 now demands 200-300 hours, transforming aspirational purchases into economically irrational investments for the middle class.

The $10,800 Chanel flap now equals three months of New York City rent, nearly half the annual cost of in-state university tuition, or more than a car down payment. For upper-middle-class professionals who once formed luxury's reliable customer base, this single accessory now requires the financial planning previously reserved for major life investments.

Most tellingly, these astronomical price increases have occurred alongside unprecedented production expansion. LVMH alone maintains over 5,600 retail locations worldwide (versus 1,300 in 2000) while generating €86 billion in 2023 revenue, hardly the output of small artisanal ateliers. The fundamental equation of supply and demand appears strategically severed, replaced by pricing divorced from traditional economic constraints.

This chasm between retail price and production cost has ruptured the psychological contract binding luxury brands and consumers. The traditional value proposition, exceptional quality, craftsmanship, and exclusivity justifying price premiums, has been stretched beyond recognition.

The collective impact of these relentless price escalations has dramatically altered the luxury landscape. According to Bain & Company's sobering 2024 Luxury Study, the personal luxury goods market experienced its first meaningful contraction since the 2008 Great Recession, as "global luxury consumers, grappling with macroeconomic uncertainty and continued price elevation among brands," began withdrawing from discretionary spending in patterns suggesting permanent recalibration.

Yet more telling than the modest market decline is the profound demographic transformation occurring beneath these surface-level statistics: the luxury consumer base contracted by approximately 50 million individual consumers between 2022 and 2024 alone. This staggering exodus represents considerably more than economic belt-tightening; it signals the mass departure of the aspirational middle-class buyer who had served as the reliable engine of luxury's remarkable growth for more than a decade.

"The democratization of luxury has reached its inflection point," explains retail analyst Marcus Wei. "These brands invested two decades expanding accessibility through entry-level products and fragrance lines that offered a taste of the luxury dream. That strategy succeeded, until they raised prices beyond what aspirational consumers could justify. We're witnessing a structural contraction as millions of once-loyal buyers walk away, their psychological contract with luxury breached."

This affordability crisis manifests differently across generations. For Boomers and older Gen X consumers who recall pre-LVMH luxury, current pricing evokes profound disbelief.

"I remember when Chanel flaps were around $2,000 in the late '90s, a significant but worthwhile investment," shares Catherine Morel, 58, a Chicago attorney. "There was a genuine sense of obtaining something truly special, expertly handcrafted pieces with substantial weight that would endure. Contemporary prices seem utterly disconnected from products that often feel marginally lighter and less substantial."

Millennials who embraced luxury during the Instagram-fueled 2010s now express buyer's remorse, betrayal, and financial anxiety.

Alicia Rodriguez, 36, a marketing director, traces her evolution: "Between 2015 and 2022, I spent nearly $30,000 on designer bags, funds that could have gone toward a down payment. I justified each purchase as an 'investment.' Now I'm watching these brands implement aggressive price increases while quality stagnates or declines. It's impossible to avoid concluding that I was manipulated by marketing that targeted my generational insecurities."

Gen Z consumers exhibit perhaps the most pronounced price sensitivity and brand skepticism among all demographic segments, with Bain's research documenting precipitously declining advocacy for traditional luxury brands particularly among this digital-native cohort.

"I observe my millennial colleagues who entered luxury five or ten years ago, and I can see how dramatically the rules have changed," explains Tyler Kim, 24, a software engineer. "Entry-level items they bought for $500-700 are now $1,200-1,500 for identical products. I'd rather allocate resources toward experiences, actual investments, or products valued for material quality rather than algorithmic visibility."

The digital landscape that once served as luxury's most powerful amplification system has undergone a remarkable metamorphosis, transforming from the industry's greatest evangelical ally into its most unforgiving critic. Social platforms once saturated with aspirational unboxing rituals now overflow with forensic quality comparisons, methodical price increase tracking, and increasingly cynical value assessments.

The hashtag #LuxuryRegrets emerged as a genuine cultural phenomenon on TikTok in early 2025, accumulating over 12 million views in just eight weeks as consumers documented purchases they no longer considered justified. The viral format typically featured the creator displaying their luxury purchase alongside its current retail price, followed by what else that sum could now purchase, from mortgage payments to investment returns to alternatives of virtually identical quality.

This transformation, from acquisition pride to ownership shame, represents perhaps the most threatening crisis luxury conglomerates have faced. When aspirational consumers no longer aspire, when desire curdles into cynicism, the psychological engine driving the business model begins to sputter.

The resulting market bifurcation has cleaved luxury into opposed segments with no middle ground. Ultra-wealthy clients with assets exceeding $30 million continue spending enthusiastically, though their preferences have evolved toward increasingly rarefied, customized pieces.

Meanwhile, the middle market has hollowed out. Former aspirational consumers have diverged: some trading down to contemporary brands, others shifting to authenticated secondhand markets offering 30-70% discounts, still others abandoning status consumption for experiences or investments.

Most revealing is the evaporation of luxury's carefully constructed "ladder," the sector's customer acquisition mechanism. Entry-level items that sold for $300-400 in 2015 now command $900-1,100, pricing out young professionals who historically formed the next generation of loyalists. A Chanel card holder jumped from $325 in 2015 to $950 today, transforming the smallest brand touchpoint from aspirational treat to significant financial commitment.

While relentless price escalation alone might have remained sustainable for many luxury consumers, the concurrent perception of declining quality standards has created a perfect storm of consumer disillusionment. Across meticulously documented social media comparisons and specialist forums, the sentiment among seasoned luxury collectors has achieved rare unanimity: prices are climbing precipitously while quality is simultaneously deteriorating.

"My 2023 Chanel double-flap, which cost $8,800 before taxes, arrived with visibly misaligned quilting, slightly asymmetrical stitching, and a subtly crooked flap closure," shares Rebecca Wong, a 42-year-old financial analyst and meticulous luxury collector. "When I respectfully pointed out these issues to my longstanding sales associate, she examined the bag briefly and informed me, 'That's within our current quality standards now.' For comparison, my carefully maintained 2009 flap exhibits perfect diamond alignment, precisely symmetrical stitching, and immaculate hardware alignment, while having cost significantly less than half today's price."

Social media has accelerated consumer awareness, functioning as documentation systems and forensic comparison tools that dismantle information asymmetries previously benefiting luxury houses. One influential video series with 8.7 million views systematically compared a 1996 Chanel flap with its 2023 counterpart. The analysis revealed thinner lambskin leather (1.2mm vs. 1.6mm), lighter-weight chain (25% reduction), simplified edge finishing, and decreased interior fabric density, despite the newer bag costing quadruple its predecessor after inflation adjustment.

"These comparison videos created a watershed moment in luxury consumer psychology," explains Dr. Elena Martinez. "Luxury houses benefited from information asymmetry: consumers lacked technical knowledge to verify quality claims. Social media shattered that imbalance. Once consumers observe measurable evidence that a $10,000 contemporary bag uses thinner materials than its $2,500 predecessor, the psychological justification architecture collapses."

Most damaging, some viral social media posts have shown stitching inconsistencies in authentic $9,000+ bags alongside the perfect stitching of $600 counterfeits, visual evidence that dramatically undermines luxury's core promise of superior craftsmanship. When a counterfeit sometimes demonstrates better construction than the authentic item it copies, the entire foundation of luxury valuation comes into question.

As traditional luxury's value proposition weakened, consumers began exploring alternative channels that offered better alignment between price and perceived value. The most dramatic beneficiary has been the secondhand luxury market, which exploded from a niche community to a mainstream shopping channel generating $40.51 billion in 2023 and projected to reach $60.55 billion by 2029.

"I used to feel that buying preloved luxury was somehow less special," explains Maya Johnson, a 34-year-old creative director. "Now I see it as the smartest option. My vintage 1990s Chanel flap cost 40% less than the current retail price, has significantly better construction quality, and carries a sense of heritage that new items lack."

This sentiment has become particularly prevalent among millennials and Gen Z, who research indicates are adopting secondhand fashion 2.5 times faster than other age groups. The psychological barriers that once made secondhand shopping seem less prestigious have completely dissolved, replaced by pride in making financially and environmentally conscious choices.

The pursuit of alternatives extends to emerging brands focused on quality and craftsmanship rather than logos. Independent designers emphasizing transparent production and direct-to-consumer models have captured former luxury clients. Brands like Polène, Cuyana, and Senreve offer high-quality leather goods at prices 30-60% below luxury products.

"I realized what I actually valued was exceptional design, materials, and craftsmanship, not necessarily a specific logo," shares former luxury collector Daniel Kim. "Once I started exploring independent brands, I discovered pieces with equal or better quality at significantly lower prices. The calculus became simple: I could own one status bag with compromised quality or three expertly crafted pieces from emerging designers."

The disillusionment with luxury's price-to-quality ratio reached a tipping point in April 2025 with what came to be known as the "Trade War TikTok" phenomenon. Amid escalating U.S.-China trade tensions, Chinese manufacturers began posting videos revealing what they claimed were the true production costs of luxury goods. One viral video alleged that a $38,000 Hermès Birkin bag cost approximately $1,000 to produce, while another claimed that 80% of luxury handbags involve Chinese manufacturing before European final assembly, despite "Made in France" credentials.

"We're witnessing information democratization catching up to luxury democratization," explains Dr. Marcus Chen. "For decades, brands controlled the narrative about their products. Social media has disrupted that asymmetry, enabling consumers to verify or challenge claims in real-time."

For consumers like Lisa Park, this evolution is already reshaping personal choices. After walking away from that $10,800 Chanel flap, Lisa began researching alternatives, not abandoning her appreciation for quality and craftsmanship, but seeking expressions that better aligned with her values.

"I found myself drawn to both ends of the spectrum," Lisa reflects. "On one hand, I discovered the joy of hunting vintage pieces from the '80s and '90s when quality standards were higher. On the other, I became fascinated by independent designers creating exceptional pieces without the conglomerate markup. What surprised me was realizing that what I valued wasn't really the logo. It was the quality, design, and how the piece made me feel."

This bifurcation appears across consumer segments. Some have migrated toward "quiet luxury," high-quality, understated pieces from brands like Loro Piana and The Row that emphasize materials over logos. Others embrace vintage pieces with superior construction quality, or regional luxury expressions offering authentic cultural connection.

What unites these paths is renewed emphasis on luxury's original promise: exceptional quality, genuine craftsmanship, and meaningful exclusivity rather than artificial scarcity through price barriers. The great price inflation of 2020-2025 wasn't just about numbers on price tags; it was the breaking point that forced consumers to question what luxury truly means and seek more authentic expressions of quality and craftsmanship.

Chapter Eighteen

The Growth Ceiling

C rystal chandeliers cast a honeyed glow across the private salon hidden on the third floor of Louis Vuitton's Avenue Montaigne headquarters. Thirty-two clients, each with annual spending exceeding €250,000, sipped Dom Pérignon as white-gloved attendants unveiled the *Meteorite Collection*: twelve timepieces featuring dials crafted from fragments of the Muonionalusta meteorite. Each €125,000 timepiece existed only in this rarefied air, accessible solely through personal invitation to clients whose spending had earned them entry into luxury's most exclusive sanctum.

Six kilometers away, on the Champs-Élysées, a queue of tourists and first-time luxury shoppers snaked outside the Louis Vuitton flagship. Security guards controlled the flow of customers entering five at a time. Inside, harried sales associates juggled multiple clients simultaneously. Amira Nassir, a 27-year-old medical resident celebrating her first career advancement with a purchase, examined a Pochette Métis bag with its recognizable monogram canvas.

"The canvas feels different from my mother's bag," she remarked, running her fingers along the surface. "And the stitching here looks a bit uneven."

The sales associate, hired three months earlier with no luxury experience, offered a practiced response about "handcrafted uniqueness" before pivoting to highlight the signature details that would make the bag recognizably Louis Vuitton to her Instagram followers. The €2,200 price tag represented six weeks of Amira's careful saving. She would never know that in the private salon across town, that same amount wouldn't cover the alligator watch strap being paired with a meteorite timepiece by clients who spent her annual salary on accessories.

Between these two worlds lay the widening chasm in luxury's growth strategy. The meteorite event would appear in no quarterly reports or press releases. The queue on the Champs-Élysées, however, would feature prominently in the brand's narrative of continued popularity and accessibility. Both were Louis Vuitton, yet they had become different brands operating under the same iconic monogram: one hidden from view, one deliberately visible; one about craftsmanship and experience, one about recognition and belonging.

For decades, luxury's growth had been predicated on democratization, bringing previously inaccessible brands to broader audiences with the promise of exceptional craftsmanship available to anyone willing to save for it. The middle class had been sold the dream that they too could own a piece of the extraordinary. Now, as luxury houses faced a formidable growth ceiling, that narrative was silently unraveling. The very clients who had fueled luxury's expansion, educated, quality-conscious middle-class professionals like Amira, were becoming casualties of a calculated shift toward the ultra-wealthy.

The spreadsheet on Bernard Arnault's desk revealed a reality few outside LVMH's executive suite were prepared to acknowledge. After years of meteoric growth, including a remarkable pandemic recovery that saw revenues soar 44% beyond pre-COVID levels in 2021, the world's largest luxury conglomerate had hit an unmistakable ceiling. The latest quarter showed organic revenue growth slowing to just 1%, with fashion and leather goods, the engine of LVMH's empire, register-ing their first decline (-5%) since the pandemic's darkest days. Across town at Kering headquarters, the numbers told an even more sobering story. Revenue had declined 11%, with EBITDA plummeting 28%, while their flagship brand Gucci had experienced a devastating 20% revenue drop with operating income down a staggering 44%.

"We convinced ourselves we had permanently expanded the luxury client base," confided a senior strategist at one major house, speaking on condition of anonymity. "The pandemic created a perfect laboratory where traditional luxury spending on travel was channeled into prod-ucts. We mistook a temporary phenomenon for a permanent shift."

That assumption had triggered production increases across the board. Factories had been running at capacity to meet projections based on pandemic spending patterns. Now, the results of that mis-judgment lay in warehouses across Europe, €3.2 billion in unsold LVMH inventory and €1.5 billion at Kering. These stockpiles represent-ed not just financial liabilities but an existential threat to brands whose identity was built on scarcity and exclusivity.

The growth ceiling manifested in other ways too. Price increases, which had accounted for a remarkable 80% of luxury sector growth between 2019 and 2023, had reached their practical limits. The canvas Louis Vuitton Speedy that had cost €760 in 2019 now commanded €1,450, a 91% increase with no discernible improvement in craftsman-ship or materials. These weren't incremental adjustments for inflation but strategic repositionings that tested the outer boundaries of per-ceived value.

In confidential strategy sessions, executives were reaching an iden-tical conclusion: the price lever had reached its mechanical limit. Any further increases risked breaking the system entirely. For the aspi-rational consumer, these price thresholds had already crossed from "worth the investment" to "impossible to justify."

"A fabulous ice cream sundae is boring by the time you have it the fifth time," noted retail analyst Simeon Siegel, capturing the ennui that had settled over once-enthusiastic luxury consumers. The relent-

less parade of similar products, combined with perceived quality declines and ubiquitous availability, had transformed objects of desire
into symbols of corporate growth strategies, luxury by algorithm rather
than artistry.

Bain & Company's luxury report quantified the phenomenon with
stark clarity: 50 million people had stopped buying luxury brands altogether, citing "broken promises" as the primary reason. This exodus
represented not a temporary market fluctuation but a seismic restructuring of luxury's consumer landscape, a silent revolt against the democratization bargain that had underpinned the industry's expansion.

For all the data visualizations filling boardroom screens, perhaps
the most telling indicator came from street level. For the first time in
recent memory, queues outside luxury stores in Paris, London, and New
York had visibly shortened. In Tokyo's Ginza district and Hong Kong's
Canton Road, where lines had once been a permanent fixture, security
guards now stood at attention before relatively quiet storefronts.

For decades, luxury houses had maintained the illusion of a monolithic brand experience. Whether you spent €500 on a perfume or
€50,000 on a crocodile handbag, you were ostensibly entering the
same brand universe. This careful balancing act had enabled luxury's extraordinary expansion while preserving its aspirational appeal.
By 2024, that façade had cracked, revealing an industry in the midst
of a calculated bifurcation into two distinct worlds: one for the ultra-wealthy and another for everyone else.

The ultra-high-net-worth strategy was transforming the summit
of luxury into an entirely different experience. Private appointments
in dedicated spaces. Exclusive collections never advertised publicly.
Personal relationships with senior design team members rather than
seasonal sales associates. Special events featuring artists and cultural
figures unavailable to regular clientele. This wasn't just preferential
treatment; it was an entirely separate brand experience operating under the same logo but in a parallel universe.

"The top 2% of luxury consumers now account for 40% of sales,
up from 35% in 2009," explained a luxury market analyst at Bain

& Company. "The math has become inescapable. When one ultra-high-net-worth client spends the equivalent of fifty aspirational customers, brands inevitably tailor their best resources to where the growth potential lies."

This strategic pivot was particularly evident in product development. For Louis Vuitton, the approach was described as "growing through mix," pricing flagship products below competitors to maintain market position, while continuously introducing new entry-level products. The casual observer might see a single unified brand, but insiders recognized two parallel product universes evolving under the same logo, one of extraordinary quality and craftsmanship, another of commercially viable approximations bearing the same signature.

At Gucci, the strategy had become even more explicit. After disappointing revenue declines, the brand was "set on moving more up-market, including by launching salons for the ultra-rich, with prices starting at $40,000." These appointment-only spaces existed in an entirely different dimension from the logo-emblazoned products that drove mass-market recognition.

The aspirational segment strategy, meanwhile, focused on maximizing margins while maintaining just enough brand signifiers to satisfy logo-driven consumers. Visible branding became more prominent as quality subtly declined. Manufacturing shifted to lower-cost facilities without public acknowledgment. The percentage of handwork decreased as mechanization increased. Materials were sourced with greater emphasis on margin than longevity, all while maintaining the narrative of exceptional craftsmanship.

These changes weren't immediately obvious to casual luxury shoppers making their first purchase. But for longtime clients who remembered the craftsmanship standards of previous decades, the evolution was unmistakable. TikTok videos dissecting construction quality went viral, including one particularly damaging example showing a former leather craftsman calculating that a €5,900 Lady Dior bag contained approximately €300 worth of materials and labor, a markup increasingly difficult to justify as quality standards evolved.

Yet even as quality concerns mounted, the houses doubled down on their bifurcation strategy. Burberry's CEO Joshua Schulman announced plans to "restore a 'good, better, best price' architecture in a luxury context across categories." This seemingly innocuous statement revealed a fundamental shift, the explicit acknowledgment of tiered quality rather than a consistent standard across all price points.

Between these two extremes, a vacuum was forming. The educated, quality-conscious middle-class luxury client, who might save for a beautifully crafted bag because they appreciated the artisanship rather than the logo, was finding themselves priced out of quality without being satisfied by conspicuous consumption. This cohort had traditionally valued discretion over display, craftsmanship over recognition. As prices rose while quality plateaued or declined, these clients began quietly slipping away, not with angry social media posts, but with a silent redirection of their appreciation toward emerging alternatives that still delivered on the original promise of luxury.

The sprawling Cheval Blanc Maison overlooking the Seine represented more than just another luxury hotel in Paris. Its pristine limestone façade housed an entirely new growth frontier for a conglomerate confronting saturation in its traditional product categories. Rooms starting at €1,500 per night featured handcrafted furnishings from the same artisans who produced leather goods for Louis Vuitton and Dior. The Dior Spa offered treatments incorporating skincare formulations unavailable at regular beauty counters.

This wasn't just diversification; it was a strategic pivot toward the last untapped frontier of luxury: the ephemeral, the experiential, the uncopyable. While handbags could be counterfeited and clothing designs replicated by fast-fashion brands within weeks, the precise sensation of waking up in a Cheval Blanc suite overlooking Paris remained stubbornly resistant to mass production, a luxury experience that couldn't be democratized without being destroyed.

"The future of luxury will not only be in luxury goods, as it's been for many years, but also in luxury experiences," Bernard Arnault had declared to investors. The hospitality industry was projected to grow at 5.8% annually between 2022 and 2032, significantly outpacing the 2.7% forecast for global economic growth. Meanwhile, the luxury products market was facing its first contraction in 15 years, suggesting a fundamental reorientation of high-end consumption.

LVMH's €3.2 billion acquisition of Belmond in 2019 had seemed curious to some analysts, a departure from the group's core expertise in retail luxury. But as the product growth ceiling materialized, this move appeared increasingly prescient. Belmond's portfolio of 46 luxury hotels, trains, river cruises, and safari lodges provided an entirely new avenue for expansion. These properties offered virtually unlimited pricing power. After all, how does one determine the "correct" price for a night aboard the only luxury sleeper train crossing the Peruvian Andes?

The experiential pivot allowed luxury houses to reclaim the scarcity that had been diluted through decades of product democratization. While factories could always produce more handbags, the Belmond Hotel Caruso in Ravello had only 50 rooms, and during peak season, demand exceeded supply by factors that would make even an Hermès Birkin waiting list seem modest. This architectural constraint provided a natural ceiling that maintained exclusivity without artificial limitations.

Perhaps most importantly, hospitality environments offered something increasingly rare in the contemporary luxury landscape: controlled contexts where the dream remained intact. Within a Cheval Blanc resort, there were no counterfeits, no unauthorized discounting, no social media dilution of the brand mystique. Guests experienced the brand exactly as its stewards intended, a purity of vision increasingly difficult to maintain in the chaotic marketplace of physical products.

The silence in LVMH's Shanghai offices was deafening. Regional executives stared at projections showing mainland China luxury sales had plummeted between 18-22%, effectively erasing half a decade of growth in a single quarter. The country that had fueled luxury's most explosive expansion, and was projected to account for 40% of global luxury purchases by 2030, had suddenly gone cold.

"We misunderstood something fundamental," admitted Michael Burke, then-CEO of Louis Vuitton, during an industry conference with rare candor. "The Chinese consumer's relationship with luxury was always more transactional than emotional." As border restrictions lifted post-pandemic, Chinese shoppers immediately resumed their pre-pandemic patterns, spending 45% more in Hong Kong and Macau and 38% more in Europe rather than continuing to shop domestically.

The exodus exposed an uncomfortable truth: the pandemic-era boom in domestic Chinese luxury sales had been largely artificial, a temporary redirection of spending rather than a fundamental shift in behavior. Even Hainan Island's duty-free paradise, once touted as the solution to overseas shopping leakage, saw sales plummet 29% in 2024. Beyond the geographic shift, a more profound transformation was occurring in Chinese consumer psychology. After years of logo-driven consumption, social media platforms like Xiaohongshu filled with discussions about "luxury fatigue" and "quiet luxury," signaling a growing sophistication that threatened the logo-centric strategy which had driven growth for years.

"The China strategy that worked for the past decade is fundamentally broken," concluded a senior luxury consultant in Shanghai. "Brands need to completely rethink their approach, moving beyond geographic expansion to cultural relevance."

The quarterly earnings call felt more like a hostage negotiation than a financial update. As LVMH executives attempted to frame a 1% organic growth rate as a "resilient performance in challenging conditions," analysts pressed relentlessly on future growth projections. The atmosphere crackled with tension between two fundamentally opposed worldviews: the shareholder demand for perpetual expansion versus the inherent constraints of genuine luxury.

"We remain focused on the long-term health of our Maisons rather than short-term market fluctuations," Bernard Arnault stated in his characteristically measured tone. The subtext was clear: luxury's growth storyline was being quietly recalibrated. After years of double-digit expansion, the conglomerate was signaling a new normal of more modest trajectories.

Hermès, with its predominantly family-controlled ownership structure, had navigated these waters differently. By maintaining extreme production discipline and resisting overexpansion, they had created a natural ceiling that preserved both exclusivity and quality. Their waiting lists for Birkin and Kelly bags weren't manufactured marketing tactics but genuine reflections of production limitations. As other houses confronted saturation, Hermès's steady trajectory appeared increasingly prescient.

The shareholder-heritage tension manifested most visibly in failed product category extensions. Fenty fashion house, launched with tremendous fanfare as LVMH's partnership with Rihanna, had been quietly shuttered after failing to gain traction. Similar cautionary tales emerged across the industry: perfume lines that diluted brand equity, diffusion labels that confused positioning, hotel concepts abandoned after initial exploration, the wreckage of growth strategies that had collided with luxury's inherent limitations.

"We're being asked to do mathematically impossible things," confided a creative director at one major house. "Maintain exclusivity while continuously expanding. Preserve craftsmanship while increasing production efficiency. Uphold heritage while constantly innovating for new markets. These are fundamental contradictions, not strategic challenges."

The tension had transformed the physical infrastructure of luxury production. Factory expansions in less publicized locations. Craftspeople being asked to increase output while maintaining quality standards. Training programs abbreviated to bring new artisans online faster. Automated processes quietly introduced into previously handcrafted techniques. These changes occurred gradually, each small compromise seemingly inconsequential in isolation, yet collectively representing a fundamental transformation, the slow erosion of craftsmanship in service of scale.

The inventory crisis of 2023-2024 brought these tensions to a head with brutal clarity. LVMH's €3.2 billion and Kering's €1.5 billion in unsold goods represented not just financial liabilities but philosophical failures, the tangible manifestation of the growth-exclusivity paradox. When production targets were set to satisfy growth projections rather than market demand, the result was warehouses filled with luxury products that couldn't be sold without damaging the very exclusivity that made them desirable.

The most revealing development was the industry's increased focus on ultra-high-net-worth individuals. When top-tier spenders accounted for 40% of revenue, maintaining their perception of exclusivity became existentially important. This led to what industry insiders called "the hidden luxury," products, experiences, and services available only to top clients, never advertised or acknowledged in public communications.

"We're operating two completely different businesses under one logo," said one anonymous former CEO. "One is about preserving a 150-year legacy of craftsmanship. The other is about meeting quarterly targets set by analysts who've never watched a craftsperson spend eight hours hand-stitching a bag. It's become impossible to serve both masters equally well."

The growth ceiling thus revealed luxury's most fundamental paradox: the business of selling exclusivity had inherent limitations that directly contradicted the growth imperatives of modern financial markets. As the industry approached this ceiling, the stress fractures became increasingly visible, not just in sales figures, but in the changing relationship between brands and the clients who had once championed them.

For luxury houses confronting their growth ceiling in 2024, the parallels to Christian Dior's pre-Arnault crisis were impossible to ignore. In both cases, periods of explosive democratization had eventually undermined the very exclusivity that made the brands desirable. The pattern established earlier, expansion, dilution, and then the inevitable search for new expressions of exclusivity, was playing out once again, but on a global scale previously unimaginable.

"We're witnessing the fundamental limits of the growth-at-all-costs model," concluded the Bain & Company luxury report with uncharacteristic bluntness. "Brands must rebuild foundations based on genuine value creation rather than financial engineering."

The path forward would require what McKinsey termed a "holistic strategic reset." Some brands would retreat to their roots, focusing on craftsmanship and exclusivity for a smaller but more dedicated customer base. Others would embrace transformation, reimagining luxury for a digital-native, sustainability-conscious generation. A third group would likely disappear, unable to navigate the transition from hyper-growth to mature market dynamics.

The signals of change were already emerging with unmistakable clarity. New luxury houses were emerging with business models deliberately designed to avoid the democratization trap, maintaining small production runs and direct client relationships, creating exclusivity through inherent limitations rather than artificial scarcity.

Meanwhile, discerning consumers who had once driven luxury's quality standards, the educated middle-class clients with genuine appreciation for craftsmanship, were quietly redirecting their attention toward smaller houses, artisanal producers, and experiences that couldn't be mass-produced. In Paris, a former leather craftsman who had spent decades at one of the leading brands now created small-batch goods for a private clientele. His waiting list stretched to eighteen months. His pieces carried no visible logo. His pricing was below the major houses' equivalent items, yet the quality was demonstrably superior.

"We spent twenty years democratizing luxury. Now we need to spend the next twenty making it luxurious again," reflected one senior executive during an off-record dinner at Paris Fashion Week. The irony was not lost on anyone present. The very success that had made them billionaires had also sown the seeds of their current predicament. The growth ceiling they had hit was of their own making, a limit not of demand but of meaning. Luxury had become so ubiquitous that it had ceased to be luxurious.

In the private salon on Avenue Montaigne, as clients examined meteorite watch dials under crystal chandeliers, this existential question remained unspoken but palpable. The exclusive experience represented both luxury's potential salvation and the acknowledgment of its fundamental limits. The financial reports would find ways to frame 1% growth as resilience. But in quiet moments, the architects of modern luxury confronted an uncomfortable truth: they had built a cathedral with no ceiling, and gravity's reckoning was finally at hand.

Chapter Nineteen

Values-Driven Exodus

Sloane Chen stood surrounded by designer shopping bags in her Manhattan apartment, the afternoon sunlight casting elongated shadows across her bedroom floor. Around her, four friends watched as she methodically examined each luxury item accumulated over the past decade, categorizing them into three piles: keep, donate, and sell.

"It started when I saw the factory footage," she explained, lifting a monogrammed handbag that had once been her prized possession. "Here I was, paying sixteen thousand dollars for something made by women earning barely enough to feed their families, in conditions I wouldn't subject my dog to." She placed it decisively in the "sell" pile.

This wasn't spring cleaning, it was what Sloane called her "luxury detox party," a gathering becoming increasingly common among former devotees of high-end brands. James, who had once queued overnight for limited-edition collaborations, showed the others a viral TikTok exposing the environmental impact behind a luxury brand's supposedly "sustainable" collection.

"The marketing campaign waxed poetic about innovative eco-materials," he said, disillusionment evident. "But it turns out they were incinerating excess inventory while trumpeting their planetary concern. That's when I felt it, this visceral discomfort, like I couldn't reconcile coveting their products while despising their practices."

That discomfort had a name: cognitive dissonance, the psychological tension that erupts when beliefs and actions collide. For these former luxury enthusiasts, growing awareness of ethical transgressions had crashed against their devotion to beloved brands, creating an internal conflict too powerful to ignore.

"I worked for twelve years at one of the big conglomerates," said Mei, a former marketing executive. "There were literally two distinct factories, one for pieces destined for high-profile clients and VIPs, and another for everyone else. This was manufactured at the second factory. The quality specifications were literally half of what they mandated for the top-tier production. Same astronomical price, though."

Sloane nodded. "That was my breaking point too. Not just the price inflation, though paying nearly eleven thousand for a bag that cost forty-three hundred when I bought my first one a decade ago stings, but realizing that as they hiked prices, they were simultaneously cutting corners. It felt like betrayal in its purest form."

David, an art director who had spent years crafting campaigns for luxury fashion, added, "The industry banked on us not noticing, or at least not caring. But something shifted after the pandemic. It's as if collectively, we all awakened from the same hypnotic trance. Now I'd rather champion craftspeople who genuinely embody their values than bankroll marketing smoke and mirrors."

The group wasn't expressing regret for past purchases so much as a palpable sense of liberation. The cognitive dissonance that had plagued them was finally resolving through deliberate action.

"You know what's funny?" Sloane mused, holding up a vintage handbag from her "keep" pile. "I still love luxury. I just realized I was worshipping at the wrong altar. This piece from the eighties was crafted by a single artisan who imbued it with pride and purpose. The luxury I crave respects the planet, honors workers with dignity, and doesn't insult my intelligence by charging more for progressively less. The magic isn't gone, it simply migrated to brands that actually deserve its custody."

The pandemic crashed into the luxury industry like a perfect storm, and in its wake emerged a more discerning, values-driven consumer. The three years between 2020 and 2023 witnessed the convergence of three formidable forces: a global health crisis that catalyzed widespread reassessment of values, accelerated digitalization that democratized information access, and heightened ethical consciousness that made consumers increasingly uncomfortable with contradictions between brand messaging and actual practice.

When COVID-19 swept across the globe, it created an unprecedented pause, a collective moment of reflection. Isolated in their homes, surrounded by possessions accumulated during years of prosperity, many consumers confronted existential questions: What truly matters? What do my purchases reveal about me? Is this accumulation of branded goods actually delivering fulfillment?

Maya Williams, a management consultant and former luxury enthusiast, described the pandemic's effect: "Sitting in lockdown, staring at a closet brimming with logoed items while watching reports of economic devastation and inequality... something just crystallized in my consciousness. The ostentatious display of wealth that once felt aspirational suddenly seemed tone-deaf, even grotesque."

This sentiment wasn't universal. For some, particularly in Asian markets, the pandemic unleashed "revenge spending," a post-lockdown surge in luxury purchases. But for a significant segment, especially those with higher cultural capital, the crisis accelerated a shift toward "quiet luxury," understated, quality-focused consumption emphasizing craftsmanship over logos and values over visibility.

Meanwhile, digital platforms morphed from convenient shopping channels into powerful information ecosystems. A viral Instagram story could expose deplorable factory conditions in seconds. TikTok videos juxtaposing vintage luxury items with their modern counterparts revealed dramatic quality deterioration. Consumer forums documented identical products being sold at wildly disparate price points across markets.

"Before, luxury brands controlled the narrative with an iron grip," explained digital strategist Amara Okereke. "Their marketing wove beautiful fantasies we all eagerly bought into. Now, with a few taps, consumers can peer behind the curtain. And that knowledge, once gained, can't be unlearned, it fundamentally alters the relationship."

This newfound transparency coincided with an unprecedented expansion in ethical consciousness. Environmental concerns transformed sustainability from niche interest to mainstream value. Labor rights gained urgency as reports emerged of garment workers abandoned when brands canceled orders during the pandemic. Social justice movements prompted consumers to scrutinize corporate practices beyond their polished diversity campaigns.

The result was explosive. Luxury brands accustomed to selling dreams found themselves under forensic examination by consumers equipped with both information and ethical frameworks to evaluate them. The financial cost of luxury had always been explicit, the price tag made that clear. But now consumers began calculating the moral cost as well, and finding many venerable houses profoundly wanting.

The luxury exodus wasn't simply a matter of price sensitivity or changing aesthetic preferences. At its core lay cognitive dissonance, the psychological discomfort that erupts when deeply held values clash with behaviors or perceptions. For luxury consumers who had cultivated emotional connections with brands over years or decades, this internal conflict manifested in distinct forms.

Maria Velasquez experienced ethical dissonance firsthand after a decade of unwavering brand loyalty. "I was at dinner with friends when someone showed me an investigative report about their sourcing practices," she recalled. "Their beautifully curated website showcased Italian craftsmen hand-cutting leather, but the report documented how they outsourced to factories where workers couldn't take bathroom breaks and earned barely subsistence wages. I felt physically ill looking at my bag, like I was complicit in something ugly while believing I was supporting exceptional artisanship."

This ethical dissonance struck particularly hard for consumers who prized sustainability and social responsibility. A comprehensive survey found that 82% of luxury consumers expect brands to uphold fair labor practices and environmental standards. When these expectations were violated, many experienced a profound misalignment between their self-image as conscientious individuals and their support of problematic companies.

Value dissonance emerged as prices climbed while quality declined, a particularly galling combination that violated the fundamental transaction promise. Gregory Tanaka, who had meticulously collected one brand's leather goods for fifteen years, documented the changes: "The same wallet increased from $450 to $1,250 over a decade, nearly triple, while simultaneously switching from full-grain to inferior corrected leather, replacing hand-stitching with machine work, and eliminating several interior features."

This dissonance intensified as consumers gained awareness of brands' two-tier strategies, creating vastly different experiences for ultra-wealthy clients versus regular customers. Learning that exceptional service and quality had become reserved for the top 2% of clients made many longtime customers feel reduced to "cash flow" rather than valued community members.

Perhaps most devastating was authenticity dissonance, the realization that a brand's carefully cultivated narrative fundamentally contradicted its actual practices. When consumers discovered that heritage brands emphasizing traditional craftsmanship were quietly shifting production to automated factories, or that companies projecting values of family and tradition were treating workers like disposable resources, the disconnection struck at the very heart of the luxury promise.

"Luxury isn't just expensive merchandise," explained consumer psychologist Dr. Sanjana Mehta. "It's a relationship built on trust and shared values. When consumers experience these dissonances, they're not simply disappointed customers, they're people in a relationship

feeling betrayed by someone they trusted. And like personal relationships, once that trust fractures, reconciliation becomes exponentially
harder."

This betrayal often manifested in what researchers identified as the
"love becomes hate" phenomenon, where formerly devoted customers
transformed into vocal critics. Unlike mere brand switching in other categories, luxury disillusionment frequently produced a sense of
having been manipulated into complicity with values they opposed,
creating not just indifference, but active rejection.

In Paolo Franchetti's wood-paneled workshop in Florence, time
seems to flow by different rules. His hands, weathered by decades of
dedication to his craft, methodically stitch a handbag that will demand
forty hours to complete. Three years ago, his small atelier served a
handful of discreet clients. Today, there's a six-month waiting list that
grows longer by the week.

"Something fundamental shifted after the pandemic," he observed.
"My new clients arrive bearing stories of disillusionment. They speak
of luxury brands they once adored but now actively avoid. They bring
photographs of their mothers' vintage bags, asking if I can create something with the same quality. They aren't abandoning luxury, they're
redefining it according to values, not labels."

Paolo's experience reflects a profound reconfiguration within the
luxury landscape: the fragmentation of the market into increasingly
divergent paths. While industry data confirmed the ultra-wealthy still
engaged in logo-driven consumption, a significant segment of traditionally loyal customers, particularly the educated upper-middle class,
were deliberately migrating their spending toward brands that demonstrated authentic alignment with their values.

This migration wasn't uniform. Research identified distinct patterns
in how consumers redirected their luxury spending when disillusionment took root. Some embraced "quiet luxury" brands like Brunello
Cucinelli, Bottega Veneta, and The Row, which emphasized craftsmanship and ethics without conspicuous branding. Others sought out in-

dependent artisans and small-scale makers offering transparency and direct relationships with creators.

Sophia Li, a former fashion magazine editor, described her own migration: "I used to chase the latest 'it' bags with almost religious devotion. Now I track down master craftspeople with the same fervor. My most treasured piece is a handbag from a small atelier in Madrid. The artisan walked me through every step of its creation, every material's origin story. It costs roughly what I used to spend on logo-heavy pieces, but the experience and values alignment deliver a completely different species of satisfaction."

What distinguished this values-based migration from previous luxury cycles was its foundation in ethics rather than aesthetics. Past oscillations between minimalism and maximalism, between logo prominence and subtlety, were primarily matters of evolving taste. This exodus was propelled by something deeper, a fundamental recalibration of what consumers considered worthy of their investment.

The digital landscape significantly enabled this migration, connecting value-driven consumers with alternatives that might have remained invisible in earlier eras. Online platforms like Craftsmanship Quarterly and Artisan & Fox curated independent makers committed to ethical practices. Instagram accounts dedicated to craftsmanship education helped consumers recognize quality beyond recognizable insignias.

"We're witnessing the emergence of distinct luxury tribes," explained cultural analyst Marcus Chen. "There remain those drawn to logos and status, particularly among new wealth. But a growing segment, often those with high cultural capital, now seek meaning beyond recognition. They crave the narrative behind the object, the ethics of its creation, the authenticity of its maker. For them, possessing something instantly recognizable to everyone has become less desirable than owning something deeply meaningful to themselves."

This values-driven migration presented luxury conglomerates with a profound dilemma. Their business models, optimized for scale and shareholder returns, often stood fundamentally at odds with the values these migrating consumers cherished: hand craftsmanship, limited production, ethical transparency, and authentic connection. The very qualities these consumers increasingly sought were precisely those that major luxury groups had often compromised in their relentless pursuit of growth.

Meanwhile, brands that had maintained integrity found themselves with unexpected momentum. They hadn't changed; the market had shifted toward what they had always championed. As Brunello Cucinelli reflected: "We never made compromises for ephemeral growth. We always believed in ethical production, in treating our artisans with dignity, in creating products of lasting value. Now the world seems to be recognizing what we have known all along, that true luxury cannot exist without humanity at its core."

When global markets tumbled in early 2024 and luxury stocks plunged amid slowing growth and consumer pullback, a handful of brands defied the downward trend. Hermès shares maintained remarkable resilience. Brunello Cucinelli reported continued strong sales that puzzled market analysts. Bottega Veneta sustained its quiet momentum without flashy marketing campaigns. Max Mara's loyal customer base seemed unfazed by economic headwinds.

Their common thread wasn't price point or product category, but an unwavering commitment to core values that aligned with what disillusioned luxury consumers increasingly sought: authentic craftsmanship, ethical production, quality without compromise, and connection to something more meaningful than transient status.

In the gentle foothills of Umbria, the medieval village of Solomeo stands as perhaps the most vivid embodiment of luxury guided by values rather than quarterly returns. Brunello Cucinelli painstakingly restored this once-crumbling hamlet to house his cashmere empire, not as a marketing backdrop, but as the living heart of his philosophy of "humanistic capitalism."

Inside the company's ateliers, artisans earn wages 20% higher than industry standard. Workdays conclude promptly at 5:30 pm, with no overtime permitted. Ninety-minute lunch breaks allow time for proper meals. Workers dine together in a company cafeteria serving local cuisine made with ingredients from the company's organic farms, the identical food served when clients or celebrities visit.

"We create beautiful clothes, yes," Cucinelli has repeatedly stated, "but our true product is dignity, the dignity of craft, the dignity of fair compensation, the dignity of balance between work and life." This philosophy manifests in cashmere knitwear of exceptional quality, but more profoundly, creates products imbued with values that resonate deeply with ethics-conscious consumers.

In stark contrast to brands that emblazoned their products with ever-more-prominent logos, Bottega Veneta charted a different course. Since 1966, the brand has championed its intrecciato technique, a distinctive leather-weaving method instantly recognizable to those "in the know" while remaining elegantly inconspicuous to others. This signature craftsmanship, rather than obvious branding, became the subtle hallmark of the house.

When the brand deleted its social media accounts in 2021, the move initially baffled industry observers accustomed to luxury's digital arms race. But the decision reflected a deeper philosophy: that true luxury thrives on discovery rather than ubiquity, on quality rather than visibility.

Hermès maintained an unwavering focus on craftsmanship over scale. The company's legendary Birkin and Kelly bags continue to be crafted by individual artisans who train for years before being entrusted with their creation. A single bag may require 20 to 25 hours of hand labor, with the artisan's personal stamp marking their work, a practice vanishingly rare in an era of industrialized luxury production.

What distinguishes Hermès is not merely its commitment to craft, but its deliberate business strategy of controlled scarcity. Rather than ramping up production to meet soaring demand, the company maintains strict limits on output, ensuring that quality never suffers for volume. This approach, prioritizing excellence over expansion, creates natural exclusivity that doesn't rely on artificial price inflation or marketing hyperbole.

What unites these diverse brands is a business approach that prioritizes intrinsic values over extrinsic growth metrics. They share an emphasis on handcraftsmanship, maintaining production predominantly
in Europe where labor standards are higher. They focus on exceptional
materials sourced responsibly. They privilege direct relationships with
clients over mass-market expansion. Most crucially, they demonstrate
coherence between their stated values and their actual practices, a
consistency increasingly rare in luxury yet increasingly demanded by
discerning consumers.

Alex Rodriguez still remembers his first luxury purchase, a wallet
from a venerable French house, bought with his first bonus as a junior
investment banker. "It wasn't just an accessory," he recalled. "It was
symbolic, a vote of confidence in myself, a membership card to a world
I aspired to join. I carried it proudly for years, watching as it developed
a patina that told the story of my professional rise."

Fifteen years later, Alex placed that same wallet beside its recently
purchased replacement. The difference was striking, the older piece
supple and rich with character, the newer one stiffer, its leather bond-
ed rather than full-grain, its stitching machine-perfect but visibly less
substantial. Both bore the same iconic logo. Both carried the same aspirational story. But the latter cost three times more while delivering
objectively less.

"That was my breaking point," he said. "Not just the obvious quality
decline, but the insult to my intelligence. They assumed brand loyalty
would blind me to what I was physically holding in my hands."

Alex's experience epitomizes a growing phenomenon across the luxury landscape: the middle-class rebellion. This transcends mere price
sensitivity, representing an active rejection by the very consumers who
fueled luxury's massive expansion over the past three decades, educated professionals with significant disposable income who once enthusiastically paid premiums for what they believed represented superior
quality, craftsmanship, and principles.

What lends this rebellion its potency is that it's led not by casual luxury dabblers, but by devoted long-term clients who had built

deep emotional connections with their chosen brands. They didn't simply shift spending elsewhere when dissatisfied; many experienced the "love becomes hate" phenomenon, where former brand advocates transform into vocal critics who actively dissuade others.

This rebellion manifests in several forms. Online communities dedicated to quality assessment have flourished, with forums filled with detailed comparisons between vintage and modern pieces, exposing quality compromises that marketing glosses over. Hashtags like #DumpTheBrand and #LuxuryDetox gain traction on social platforms, where once-loyal consumers document their disillusionment in meticulous detail.

Many middle-class luxury consumers have redirected their spending toward vintage pieces from the brands' "golden eras" before quality compromises, fueling unprecedented growth in the luxury resale market. Others have discovered independent craftspeople and smaller luxury houses that maintain the standards the conglomerates have abandoned.

What makes this rebellion particularly potent is that middle-class luxury consumers often possess high cultural capital, the knowledge, education, and taste that enables them to evaluate quality beyond superficial brand names. They're typically well-informed, digitally connected, and influential within their social circles. When they speak, others listen and purchasing behaviors shift.

"These aren't just lost sales," explained luxury retail analyst Sophia Chen. "These are lost evangelists. The middle-class luxury consumer has traditionally been the unpaid brand ambassador who introduces friends to the brand, who posts enthusiastically about purchases, who creates the aspiration that drives entry-level sales. When they turn against a brand, the damage extends far beyond their individual spending power."

In a sunlit workshop on the outskirts of Madrid, master leatherworker Elena Suárez places her latest creation, a meticulously crafted handbag, on a small wooden table. With practiced movements, she attaches a small medallion to the interior. It's not her brand logo, but something more revolutionary: a QR code linking to a blockchain record documenting every aspect of the bag's creation, from the Italian tannery where the leather was processed using vegetable-based methods, to the names of the three artisans involved in its construction, to the precise environmental impact of its production.

"My grandmother would have considered this absolute madness," Elena laughs. "In her day, luxury was about mystique, the less the customer knew about production, the more magical it seemed. Today, that opacity feels suspicious, even deceptive. My clients don't want elaborately constructed fairy tales; they want verifiable facts."

Elena's approach represents a fundamental paradigm shift: transparency has become the new currency of authentic luxury. As traditional markers of exclusivity lose their power to signal true value, detailed knowledge about how, where, and by whom products are made has emerged as the ultimate differentiator for discerning consumers.

This transformation accelerated dramatically after the pandemic, when heightened ethical awareness coincided with unprecedented digital information access. Suddenly, questions once considered impolite or irrelevant in luxury boutiques became central to purchasing decisions: Who made this? Under what conditions? With what environmental impact? At what true cost?

"Transparency isn't just about ethics," explained consumer psychologist Dr. Nathan Park. "It's fundamentally about power. Historically, luxury brands held informational advantages that allowed them to charge extraordinary premiums based partly on consumers' inability to accurately assess value. Digital transparency has fundamentally altered that dynamic, shifting power toward informed consumers who can verify claims and compare alternatives in ways previously unimaginable."

The rise of transparency as luxury currency takes concrete shape across the industry. Blockchain technology has evolved into practical applications like digital product passports that verify authenticity while documenting ethical claims. Independent certification systems have gained unprecedented prominence, with standards like B Corp certification functioning as trusted third-party validation of ethical claims.

Perhaps most significantly, direct-to-consumer models connecting clients directly with makers have flourished. Small-scale artisans previously limited to local markets now reach global audiences through platforms that curate craftspeople committed to transparent, ethical practices.

As Maya Winters entered Elysian, a small San Francisco boutique showcasing ethical luxury, the experience bore little resemblance to the flagships of major houses she had frequented a decade earlier. There were no intimidating security guards, no products displayed like untouchable museum artifacts. Instead, craftspeople worked in an open studio visible from the retail space. Price tags included not just costs but wage information for the makers. Materials were documented with environmental impact assessments.

"This feels like coming home," Maya said, running her fingers across a handwoven textile. "I never stopped loving luxury, I just needed to find luxury that loves the world back."

Maya's journey, from aspiration to disillusionment to rediscovery, embodies the evolution of luxury appreciation in our time. The principled departure she represents transcends a simple pendulum swing between minimalism and maximalism. Evidence suggests we're witnessing something more profound: a fundamental transformation in how luxury is defined, created, and consumed.

The patterns of decline and renewal visible in today's luxury landscape echo historical precedents. However, three critical factors distinguish the current transformation: its foundation in ethics rather than aesthetics, the irreversible transparency created by digital information flow, and the generational shifts driving demand for principled alignment.

Perhaps most significantly, generational succession points toward lasting change. Millennials and Gen Z, who will constitute approximately 70% of the global luxury market by 2025, consistently demonstrate stronger preferences for sustainability, authenticity, and transparent ethics than previous generations. As their purchasing power increases, their values increasingly shape market demands.

"What we're witnessing isn't just a temporary shift in consumer preferences," explained luxury industry analyst Sophia Chen. "It's a fundamental redefinition of what luxury means at its core. The old equation of high price plus exclusivity plus status signaling is giving way to a more complex formula where ethical integrity, authentic craftsmanship, and values alignment are equally essential components."

As Maya left the boutique with her purchase, a cashmere sweater made by a cooperative of Mongolian herders practicing regenerative grazing, she reflected on her own evolution: "The magic didn't disappear into thin air. It just migrated to places where craftsmanship, ethics, and authenticity align in perfect harmony. I feel the same excitement I felt with my first luxury purchase years ago, but without the cognitive dissonance, without compromising my values. That's the true luxury, something beautiful that you can love completely, without reservation or justification."

Her experience embodies a fundamental truth about luxury: Its essence doesn't disappear, it transforms and finds new expressions of exclusivity, craftsmanship, and aspiration. In today's transformation, this evolution follows pathways defined by ethics and principles alongside aesthetics and status. The result isn't luxury's end, but its metamorphosis into something potentially more authentic, sustainable, and ultimately meaningful than what came before.

Chapter Twenty

The Regional Rebellion

The SKP mall in Beijing had long served as a shrine to Western luxury. A decade earlier, Chinese shoppers would form serpentine queues outside Louis Vuitton, Burberry's signature check adorned every third handbag, and Gucci logos crowned both the aspiring middle class and ultra-wealthy alike. The symbolism spoke volumes: Western luxury represented arrival, sophistication, cosmopolitan identity.

But on this crystalline autumn morning in 2024, Mei Lin, a 32-year-old tech executive, barely acknowledged the Dior boutique as she strode past with quiet purpose. The uniformed attendant's hopeful smile faded as she continued toward a minimalist storefront several doors down. Inside, the space resonated with a different energy, eschewing gilt-edged European opulence for something more restrained, contemplative, unmistakably Chinese.

"Welcome back, Ms. Lin," said the sales associate at ICICLE, recognizing her immediately. "Would you like to see our new collection? The cashmere has just arrived from Inner Mongolia."

Mei traced her fingers along a row of impeccably tailored garments in hushed tones of ivory, celadon, and charcoal. No logos disrupted their surfaces; the quality communicated through the material itself, double-faced cashmere, hand-finished edges, silhouettes that evoked traditional Chinese garments without literal reproduction.

"It's beautiful," she murmured, pausing at a structured cashmere coat. "And made here?"

"Of course," the associate replied. "Designed in Shanghai, crafted in our ateliers in Suzhou. We take particular pride in the interior finishings."

He turned the sleeve to reveal exquisite hand-stitching inside. Mei nodded appreciatively. Ten years ago, she would have instinctively sought a European brand label, convinced only Western houses could achieve this caliber of craftsmanship. Now, the knowledge that this piece emerged from her own cultural heritage added dimensions of meaning no imported brand could match.

As Mei tried on the coat, she caught her reflection. The mirror revealed not merely a woman in elegant clothing but someone wearing the physical manifestation of cultural confidence cultivated over a decade. In this Chinese luxury brand's quiet sophistication, she discovered something Western houses had once promised but no longer delivered: genuine distinction, cultural resonance, understated knowledge that transcended mere logos or heritage marketing.

Outside the fitting room, European tourists posed with shopping bags emblazoned with Chanel and Louis Vuitton insignia. Mei smiled faintly, remembering when she too had sought validation through those iconic packages. Now, as she decided to purchase the ICICLE coat, she contemplated how profoundly the landscape had transformed. Luxury's essence remained vibrant but had found new expression in brands that resonated authentically with a new generation's values and cultural identity.

The transformation evident in Mei Lin's shopping preferences wasn't an isolated shift but the visible crest of a profound nationwide movement. "Guochao" (国潮), literally "national wave" or "China chic," represented a seismic realignment in Chinese consumer psychology. This was no mere fashion trend but a fundamental recalibration of value perception that upended decades of Western luxury dominance.

Consumer preference for domestic brands over foreign alternatives among Chinese consumers had surged from a mere 15% in 2011 to an astonishing 85% by 2020. Yet numbers alone couldn't capture the emotional and cultural dimensions of this shift, the pride, rediscovery, and cultural homecoming that propelled it forward.

Li-Ning's metamorphosis embodied this journey perfectly. Founded in 1990 by the Olympic gymnast of the same name, the sportswear company had languished for decades as a domestic also-ran, perpetually eclipsed by Nike and Adidas. Then came its watershed moment at New York Fashion Week 2018, where the brand unveiled its "Wu Dao" collection, steeped in Taoist philosophy. Models traversed the runway in garments adorned with bold Chinese characters and design elements that honored traditional clothing without pastiche. The international fashion press took notice; Chinese consumers ignited with recognition.

In the months that followed, the crimson and white "中国李宁" (China Li-Ning) logo transformed into a badge of honor among young Chinese urbanites who had previously dismissed domestic brands. By 2023, Li-Ning had dramatically expanded its market share, competing shoulder-to-shoulder with global giants on both innovation and cultural resonance.

Beyond fashion, this cultural resurgence flourished through diverse creative channels. Shang Xia, established in 2009 as a Hermès initiative, exemplified a thoughtful approach to Chinese luxury renaissance. The brand devoted itself to revitalizing traditional Chinese craftsmanship, from intricate bamboo weaving to sophisticated porcelain, through a contemporary aesthetic vision.

"The objective wasn't simply to create another luxury brand, but to resurrect craft traditions that risked disappearing," explained Jiang Qiong'er, Shang Xia's CEO and creative director. "We're providing a contemporary context for ancient knowledge, making it relevant for modern lives while honoring its origins."

This cultural confidence gained momentum through a generational shift. For China's Millennials and Gen Z consumers, who matured during their country's emergence as a global power, no inherent inferiority complex colored their perception of Chinese products or aesthetics. Unlike their parents, who had witnessed China's transition from isolation to openness, these younger consumers identified as citizens of a culturally rich nation with valuable contributions to the global luxury conversation.

Social media platforms like Xiaohongshu (Little Red Book) and Douyin (TikTok) became catalysts for this movement, with influencers championing domestic brands and traditional design elements. The digital-native quality of Guochao accelerated its spread; content celebrating Chinese craftsmanship and design could reach millions overnight, creating instant demand for previously obscure local brands.

While government support for domestic enterprises created favorable conditions, Guochao's appeal transcended policy considerations. Its core revelation proved more fundamental: authentic luxury could arise organically from China's rich aesthetic traditions and cultural values without seeking validation from European fashion capitals.

While China's Guochao movement represented the most dramatic manifestation of regional luxury rebellion, similar currents were transforming landscapes across Asia and beyond. In India, designer Sabyasachi Mukherjee had established a luxury house that rivaled Western brands in prestige while remaining deeply anchored in Indian cultural heritage. His opulent bridal wear, featuring traditional embroidery techniques like *zardozi* and *gota patti*, had transformed the Indian luxury landscape by elevating indigenous craftsmanship to global standards.

"I wanted to create luxury that speaks of India's heritage without apology or dilution," Sabyasachi explained in a 2023 interview. "Why should we look to Paris for validation when we have five thousand years of design history? Our embroidery traditions alone represent craft lineages older than many European countries."

This confidence manifested beyond rhetoric. When Hermès attempted to introduce its interpretation of the saree to the Indian market, it encountered limited success despite the brand's global prestige. For this culturally significant garment, Indian consumers gravitated toward domestic designers who possessed deeper understanding of the saree's cultural context and traditional techniques.

The Middle East was composing its own chapter in this global story of luxury regionalization. Rather than simply adopting Western luxury codes, the region had begun asserting its distinct aesthetic preferences and cultural values. The rise of modest luxury exemplified this shift, with many global brands creating special Ramadan collections featuring longer hemlines, looser silhouettes, and designs that honored religious and cultural norms. Dubai-based brand Taller Marmo had flourished by blending Italian craftsmanship with distinctly Middle Eastern silhouettes.

Even Japan, long a sophisticated luxury market with distinctive sensibilities, was experiencing renewed appreciation for domestic craft traditions. Brands like Visvim had cultivated global followings by combining meticulous Japanese artisanal techniques with contemporary design.

This global regionalization of luxury transcended mere market expansion; it signified a fundamental redefinition of luxury's essence. Traditional luxury capitals like Paris and Milan no longer exclusively determined what constituted prestige or desirability. Consumer preferences were fragmenting along regional lines, with cultural specificity and authenticity increasingly valued alongside, or even above, Western heritage narratives.

As one luxury industry veteran observed, "We're witnessing the decentralization of luxury. The flow of influence is no longer one-directional, from Europe outward, but multidirectional, with regional traditions informing global trends as much as they're influenced by them."

While regional luxury houses represented one facet of the rebellion against Western luxury dominance, another powerful front emerged through accessible luxury alternatives. These brands, positioned be-

tween mass market and traditional luxury segments, offered compelling value propositions based on quality, design intelligence, and
transparency rather than centuries-old heritage or extreme exclusivity.

On a luminous spring morning in Paris, the Polène flagship store
near the Seine welcomed a steady stream of visitors. Unlike the intimidating formality of neighboring heritage luxury boutiques, the atmosphere felt warm and inviting. Founded by siblings Mathieu, Elsa, and
Antoine Mothay in 2016, Polène had quickly risen from obscurity to
become a globally recognized name in accessible luxury leather goods.

The brand's sculptural handbags, with their distinctive curved silhouettes and architectural precision, graced glass vitrines throughout the space. Crafted from full-grain leather sourced from Italian and
Spanish tanneries and priced between €300-500, they represented a
new luxury equation: exceptional design and materials at prices significantly below heritage luxury houses, whose comparable products had
climbed well above the €2,000 threshold.

"We don't need to charge €3,000 for a bag to deliver quality," Mathieu Mothay explained in an interview. "By controlling our distribution
and focusing on direct relationships with customers, we eliminate un-
necessary markups. Our value proposition is straightforward: excellent
materials, innovative design, transparent pricing."

This philosophy resonated powerfully with consumers who had
grown increasingly skeptical of traditional luxury's price-value equation. In just seven years, Polène had cultivated a devoted global following without conventional advertising, relying instead on the visual
distinctiveness of its designs and word-of-mouth from satisfied customers.

Across the Atlantic, American brand Senreve pioneered a different
approach to accessible luxury. Founded in 2016 by Stanford graduates
Coral Chung and Wendy Wen, the brand targeted professional women
seeking bags that seamlessly blended functionality with luxury aesthetics. Its signature Maestra bag transformed from tote to backpack
to crossbody, accommodating a laptop while maintaining an elegantly
structured silhouette.

Like Polène, Senreve employed a direct-to-consumer model that eliminated traditional retail markups, allowing it to offer Italian-made products in the $500-1,500 range, significantly below comparable heritage luxury offerings. The brand's focus on both quality and functionality, combined with relatively accessible pricing, provided a compelling alternative for consumers seeking tangible value beyond brand prestige alone.

What united these diverse brands was their commitment to delivering tangible, perceptible value rather than trading primarily on heritage or exclusivity. They recognized that for many contemporary consumers, particularly Millennials and Gen Z, luxury was evolving beyond traditional status markers toward nuanced evaluation balancing quality, design intelligence, brand values, and price.

This accessible luxury segment posed a subtle yet significant threat to traditional luxury houses by challenging the fundamental premise that extraordinary prices were necessary for extraordinary products. By demonstrating that exceptional design and materials could be delivered at moderate price points through streamlined business models, these brands forced heritage houses to articulate more clearly what justified their premium beyond historical legacy alone.

As one industry analyst noted, "These brands are creating a new middle way in luxury, neither fast fashion nor heritage houses, but a category that prioritizes honest value, whether through cultural authenticity, quality craftsmanship, or innovative design. For many consumers, this offers a more meaningful luxury experience than logo-heavy products at extreme price points."

The boardroom at LVMH's Parisian headquarters hummed with tension as executives reviewed regional performance metrics. The numbers from China spoke volumes: while some brands in the conglomerate's portfolio maintained growth, others showed concerning deceleration despite massive marketing investments. The emergence of domestic Chinese luxury players and shifting consumer preferences toward cultural authenticity had created unprecedented competitive challenges.

"We need to go beyond seasonal collections and superficial local-ization," argued one senior executive who had spent years in Shanghai. "Chinese consumers can distinguish between genuine cultural engagement and tokenistic gestures. Our strategies must evolve."

This conversation echoed in luxury boardrooms worldwide as Western luxury houses confronted the regional rebellion reshaping their industry. Their responses ranged from sophisticated adaptation to problematic appropriation, with varying degrees of success.

Louis Vuitton demonstrated one approach through its collaboration with Japanese designer NIGO for the LV² collection. Rather than simply applying Japanese motifs to existing designs, this partnership represented a genuine creative dialogue between Western luxury codes and Japanese streetwear sensibilities. The resulting products felt authentic to both traditions while creating something fresh, and the collection resonated strongly with consumers seeking cultural cross-pollination rather than superficial adaptation.

Some legacy houses pursued strategic investments as a path to cultural relevance. Kering's acquisition of Chinese jewelry brand Qeelin in 2012 exemplified this approach. Founded in 2004, Qeelin was known for contemporary jewelry that incorporated traditional Chinese symbols and aesthetics. Under Kering, the brand maintained its cultural roots while gained access to global resources and distribution.

The appointment of local creative talent to leadership positions marked perhaps the most substantive response by some houses. When these appointments conferred genuine creative authority rather than symbolic representation, they could transform a brand's relationship with regional markets by bringing authentic cultural perspectives to the design process itself.

However, success required more than technical execution; it demanded genuine cultural fluency. Brands that approached regional markets with curiosity rather than assumption, hiring local talent not just for execution but for strategic guidance, generally fared better than those applying standardized global approaches.

"True adaptation requires understanding the fundamental values and worldview of a culture, how beauty is defined, how status functions, how history is interpreted," observed luxury analyst Wei Zhang. "Brands that invest in this deeper understanding create authentic connections that superficial localization can never achieve."

In a tranquil studio on Shanghai's outskirts, master craftsman Li Xiaofeng bent over a table of raw zitan wood, the legendary "purple sandalwood" once reserved exclusively for imperial furniture. His weathered hands moved with consummate precision, shaping the material using techniques passed through generations. For decades, he had created pieces for anonymous export to global luxury houses. Now, at sixty-eight, he served as the principal artisan for an emerging Chinese luxury furniture brand that prominently featured his name and story in its marketing.

"For most of my career, my craftsmanship was valued but my cultural understanding was not," he explained, carefully measuring a joint that would be assembled without nails or screws. "Western designers would send blueprints, and I would execute them. Now I contribute not just technique but knowledge, the philosophy behind traditional Chinese furniture design, why certain proportions matter, how the wood should interact with its environment."

Li's journey embodied the profound transformation reshaping the luxury landscape: a recalibration of cultural authority and creative leadership from West to East, from established houses to emerging regional voices, from outsourced production to authentic expression anchored in local heritage.

Evidence of this migration appeared across multiple domains. Auction results revealed growing premiums for exceptional examples of Asian craftsmanship, with Chinese ceramics and Japanese lacquerware commanding prices that rivaled or exceeded their European counterparts. Museum exhibitions increasingly featured Asian luxury traditions as subjects worthy of scholarly attention, not merely as influences on European design.

This gradual eastward shift in luxury's center of gravity reflected the historical pattern of aesthetic evolution. Throughout time, expressions of exceptional quality and prestige have never remained fixed; they've continually transformed in response to shifting market forces, cultural values, and consumer sensibilities.

For Western luxury conglomerates, this presented both challenge and opportunity. Those who recognized the migration as inevitable rather than temporary could participate in it through strategic partnerships, genuine cultural exchange, and respect for regional creative leadership. Those who clung to outmoded notions of European cultural supremacy in luxury definition risked increasing irrelevance as consumer preferences evolved.

The most dynamic aspect of this migration was its polycentric nature. Rather than simply shifting from one dominant center (Paris/Milan) to another (Shanghai/Tokyo), luxury's essence was dispersing across multiple regional expressions, each with its own authentic cultural foundations. This created a richer, more diverse luxury ecosystem where different traditions could engage in meaningful dialogue rather than hierarchical imitation.

"What we're observing isn't a simple substitution but rather an expansion," noted cultural historian Dr. Aimee Wong. "Our understanding of what constitutes 'exceptional' is broadening to embrace diverse cultural traditions, aesthetic philosophies, and craftsmanship legacies previously marginalized in the global conversation."

In this evolving context, consumers benefited from unprecedented choice. Those seeking the understated elegance of Japanese minimalism, the vibrant expressiveness of Indian craftsmanship, the philosophical depth of Chinese design traditions, or the heritage narratives of European houses could find authentic expressions of each. Luxury was becoming less monolithic and more personalized, allowing consumers to align their purchases with their individual cultural values and aesthetic preferences.

The regional rebellion had fundamentally altered luxury's trajectory. Western houses would continue to play important roles, indeed, many would thrive by embracing meaningful cultural exchange, but the era of unquestioned European dominance had conclusively ended. The future belonged to brands that understood luxury as a conversation between cultures rather than a monologue from established centers to emerging markets.

As evidence of this transformation, some regional luxury houses were beginning to influence global trends rather than merely responding to them. Chinese designers featured prominently in global fashion publications, Japanese minimalism served as a reference point for architects and interior designers worldwide, and Indian textile techniques inspired Western fashion houses. The flow of influence had become multidirectional.

This transformation heralds rich possibilities for luxury's future. As definitional authority diversifies across cultural contexts, innovative interpretations emerge that honor heritage while remaining relevant to contemporary life. The qualities that have always defined exceptional luxury, the ability to inspire desire, demonstrate discernment, and express distinction, continue to thrive, finding expression through diverse traditions once marginalized by Western-centric narratives.

Chapter Twenty-One

A Quiet Kind of Luxury

The Madison Avenue flagship of The Row seemed designed to whisper rather than shout. Unlike the gleaming, logo-emblazoned temples that had become luxury's norm, this space breathed with minimalist restraint: cream walls, pale oak floors, and carefully curated furniture pieces that read more as museum installation than retail display. The clothing hung with deliberate space between each item, a tableau of neutral tones and immaculate construction.

I observed two women browsing the store that afternoon. The first, caressing a caramel cashmere coat devoid of visible branding, wore a simple white shirt tucked into high-waisted trousers, accessorized only with a butter-soft leather bag bearing no logo. The second woman traced her fingers along the sleeve of an oversized black blazer, her outfit similarly understated. Neither outfit announced its undoubtedly steep price through conspicuous branding, yet when their eyes met across the room, something passed between them: a flicker of recognition, a subtle nod.

In that silent exchange lay an entirely different language of luxury. These women recognized in each other not the flash of logos, but the fall of fabric, the precision of a seam, the quality of materials that only the educated eye could discern. They belonged to a quiet club where wealth whispered rather than shouted, where status came through knowledge rather than badges.

The Row epitomized this new approach. Founded by Mary-Kate and Ashley Olsen in 2006 (named after London's Savile Row to signal their focus on tailoring), the brand had deliberately distanced itself from the founders' celebrity status. Instead, they let their creations speak through exceptional fabrics, impeccable details, and precise tailoring, combining timeless perspective with subtle attitudes to create what they termed an "irreverent classic signature." Unlike typical celebrity-founded lines, the Olsens chose to let their work stand on intrinsic merit rather than association, embodying quiet luxury through sophistication and substance over spectacle and symbols.

What made the exchange between these women so fascinating was how it represented the antithesis of what luxury had become. Here, recognition required connoisseurship: the ability to discern quality without obvious markers, to appreciate craftsmanship through educated eyes rather than brand associations.

The magic hadn't disappeared from luxury; it had merely migrated to places where only those with cultural capital could find it. And in this serene space, far from the clamor of logo-emblazoned flagships, these women had found their tribe.

When Rebecca sold her extensive collection of logo-covered handbags in 2019, her friends were baffled. "You spent a decade building that collection," they protested. But as she carefully photographed and listed each monogrammed piece, she felt not loss but liberation. "It was like clearing out mental clutter," she told me over coffee, now dressed in a perfectly tailored navy blazer without visible branding. "I realized I'd been carrying advertisements, not investments."

Rebecca's journey from logo devotee to quality connoisseur mirrored a broader shift among luxury consumers. After years of democratization had rendered luxury symbols commonplace, many experienced a profound status anxiety: our carefully curated symbols no longer carried the distinction they once promised. The dilution of exclusivity through broader accessibility had hollowed the emotional reward traditionally associated with luxury purchases.

For some, like Rebecca, this disappointment sparked not rejection but rediscovery, a quest to reconnect with luxury's original promise of exceptional quality and craftsmanship. "I replaced twelve logo bags with one Loro Piana Sesia bag," she explained. "When I first held it, I understood immediately what I'd been missing. It was like trading processed food for a meal crafted from farmer's market ingredients."

The sensory awakening she described was common among those making this transition. After years of evaluating luxury primarily through visual signals (logos, recognizable patterns, distinctive hardware), many were rediscovering the tactile pleasures that had traditionally defined luxury: the substantial weight of properly loomed cashmere, the supple hand of vegetable-tanned leather, the perfect tension of hand-stitched seams.

Michael, a 42-year-old architect, described his first experience with a Brunello Cucinelli sweater in almost spiritual terms: "It sounds ridiculous, but touching it was a revelation. I'd spent thousands on branded clothing, but this was different; the cashmere felt alive somehow." The piece cost more than any sweater he'd previously purchased, yet contained no visible branding. "The only people who recognize it are those who own one themselves," he noted with evident satisfaction. "That feels more exclusive than any logo ever could."

For younger consumers like Amelia, 28, who bypassed logo luxury entirely, the journey often began online. "I spent months in forums learning about construction techniques before making my first purchase," she explained. Her education centered not on brand recognition but on identifying quality markers: full-canvas construction in suits, hand-rolled hems on scarves, the suppleness of different leather tannages. This knowledge-based approach connected to a broader trend of "consumer maturity," where advanced consumers evolved toward more subtle, inconspicuous forms of consumption based on deeper understanding of product attributes.

The transition wasn't just about aesthetics but increasingly about values alignment. For many, quiet luxury brands offered not only superior craftsmanship but also more ethical and sustainable approaches. Rebecca pointed to Brunello Cucinelli's "humanistic capitalism" philosophy, where workers received wages significantly above industry standards and worked in beautifully restored buildings in Solomeo, Italy. "When I buy from them, I'm supporting a vision I believe in, not just acquiring another status symbol."

What united these diverse journeys was a fundamental shift in how value was perceived: from external validation to personal knowledge, from conspicuous branding to inconspicuous quality. The satisfaction derived not from others recognizing the purchase but from the consumer's own ability to discern and appreciate craftsmanship. In this new paradigm, the most sophisticated status signal wasn't displaying recognizable luxury but demonstrating the cultural capital necessary to appreciate its more subtle expressions.

"That's the same shirt my father was buried in," Tom Wambsgans sneered at cousin Greg in HBO's "Succession," mocking Greg's Burberry purchase while himself wearing what appeared to be a plain navy sweater, deceptively simple with its perfect drape and barely perceptible depth of color that viewers later identified as Loro Piana cashmere, retailing for approximately $2,000. In this iconic scene, the show crystallized what would become known as the "Succession effect," a cultural moment that thrust "stealth wealth" fashion into mainstream consciousness.

The series provided a masterclass in distinguishing old-money style from nouveau riche fashion through meticulous costume design. The Roy family's wardrobe became a character itself, telegraphing quiet luxury through whisper-not-shout clothing devoid of logos but stratospheric in price. Costume designer Michelle Matland deliberately chose pieces from Loro Piana, Brunello Cucinelli, Zegna, and The Row, creating what fashion observers termed "quiet luxury" or "stealth wealth," clothing that signaled status only to those educated enough to recognize its quality.

The impact proved measurable. Google searches for "quiet luxury" and "stealth wealth" skyrocketed during the show's final season in 2023. Luxury retailers reported unprecedented interest in logo-free pieces from brands featured in the series. The Row saw such demand increase for its minimalist designs that certain items remained sold out for months.

What made "Succession" particularly influential was how it educated viewers on the subtle codes of wealth signaling. The characters' clothing never featured prominent branding, yet each outfit conveyed precise information about power, taste, and status. The timing coincided with and accelerated growing weariness with logo-heavy consumption, providing a compelling visual lexicon that catalyzed mainstream recognition of this alternative approach.

The unassuming medieval village of Solomeo, perched atop a gentle Umbrian hill, seemed an unlikely epicenter for luxury's reinvention. Yet here Brunello Cucinelli established his humanistic approach to cashmere production, an approach that would help redefine luxury for a generation seeking meaning beyond logos.

The Italian approach to luxury maintained connections to preindustrial craft traditions. At Bottega Veneta's atelier in the Veneto region, the signature intrecciato weave, leather strips interlaced in a distinctive pattern, required dozens of precise hand movements. The technique, originally developed in the 1970s when the house had limited sewing machinery available, created bags with distinctive tactile signatures. The subtle irregularities in tension and pattern that accompanied handweaving meant each piece carried unique sensory fingerprints, the antithesis of mass production's standardization.

Daniel Lee's tenure as creative director at Bottega Veneta (2018-2021) exemplified this shift. His work maintained the house's craft foundations while creating designs that became instantly recognizable to fashion cognoscenti despite their logo-free presentation. The Pouch bag, unveiled in his first collection, featured no external branding but became immediately identifiable through its distinctive gathered leather form, demonstrating how shape, material, and construction could create recognition without monograms.

The emphasis on materiality over marketing reflected in these houses' business practices. Cucinelli's dedication to maintaining manufacturing in Solomeo, paying workers above-market wages, and preserving craftsmanship was not just ethical positioning but recognition that human skill created distinct quality impossible to replicate through automation.

For consumers rediscovering craftsmanship, these experiences often proved transformative. "I used to buy luxury for how it photographed on Instagram," admitted Caroline, a former influencer. "Now I buy for how it feels against my skin, how it changes with me over time. My Bottega bag has developed a patina that tells our story together, something a logo-covered piece could never do."

While Italian craftsmanship had deep historical roots, the new global stealth wealth landscape encompassed diverse approaches united by understated aesthetics and quality-first philosophy. Beyond The Row's American minimalism, houses like Gabriela Hearst brought Uruguayan craft traditions and sustainability focus to luxury, while European heritage guardians like Delvaux and Moynat revived historical craft techniques for contemporary connoisseurs.

The Row exemplified American minimalism within this movement. Their approach centered on impeccable materials and silhouettes that conveyed sophistication through restraint. "The Row's pieces make you feel like you're in on a secret," observed Rachel, a devoted customer. "The knowledge that the plain white shirt you're wearing costs nearly $1,000 and is recognized by only those who understand quality, that's the new exclusivity." The brand's extreme anti-marketing stance, no splashy campaigns, minimal social media, a resistance to celebrity associations despite its celebrity founders, created mystique through absence rather than presence.

Gabriela Hearst brought different cultural influences to quiet luxury. Founded in 2015, the brand blended Hearst's Uruguayan ranching background with luxury craftsmanship. Her "honest luxury" philosophy emphasized sustainability alongside quality, incorporating materials like deadstock fabrics, wool from her family's ranch, and collaborations with nonprofits like Manos del Uruguay, a women's weaving collective.

European heritage brands offered another expression of stealth wealth. Belgium's Delvaux, founded in 1829 and the oldest fine leather luxury goods house in the world, maintained exceptional craftsmanship while remaining largely unknown outside connoisseur circles. Similarly, Moynat, a French trunk maker founded in 1849 and revived by LVMH in 2010, continued traditional techniques while maintaining deliberate obscurity.

This global movement maintained exclusivity not primarily through limited production but through knowledge barriers. Without education about artisanal indicators, consumers couldn't recognize or fully appreciate these pieces. This created natural limitation that preserved exclusivity while allowing growth.

When Thomas first purchased a Brunello Cucinelli cashmere sweater, he experienced something unexpected: the garment's absence of visible branding actually heightened his satisfaction. "There's something deeply gratifying about owning something exceptional that can only be recognized by others who share your knowledge," he reflected. "It creates a more meaningful form of connection than logo recognition ever did."

This psychological shift, from wanting everyone to recognize your purchases to preferring recognition only from select individuals, lay at the heart of quiet luxury's appeal. It represented an evolution in status signaling from conspicuous to inconspicuous consumption, where the marker of sophistication became not displaying luxury but having the connoisseurship to recognize it in its unmarked form.

Research in consumer psychology identified this as a form of "consumer maturity," where experienced luxury consumers often preferred inconspicuous products while less experienced ones favored more obvious branding. This pattern appeared across cultures but intensified in mature luxury markets where consumers had moved beyond initial status-seeking to more nuanced appreciation of craftsmanship and quality.

The psychological rewards of this knowledge-based approach operated on multiple levels. First came the satisfaction of educational attainment, the pride in developing expertise previously limited to industry insiders. Second, connoisseurship created a form of community through shared recognition. "There's this moment when you notice someone else carrying Delvaux or wearing The Row," explained Richard, a finance executive. "Your eyes meet, and there's this flutter of mutual recognition, not just of the brand but of each other as people who value the same things."

Beyond individual psychology, quiet luxury participation conferred what sociologist Pierre Bourdieu termed "cultural capital," knowledge and taste that function as status markers within specific social contexts.

Online communities played crucial roles in this knowledge development. Forums dedicated to specific crafts or brands became spaces where enthusiasts shared expertise and reinforced valuation of subtle quality markers. These communities established shared vocabulary for discussing craftsmanship features invisible to untrained observers: the tension of hand-stitches, the appropriate drape of properly milled fabrics, the correct patination of vegetable-tanned leather.

Here lay one of quiet luxury's central paradoxes: items with minimal or absent branding frequently commanded higher prices than their logo-emblazoned counterparts. A plain Loro Piana cashmere sweater often cost more than a logo-covered Gucci equivalent; an unmarked Valextra bag typically exceeded the price of a monogrammed Louis Vuitton piece.

"It's actually quite logical," explained luxury retail analyst Marcus Chen. "The logo itself adds no material value; it's marketing. When a brand invests those resources instead in superior materials and craftsmanship, the cost naturally increases while visible branding decreases." This created what Chen termed "inverse logo pricing," as logo prominence decreased, price typically increased.

Perhaps the most intriguing paradox lay in ownership structures. Many paragon quiet luxury brands belonged to the same conglomerates dominating logo-heavy luxury. LVMH, better known for Louis Vuitton's prominent monograms, owned Loro Piana (acquired 2013) and Moynat (revived 2010). Kering, parent company of logo-prominent Gucci, controlled Bottega Veneta.

Genuinely independent quiet luxury houses offered alternatives for those seeking complete separation from conglomerates. The Row remained privately owned by its founders, maintaining complete creative and strategic control. Brunello Cucinelli operated as a public company but with the founder maintaining significant ownership and philosophical direction.

The allure hadn't disappeared from luxury; it had migrated to new expressions that preserved the original values that had made luxury compelling in the first place: exceptional craftsmanship, material quality, aesthetic refinement, and true exclusivity.

This cyclical pattern, where luxury houses democratize to grow, diluting their exclusivity, while new custodians of artisanal excellence emerge to capture the mystique, revealed itself as a perpetual rhythm in luxury's evolution. What we were witnessing wasn't the death of luxury but its renewal through houses committed to quality over ubiquity, substance over symbolism.

For individual consumers, this evolution often manifested as a personal journey. Many described an evolution from logo-heavy purchases that delivered short-lived excitement to fewer, more considered acquisitions that provided lasting satisfaction through quality appreciation.

This evolution wasn't about rejecting luxury but rediscovering its essence. The emotional journey from enchantment to disillusionment to rediscovery reflected not cynicism but a more sophisticated engagement with quality and craft. For many, quiet luxury represented not the abandonment of luxury's promise but its fulfillment in more meaningful form.

Perhaps most significantly, this evolution demonstrated consumer agency in shaping luxury's direction. As discerning consumers shifted their spending toward quality-focused houses, they created market validation for approaches prioritizing craftsmanship over marketing, substance over symbolism.

"I don't worry about which specific brands will maintain their standards," a young woman at The Row reflected. "I've learned to recognize quality beyond labels. If a house dilutes its craftsmanship for growth, the magic will simply migrate somewhere new, and those of us who've educated our eyes and hands will follow it."

Chapter Twenty-Two

The New Custodians

In the northern Italian region of Umbria, golden morning light spills across the medieval village of Solomeo as artisans make their way through cobblestone streets to work. Inside a restored 14th-century castle, master cashmere knitter Gabriella guides her apprentice through the final stitches of a sweater that will command €2,800 at completion. No logo will announce its provenance; its exquisite construction alone will identify it to those with the sensory education to recognize artisanal mastery.

"My grandfather taught my father, who taught me," Gabriella explains, her fingers dancing with practiced precision. "This garment will outlive its first owner if cared for properly."

In Paris, leather artisan Pascal bends over a Moynat handbag, demanding forty hours of handwork using techniques that trace their lineage to the 19th century. And in a minimalist New York studio, designers at The Row sift through fabric samples, rejecting dozens that fall short of their exacting standards.

These vignettes represent a powerful counternarrative to luxury's mass democratization. While conglomerate flagships push logo-heavy accessories and increasingly accessible price points, a different approach thrives in these quieter spaces. These brands, Brunello Cucinelli, Moynat, The Row, Loro Piana, Bottega Veneta, and others, have become the new custodians of luxury's original essence: exceptional craftsmanship, material integrity, and timeless design that transcends seasonal whims.

As established luxury houses expand to capture broader markets, they inevitably dilute the rarity and exclusivity that defined their initial allure. This creates space for new or revitalized brands to capture the essence that migrates away from mass luxury, to become guardians of the "magic" that defined luxury's original promise.

What distinguishes these custodians isn't primarily aesthetic but philosophical. They approach luxury as a commitment to excellence rather than a marketing category, building business models that prioritize quality over quantity, connoisseurship over conspicuousness, and enduring value over ephemeral trends.

"When an object emerges from hands that have mastered their craft over decades, with attention to every minute detail, it contains something beyond its material components," explains Brunello Cucinelli, whose eponymous brand revitalized Solomeo while building a global enterprise founded on "humanistic capitalism" and exceptional cashmere. "Human dignity lives within the object itself."

This dignity manifests throughout the entire creation process. In Solomeo, Cucinelli's artisans work in light-flooded studios converted from medieval buildings, earning wages that significantly exceed industry standards. At Bottega Veneta's atelier in the Veneto region, craftspeople trained through the company's Accademia Labor et Ingenium preserve the distinctive intrecciato weaving technique that has become the brand's unspoken signature. At Moynat, each bag evolves under a single artisan from inception to completion.

What unites these diverse caretakers isn't a rejection of commercial success but a fundamentally different philosophy for achieving it.

They've discovered how to build enduring enterprises by safeguarding techniques that might otherwise vanish, creating value through extraordinary expertise rather than artificial scarcity.

At dawn in the Peruvian Andes, above 3,500 meters where the air thins and the sky deepens to cobalt, Loro Piana's field teams prepare for a vicuña gathering. Working with local communities, they carefully herd these wild camelids into temporary corrals, where the animals will be shorn of their precious undercoat before returning to their mountainous freedom.

Each vicuña yields a mere 250 grams of usable fiber, and the animals can only be shorn every two years. A single coat crafted from this golden fleece requires the yield from twenty-five to thirty-five animals and commands prices starting at €20,000.

"The fiber almost breathes in your hands," says Marco Pozzoli, who oversees Loro Piana's fiber sourcing. "Its warmth comes not just from insulating properties but seems to carry something of the living animal, the altitude, the particular grasses of the high plains."

This devotion to extraordinary materials forms the cornerstone of quiet luxury's value proposition. While logo-heavy brands increasingly incorporate synthetic components and cost-cutting production methods, these artisanal stewards invest ever more deeply in material excellence, often controlling entire supply chains from source to finished product to ensure uncompromised quality.

Brunello Cucinelli approaches cashmere with similar reverence, sourcing the finest fibers from Mongolia and Inner Mongolia through decades-long relationships with herders. At The Row, material sourcing becomes an exercise in global treasure hunting. Buyers travel extensively to discover small-batch textiles from specialized mills: Japanese denims woven on vintage shuttle looms, Scottish cashmeres from establishments dating to the 18th century, Italian silks produced by families who have perfected their craft over centuries.

These extraordinary materials command commensurate prices, not as arbitrary luxury markups but as reflections of genuine resource scarcity and extensive processes required to transform raw materials into exceptional components. What distinguishes these custodians' approach extends beyond quality to sustainability, both environmental and cultural. By investing in traditional production methods and the communities that preserve them, these brands maintain supply chains that can continue indefinitely.

The result is a material vocabulary that speaks in whispers rather than shouts: fabrics, leathers, and fibers whose exceptional qualities reveal themselves through sensory experience rather than visual branding. For the educated luxury consumer, the hand of a Cucinelli cashmere or the drape of a garment from The Row has become luxury's new signature, recognizable not through logos but through developed connoisseurship.

On the northern edge of Bottega Veneta's atelier in Montebello Vicentino, master artisan Roberto Bonaventura guides a new apprentice through the complex intrecciato technique that has defined the house since 1966. The trademark leather weave involves cutting leather into precise strips, then interlacing them to create a distinctive three-dimensional pattern requiring extraordinary manual dexterity.

"It takes three years to become proficient," Bonaventura explains, adjusting the apprentice's grip while demonstrating the precise tension needed at a challenging corner. "Five years to achieve true mastery. We cannot rush this process any more than a violinist can rush learning Paganini."

This deliberate pace forms the foundation of an alternative business model, one that inverts conventional luxury strategy. While democratized luxury houses race toward greater volume through accessible products, these custodian brands have developed a counterintuitive approach: producing less, charging more, and creating enduring value that transcends fashion's cycles.

The economic equation differs fundamentally from mass luxury. A Louis Vuitton canvas bag might sell for €1,500 with materials costing less than €100 and assembly completed in 2-3 hours, creating dramatic margins multiplied across hundreds of thousands of units. In contrast, a Bottega Veneta intrecciato bag might require 8-12 hours of skilled labor with more expensive materials, commanding €3,500-5,000 but selling in quantities measured in thousands rather than hundreds of thousands.

"We embrace the natural limitations imposed by our commitment to craftsmanship," explains Lisa Attia, CEO of Moynat. "Our artisans require proper time to create pieces worthy of our heritage. This means our growth will never match brands producing in high volume, but it ensures our pieces maintain their value and integrity."

This artisanal-focused approach extends beyond production to inform every dimension of these houses' operations. Retail environments become intimate spaces for education rather than high-volume sales channels. Product assortments remain tightly edited rather than expanding endlessly into new categories.

The approach demands courage that runs counter to conventional business wisdom, particularly for publicly traded companies under constant growth pressure. Brunello Cucinelli pioneered what he terms "gracious growth," targeting steady, sustainable expansion of 8-10% annually rather than the dramatic escalation expected of luxury darlings.

For these heritage champions, technical virtuosity isn't merely marketing narrative but foundational business strategy. They invest heavily in preserving specialized skills through formal training programs. Bottega Veneta established its Accademia Labor et Ingenium to train new generations in traditional leather crafts. Brunello Cucinelli's School of Contemporary High Craftsmanship offers programs in tailoring, cutting, mending, and knitting.

This expertise-driven paradigm redefines the very essence of exclusivity. Rather than manufacturing scarcity through artificial limitations, these brands embrace the natural constraints imposed by their commitment to quality. A Cucinelli sweater's exclusivity stems not from deliberately constrained production but from the genuine scarcity of artisans capable of creating it to the company's standards.

In a sleek Milanese conference room in 2013, the leadership of Loro Piana finalized the sale of an 80% stake to luxury conglomerate

LVMH for €2 billion. The acquisition represented a curious paradox: the world's largest luxury group, known for democratizing brands like Louis Vuitton through massive scale, now owned one of the quintessential custodians of quiet luxury.

This revealed a sophisticated portfolio strategy. LVMH, Kering, and Richemont had built multi-tiered luxury ecosystems where different brands served different market segments and consumer journey stages, from entry-level luxury accessible to middle-class consumers to ultra-exclusive houses serving the genuinely wealthy.

For the quiet luxury custodians, conglomerate ownership brought substantial advantages alongside potential risks. Loro Piana gained access to LVMH's unparalleled global distribution network, financial resources for expansion, and operational expertise.

Yet tensions inevitably arose between growth expectations and craft preservation. In contrast, independently owned custodians maintained complete autonomy over their business approaches. The Row, privately owned by Mary-Kate and Ashley Olsen despite its extraordinary success, answered to no shareholders beyond its founders.

Similarly, Brunello Cucinelli maintained controlling interest in his public company, allowing him to pursue his "humanistic capitalism" without shareholder revolt. When questioned about modest growth targets during investor calls, he firmly defended his philosophy: "We are growing at what I believe to be a healthy, sustainable pace. I have always been wary of brands that grow too quickly, they risk losing their soul in the process."

This segmentation ensured that regardless of ownership structure, the "magic" of luxury would always find appropriate vessels. As some houses inevitably grew toward greater accessibility, others would emerge to capture the essence that had migrated away.

On a February morning in 2021, devoted followers of Bottega Veneta's Instagram account, which had accumulated 2.5 million followers, discovered it had vanished overnight. The brand, under creative director Daniel Lee, had taken the unprecedented step of deleting its social media presence entirely while at the height of its renaissance.

"The decision reflected Daniel Lee's belief that social media homogenizes luxury, forcing brands into a constant stream of content that undermines exclusivity and mystery," explained a former Bottega Veneta digital strategist. "He wanted the products to be experienced physically, not flattened into Instagram squares."

This dramatic move highlighted the core challenge facing quiet luxury custodians in the digital age: how to maintain their essence, exclusivity, craft appreciation, sensory experience, within platforms designed for mass visibility, instant gratification, and two-dimensional representation.

The Row epitomized the minimalist approach. Its Instagram account functioned more as curated mood board than marketing channel, featuring art, architecture, and design influences alongside sparse product imagery. Posts appeared irregularly, without captions or calls to action.

Brunello Cucinelli adopted a storytelling-rich approach that emphasized craft, philosophy, and place over product promotion. The brand's digital content delved deeply into the restoration of Solomeo, the humanistic philosophy guiding the company, and the craftsmanship behind its creations.

These varied approaches shared common elements distinguishing them from mainstream luxury's digital strategies. Product launches received minimal fanfare rather than countdown campaigns. Influencer partnerships were highly selective or entirely absent. Pricing rarely appeared in social content, reinforcing the "if you have to ask" exclusivity principle.

This digital discretion extended to customer relationships. Rather than mass email marketing, these brands favored personalized digital clienteling with remarkable specificity.

"Our digital strategy is less about maximizing impressions and more about deepening connection with those who already appreciate what we do," explained a Valextra digital executive. "We would rather have 10,000 genuinely engaged followers who understand our values than a million who simply like our aesthetic."

The approach required confidence to resist industry pressure toward digital overexposure. Yet their selective presence created distinctive value in an overcrowded attention economy, the luxury of absence in a world of omnipresence.

In a sunlit workshop within Hermès's leather goods facility in Pantin, just outside Paris, master saddle maker Jean-Luc Parisot performed a ritual unchanged since the house's founding in 1837: hand-stitching a saddle using techniques developed for 19th-century European cavalry officers.

"We are not merely producing objects but preserving a cultural heritage," explained Axel Dumas, CEO of Hermès and sixth-generation member of the founding family. "These techniques exist only because we continue to practice them. Once interrupted, such knowledge chains are nearly impossible to reconstruct."

This preservation manifested most visibly in the apprenticeship systems these houses maintained. At Moynat, new leather workers underwent a three-year training program under master artisans before working independently. Brunello Cucinelli's School of Contemporary High Craftsmanship formalized knowledge transfer across multiple disciplines.

The approach contrasted sharply with manufacturing trends in mass luxury, where production increasingly relied on semi-skilled workers performing standardized tasks. Even at premium price points, many luxury goods were now produced through fragmented processes where no single artisan maintained comprehensive knowledge of the entire creation.

Beyond formal apprenticeships, quiet luxury custodians invested in documenting endangered techniques. Delvaux maintained extensive archives of historical leather-working methods dating back to the 19th century. Bottega Veneta created detailed records of regional variations in the intrecciato technique.

The most visionary among these houses recognized that genuine preservation demanded evolution rather than stagnation. Hermès continuously developed new applications for traditional saddle-stitching.

Loro Piana invested in research to apply ancient fiber-processing techniques to newly developed materials.

"The greatest risk to craft preservation isn't change but irrelevance," observed a master patternmaker at Brunello Cucinelli. "If traditional techniques produce only museum pieces disconnected from contemporary life, they become curiosities rather than living traditions. Our responsibility is finding meaningful applications for ancient knowledge in modern contexts."

This philosophy, preservation through evolution rather than stagnation, distinguished genuine craft custodians from brands trading in empty heritage narratives.

Atop the Umbrian hill where Brunello Cucinelli had revitalized Solomeo, the evening light gilded a scene that defied conventional business logic. Stone buildings housing workshops stood alongside a theater, library, and vineyard. Employees departed at reasonable hours to spend time with their families.

"I believe that profit and human dignity can coexist, must coexist," Cucinelli explained from his office overlooking the village. "We have demonstrated that a business respecting human limits and natural rhythms can still be commercially successful."

This balance between commercial viability and human-centered values defined the unique approach of quiet luxury's custodians. During the 2008 financial crisis, while logo-heavy luxury suffered double-digit declines, Hermès and Brunello Cucinelli demonstrated remarkable resilience.

This resilience stemmed from multiple factors: client relationships emphasizing genuine quality appreciation rather than trend participation; products that maintained value over time; and controlled growth that prevented overexpansion.

Most fundamentally, their business models prioritized enduring value over quarterly metrics. Beyond business resilience, these quality-focused houses increasingly embedded environmental stewardship into their core operations. Brunello Cucinelli implemented regenerative farming practices around Solomeo. Gabriela Hearst pioneered car-bon-neutral fashion shows. Loro Piana's vicuña conservation program helped restore a species once threatened with extinction.

"True luxury should consider all costs, environmental, social, and cultural, not just financial ones," explained Gabriela Hearst. "When we speak of sustainability, we must include the sustainability of craft traditions, rural communities, and environmental systems that make our work possible."

Perhaps the most profound sustainability these houses embodied was cultural, preserving approaches to creation threatened by industrial efficiency. In a market increasingly defined by algorithm-driven design and quarterly profit pressure, they maintained space for human judgment, craft tradition, and long-term thinking.

The pattern was evident throughout luxury's history. When Dior diluted its exclusivity through excessive licensing in the 1970s and early 1980s, Hermès gained prominence among consumers seeking genuine quality. As Louis Vuitton expanded broadly in the 1990s and 2000s, Bottega Veneta found renewed relevance under Tomas Maier's quiet luxury approach. The more recent democratization of Gucci created space for The Row's minimalist perfection.

"The essence of luxury is eternal, though its vessels change," reflected François-Henri Pinault, CEO of Kering. "In every generation, certain houses maintain the highest standards while others evolve toward broader markets."

For the custodians themselves, this understanding brought both responsibility and opportunity. Their role was not merely commercial but cultural, maintaining traditions, techniques, and values that created meaning beyond status or fashion.

"We don't think in quarters or even years, but generations," Axel Dumas explained of Hermès's approach. "This perspective changes everything: how we train our artisans, how we source our materials, how we design our products."

In this extended vision lay perhaps the greatest sustainability of all, the ability to maintain luxury's essential promise across changing conditions, preserving its magic not as static tradition but as living practice adapting to each era without compromising its core values.

Chapter Twenty-Three

The Magic Migrates

The exhibition space in Milan's Brera district hummed with quiet conversation as attendees drifted between displays of contemporary craft. I observed two women who had been circling the room, their paths finally converging before a glass case housing a leather portfolio. No logos marked its surface; only the subtle perfection of its construction proclaimed its value.

The first woman, perhaps in her early forties with silver-streaked hair, wore a cashmere coat in a shade hovering between camel and sand, the kind of elusive color that demanded exquisite natural dyeing. The second, younger by a decade and dressed in a perfectly tailored linen jacket, carried a handbag whose leather seemed to absorb rather than reflect light.

"The edge finishing is remarkable," the younger woman said.

The older woman nodded. "Burnished by hand. You can tell by the slight variations in the patina. Probably used traditional pine resin."

They continued analyzing the piece with the effortless shorthand of connoisseurs, discussing techniques I'd never encountered, referencing traditions from regions I couldn't place. Neither mentioned price or brand. Their appreciation centered entirely on the craft itself, the artisan's decisions, the materials, the evidence of time devoted to creation.

This exchange would have been unthinkable a decade earlier, when luxury meant recognizable monograms and status-signaling logos. These women embodied a new tribe of luxury consumers who had completed the journey from conspicuous consumption to something more nuanced, a relationship with craftsmanship that demanded education, sensory development, and a reimagining of value.

As they moved to examine a series of hand-blown glass vessels, I realized I was witnessing the completion of luxury's cycle. The magic hadn't vanished when traditional luxury houses expanded and democratized; it had simply migrated to new expressions that those with cultivated taste could recognize. For these women, the thrill came not from displaying status through familiar symbols but from their ability to recognize quality through educated eyes and fingertips, a form of discernment far more exclusive than the ability to purchase a logo-covered handbag.

In their quiet appreciation, in their careful assessment of craft details invisible to untrained eyes, they had discovered what so many of us sought since logo fatigue set in: enchantment restored through knowledge, sensory engagement, and connection to human skill.

After the logo-laden binge of the 2010s came the inevitable hangover. We'd gorged on monograms, on hardware embossed with recognizable initials, on items whose primary function seemed to be announcing their price tag rather than serving any practical purpose. The brands we once coveted had become ubiquitous. What had once felt exclusive now felt commonplace; what had once seemed special now seemed mass-manufactured.

"I looked at my closet one morning and felt physically ill," Rebecca told me over coffee in a Paris café. Once an enthusiastic luxury consumer with a collection of logo-heavy bags spanning every major house, she had recently divested herself of nearly everything bearing a conspicuous brand mark. "Beyond the money I'd spent, I realized I'd been participating in something that had lost its soul. These objects had ceased to be expressions of craftsmanship; they'd become walking advertisements. And I had paid thousands for the privilege of serving as a billboard."

Rebecca's disillusionment wasn't isolated. By 2024, approximately 50 million consumers had retreated from purchasing traditional luxury goods over the previous two years. This unprecedented exodus reflected a profound disconnection between what mainstream luxury houses were offering and what consumers were seeking.

Part of this stemmed from the widening gap between price and perceived value. As luxury conglomerates pushed prices ever higher, with increases of up to 400% on certain iconic pieces over a two-decade period, without corresponding quality improvements, consumers began questioning what exactly they were paying for. As Andrea Guerra, CEO of Prada, noted in a moment of surprising candor, the industry had experienced "hyperinflation [of handbag prices] that was not linked to the value of the dream offered to consumers."

But price inflation wasn't the sole catalyst for disillusionment. A deeper emotional current flowed beneath, the sense that luxury's enchantment had evaporated through sheer ubiquity. Michael, who once embraced logo-driven luxury, pinpointed the moment his relationship with traditional luxury brands transformed: "I was waiting for a flight at Heathrow when I realized nearly every person in the lounge carried the same designer bag I'd just purchased. I'd invested a small fortune to become indistinguishable from everyone else."

This discomfort, the dawning recognition that mass luxury contained an inherent contradiction, created a void. We had invested emotionally and financially in luxury's promise: the belief that exceptional objects could transform our experience, connecting us to tradition, craft, and beauty. When that promise fractured, many entered a searching phase, wondering where to find the enchantment that had initially drawn them to luxury.

For some, this searching took shape as wholesale rejection of material luxury in favor of experiences. "I traded bags for memories," explained Sophia, who now directed her resources toward experiencing traditional crafts worldwide rather than acquiring finished products. "Learning weaving techniques directly from Peruvian artisans brings me far more satisfaction than purchasing another designer scarf."

Others ventured into previously unexplored territories where knowledge itself created natural barriers to entry. Vintage timepieces, first-edition literature, small-batch spirits, and heritage food traditions attracted waves of consumers seeking depth rather than display.

As consumers moved beyond logo disillusionment, their journeys didn't follow a single trajectory. Wei Zhang, a marketing executive based in Shanghai, found his path through cultural heritage. After years of collecting Western luxury brands, he experienced what he described as "a moment of cultural awakening" while visiting an exhibition of traditional Chinese crafts. "I stood before a display of Yixing clay teapots, simple, unadorned, yet possessing a depth of artistry that made the designer items in my home feel hollow by comparison," he recalled.

This encounter led Wei to divest most of his logo-heavy collection and redirect his resources toward supporting the revival of Chinese craft traditions. "What I value now isn't the status a recognizable brand confers, but the connection to cultural continuity these pieces represent," he explained.

A different path emerged for consumers like Aisha, a London-based physician who found meaning through alignment with personal values. "I reached a point where I couldn't reconcile my concerns about climate change with my consumption habits," she explained. Her turning point came after researching the environmental impact of her favorite fashion brands.

Aisha's journey led her toward brands with genuine sustainability commitments. She began focusing on circulation rather than accumulation, investing in pieces designed to be repaired and eventually biodegraded or recycled. "What feels luxurious to me now is knowing the complete story of what I own, where the materials came from, who made it, under what conditions, and what will happen when I'm finished with it," she explained.

What united these divergent paths, whether through cultural heritage or values alignment, was a fundamental shift from passive consumption to active engagement. Each required investment beyond financial resources; they demanded time, attention, education, and personal growth.

Perhaps most telling was that none of these paths led back to the abandoned territory of logo luxury. Once consumers had experienced the deeper satisfaction of knowledge-based appreciation, the thin pleasure of brand recognition rarely proved enticing enough to draw them back.

The most striking transformation in post-logo luxury wasn't just where consumers directed their attention but how they engaged with the objects of their desire. The fundamental nature of luxury consumption was evolving from a focus on ownership to an emphasis on knowledge, a shift that changed not just what people bought but how they experienced luxury itself.

Thomas, who previously quantified success through his inventory of designer acquisitions, now conversed more passionately about his accumulated knowledge than his material possessions. In his Amsterdam apartment, he led me through a collection transformed, once dominated by logo-emblazoned statement pieces, now composed of understated expressions of masterful craft. Pausing before an unbranded leather briefcase, he lifted it with reverent hands.

"Look at the stitching here," he said, pointing to nearly invisible seams. "This is saddle stitching, each hole is punched by hand, then the artisan passes needles from both directions, creating a stitch that won't unravel even if the thread breaks in one place." His fingers traced the edge of the leather, which gleamed with a subtle polish. "And this edge finishing, they've beveled the leather, then burnished it with natural gum arabic and beeswax. It takes hours of patient work, but the result is an edge that will never fray or separate."

More compelling than Thomas's expertise was his palpable delight in it. The spark in his eyes while explaining these nuances revealed a profound transformation: luxury consumption had evolved from a predominantly social activity (centered on external validation) into an intensely personal pursuit.

This shift toward connoisseurship flourished within an ecosystem of digital connection. Online platforms democratized specialized knowledge once exclusively held by industry insiders. Virtual communities fostered spaces where enthusiasts exchanged insights, evaluated products, and collaboratively developed assessment criteria that frequently challenged established marketing narratives.

This shift from ownership to knowledge created a form of exclusivity potentially more meaningful than price barriers. While financial resources could be acquired suddenly, developing true connoisseurship required time, dedication, and personal investment that couldn't be purchased or faked. "You can buy a Birkin with a credit card in an afternoon," Thomas observed, "but you can't buy the ability to recognize quality craftsmanship without years of study and experience."

For many, this knowledge-based approach to luxury provided deeper, more lasting satisfaction than the cycle of acquisition and display that had characterized their previous relationship with luxury. "There's something profoundly different about appreciation based on understanding rather than recognition," explained Miranda, who had transitioned from collecting logo-marked luxury items to seeking out the work of master artisans. "When you recognize quality through educated senses rather than through marketing cues, the relationship becomes intimate rather than performative."

Against the backdrop of digital saturation and virtual living, luxury's migration toward sensory richness emerged as a powerful countercurrent. While our daily existence became increasingly screen-mediated, a revival of tactile appreciation blossomed among consumers craving authentic material connection.

I watched as Maria ran her fingers across the surface of a wooden table in the showroom of a small Japanese-influenced furniture maker in Copenhagen. Her eyes closed briefly as she concentrated on the sensation. "Feel this," she said, guiding my hand to the edge. "There's a subtle roundness that welcomes your touch, not machine-perfect like factory furniture, but shaped by hand-planes to follow the natural grain of the wood."

Maria, an architect who had once furnished her home with recognizable designer pieces, now sought out craft studios producing work of exceptional tactile quality. "I became aware that I was living in a visually impressive but sensually impoverished environment," she explained. "Everything looked good in photographs but offered little pleasure to touch. Now I select things primarily for how they feel when I interact with them: the temperature of ceramic against my lips, the weight of hand-forged cutlery, the gentle give of wood that responds to humidity and use."

This turn toward sensory engagement wasn't merely aesthetic preference; it represented a fundamental shift in how these consumers experienced luxury. Research indicated a significant 188% increase in demand for tactile luxury experiences over an 18-month period in the early 2020s, suggesting a collective hunger for physical engagement in our increasingly virtual world.

The heightened value placed on sensory quality created natural scarcity that logo recognition could no longer provide. While logos could be replicated and mass-produced, the subtle tactile properties of hand-planed wood, hand-stitched leather, or hand-loomed textiles couldn't be convincingly mechanized.

"The most exclusive experiences now are those that can't be digitized," observed Emily, who sourced rare textiles for interior designers. "These sensory qualities can't be mass-produced, can't be faked with technology, and can't be fully appreciated through a screen. They create a form of exclusivity based not on artificial scarcity but on genuine material qualities and the education required to appreciate them."

The deepest transformation in luxury's evolution wasn't merely about where the enchantment migrated, but how consumers wove it into the fabric of their lives. As conventional luxury narratives weakened their grip, consumers started authoring their own definitions of what luxury signified to them personally.

Lauren's Brooklyn apartment expressed this narrative with quiet eloquence. Nothing in the space broadcast wealth or status at first glance. Her furnishings formed an eclectic collection, vintage pieces mingled with contemporary elements, all understated in their presentation. Closer examination, however, unveiled exceptional quality in surprising locations: ceramic tableware thrown by a Japanese master potter, textiles meticulously woven on Guatemalan looms, kitchen knives smithed by a third-generation Portland blademaker.

"I used to furnish my home according to what I thought would impress visitors," Lauren explained, running her hand along the edge of a walnut dining table made by a woodworker in Vermont. "Now I choose things based on their story and how they connect to my values and experiences. This table comes from trees harvested sustainably from a family forest. I've visited the workshop, seen how they work with the natural grain patterns rather than forcing uniformity. When I eat here, that knowledge is part of the experience."

Lauren's approach exemplified a broader transition toward personalized luxury narratives, expressions of taste and values that couldn't be captured by conventional status signifiers. This fragmentation of luxury into personal narratives represented perhaps the most significant challenge to traditional luxury marketing, which had relied on universal status codes and aspirational messaging.

The personal luxury narrative typically wove together multiple elements that traditional marketing treated separately: individual taste, values alignment, cultural connection, and life experience. Perhaps the most significant aspect of this evolution was how it changed the social function of luxury. Traditional luxury consumption had operated primarily as external communication, signaling status, taste, and belonging to others through recognizable markers. The personal luxury narrative, by contrast, served a more internal purpose, reinforcing the individual's sense of identity, values, and connection to what they found meaningful.

This shift toward personal meaning created a form of luxury that was potentially more resilient than status-based consumption. While positional goods derived value primarily from their exclusivity (which could be eroded through democratization), personally meaningful objects maintained their value regardless of market trends or brand dilution.

As I followed the threads of how luxury's essence had evolved over the past decades, patterns emerged that suggested not a final destination but an ongoing cycle of transformation. To comprehend this perpetual evolution, I reconnected with Catherine, my interview subject from fifteen years prior when she was deeply immersed in logo fascination. During that original meeting, she'd proudly displayed her collection of monogrammed accessories. Today, in her garden outside Paris, she spoke with matching enthusiasm but about entirely different possessions, objects chosen not for their instant recognition value but for their connection to craft traditions she had dedicated years to understanding.

"Looking back, I can see I've completed a full cycle," she reflected, tracing her finger along the rim of a ceramic cup made by a potter whose work she collected. "From initial enchantment with luxury brands to disillusionment as they became ubiquitous, then searching for alternatives, discovering craft and connoisseurship, and finally finding a new kind of enchantment in knowledge and sensory appreciation. But I'm not naive enough to think this is the end of the story."

Her awareness that this evolution wasn't final but cyclical echoed through conversations with other consumers who had made similar journeys. They recognized that the alternatives they'd embraced, whether quiet luxury brands focused on craftsmanship, small-scale artisans creating exceptional work, or regional craft traditions experiencing revival, carried the seeds of the same cycle that had transformed the brands they'd abandoned.

What made the current cycle distinct was the speed and transparency with which it unfolded. Digital platforms allowed consumers to witness brand evolution in real-time and to share their observations collectively. Information about changes in production methods, materials, or business models spread rapidly through forums and social media, accelerating both the disillusionment phase when brands compromised and the discovery phase when alternatives emerged.

Despite these compressed timeframes, the fundamental human desires driving the cycle remained constant: the desire for distinction, for meaning beyond functionality, for sensory pleasure, for connection to skill and intention, for objects that reflect and reinforce identity. These needs seemed woven into human psychology, ensuring that even as particular expressions of luxury rose and fell, the search for enchantment would continue.

"Understanding this cycle doesn't make me cynical," Catherine said as our conversation drew to a close. "If anything, it makes me more appreciative of where each brand or maker stands in their own evolution. I can value a house that has maintained some core of integrity even through growth, while still searching for those emerging voices that represent the purest expression of craft in the present moment."

Her perspective suggested a maturity in luxury consumption that transcended the simplistic patterns of falling in love with brands and then rejecting them when they changed. It acknowledged that luxury's essence was never static but always in motion, always seeking new vessels when old ones could no longer contain it.

As luxury consumers, our personal journeys often parallel this broader cycle, progressing from initial uncritical enthusiasm through disillusionment toward a more sophisticated understanding that acknowledges both luxury's inherent constraints and its enduring potential. The essence never truly vanished; rather, it evolved to demand more from us, developing finer sensory perception, training discerning eyes, crystallizing personal values, and engaging with material culture at deeper levels. In this challenge to grow lies what may be contemporary luxury's greatest gift: not the passive collection of status markers but the active cultivation of discernment that ultimately transforms both our chosen objects and our very selves.

Chapter Twenty-Four

An Eternal Cycle

M orning light splintered through Baccarat crystal as it danced across LVMH's Avenue Montaigne headquarters. Twelve executives maintained a studied silence around an immaculate marble table. At the head, a silver-haired figure scrutinized projected images of a Florentine leather atelier, a modest workshop whose handcrafted bags had cultivated a devoted following among those who had abandoned mainstream luxury labels.

"They've maintained a three-year waitlist without a euro spent on marketing," noted a sharp-featured woman with an impeccably tailored suit. "Their clientele includes numerous collectors who've divested their pieces from our flagship brands since 2020." She gestured toward a revenue projection, modest in scale but with an unwavering upward trajectory. "Despite deliberately constrained production, they achieve extraordinary margins, and more tellingly, they've captured precisely the consumers we're losing, those pursuing genuine craft excellence and authentic connection."

The chairman's expression remained inscrutable as he examined photographs of the workshop, housed in a restored 19th-century Florentine building where seven artisans practiced techniques preserved across centuries. His gaze lingered on images highlighting signature elements: edges burnished with heritage pine resin, saddle-stitching executed by hand rather than machine, and hardware pieces individually forged by a local foundry operated by the same family for five generations.

"How do the founders view acquisition possibilities?" he inquired.

"Previously resistant," responded a silver-templed executive. "They've declined three competitor approaches already. But circumstances might have created vulnerability. Their current atelier has reached capacity limits, and their master craftsman celebrates his seventieth birthday next month with no clear succession plan established."

The chairman considered the integration financials on screen. Though the numbers promised favorable returns, his attention fixed on a customer testimonial highlighted below: "After a decade collecting prestigious labels, I've rediscovered the enchantment I thought lost."

"Enchantment," he echoed, the word hanging in the air.

"Evokes early Dior," ventured a white-haired board member. "Before the licensing proliferation. During Christian's era."

A whisper of a smile crossed the chairman's face. "Just as Vuitton existed before our intervention." With a decisive motion, he closed his leather folio. "This narrative repeats with remarkable precision, doesn't it? The dedicated workshop elevating craft above commerce. Production deliberately limited. Clientele valuing intrinsic excellence over conspicuous status." His gaze swept across the assembled executives. "We recognize this moment in the evolutionary sequence. We've encountered it repeatedly."

"Our fundamental challenge," interjected the woman who had initiated the presentation, "lies in whether we can integrate their operation without extinguishing the very magic that makes them extraordinary."

The chairman maintained his composed exterior, though longtime colleagues might have detected momentary irony in his expression. These discussions had recurred throughout his career, only the brand

names changing: Dior yielding to Fendi, then Bulgari, most recently
Tiffany, while the underlying rhythm remained unchanged.

"Proceed with an approach," he announced after measured deliber-
ation. "But with sophisticated refinement. Offer resources while guar-
anteeing independence, expertise without demanding standardization. Structure this as genuine partnership rather than absorption."
Rising to his feet, he effectively concluded the meeting. "What we're
securing transcends a mere brand. We're acquiring luxury's next evolutionary phase, this incarnation of it, at least."

As colleagues dispersed, he lingered by the panoramic window, observing Avenue Montaigne below where crowds streamed into flagship
stores whose namesakes had once been modest workshops like the
Florentine atelier under discussion. The perpetual motion continued,
precisely as anticipated. Luxury's essence remained intact; it had merely migrated, following its timeless choreography of emergence, capture,
diffusion, and rebirth.

Luxury's revolutionary movements preceded Silicon Valley's fascination with "disruption" by centuries. Each generation witnesses what
appears to be unprecedented transformation, consumers abandoning
established houses for emerging artisanal workshops, without recognizing this as merely the latest movement in luxury's ancient choreography. Throughout history, this sector has followed a remarkably
consistent sequence: artisanal houses rise through craft excellence, expand to reach broader markets, inevitably democratize their offerings,
creating space for new specialists who restore exclusivity and authentic
craftsmanship.

Dior's trajectory provides the definitive case study of this phenomenon. Following its founder's death in 1957, the maison aggressively
pursued licensing agreements that generated immediate financial rewards. By the late 1970s, the Dior signature adorned everything from
haute couture to bathroom accessories. This proliferation delivered
short-term profits while creating an existential contradiction: a prestige label predicated on exclusivity had become ubiquitous. The confluence of overlicensing and counterfeit products led the Boussac Group,

Dior's parent company, to bankruptcy by 1978, marking the nadir in the brand's trajectory.

Today's luxury landscape mirrors these historical precedents with uncanny precision. The dominant luxury groups that once embodied exclusivity now face criticisms about overexposure and dilution that echo Dior's challenges from half a century ago. A market recalibration beginning in 2024 marked the first significant non-pandemic slowdown in luxury growth in 15 years, potentially signaling a pivotal moment in the sector's trajectory.

Walk through any international transportation hub and witness luxury's fundamental contradiction made manifest. Airport concourses feature virtually identical storefronts offering logo-laden merchandise to harried travelers of every description. From Singapore to Seoul to Dubai, perfectly arranged displays showcase indistinguishable assortments of branded accessories, available to anyone possessing sufficient credit limit. What would the originators of these houses think: Cristóbal Balenciaga meticulously adjusting a sleeve's drape, Guccio Gucci selecting leathers for aristocratic clients, or Louis Vuitton personally constructing travel pieces for nobility?

The intensified pace of this evolution stems largely from structural industry transformations. While Dior's metamorphosis stretched across decades, contemporary labels experience accelerated lifecycles driven by shareholder expectations, instantaneous global exposure through digital channels, and conglomerate-imposed growth mandates. What historically required generations now transpires within mere years.

These recurring evolutionary phases stem from luxury's inherent contradiction: the simultaneous requirements for exclusivity and commercial expansion. This fundamental tension, the same force that propelled Dior's expansion and subsequent decline, continues orchestrating luxury's transformation today, often within the very organizations that previously navigated these challenges.

Behind the pristine storefronts and runway spectacles operates an intricate strategic infrastructure specifically engineered to harness luxury's cyclical nature. The dominant luxury conglomerates, LVMH, Kering, and Richemont, have each cultivated distinctive methodologies for addressing luxury's intrinsic contradictions.

Under Arnault's stewardship, LVMH established the archetype for luxury consolidation through methodical acquisition across diverse categories. This framework emerged directly from his formative experience revitalizing Dior. As part of a major restructuring, more than 300 licenses were bought back to regain control of the brand's image and distribution. This meticulous reclamation of brand authority subsequently became part of the Arnault playbook on dozens of luxury acquisitions over the next 30 years.

LVMH's vast constellation, encompassing over 75 distinct brands, functions as an ecosystem with houses strategically positioned at various points in luxury's evolutionary sequence. Within this structure, anchor properties like Louis Vuitton and Dior generate significant revenue streams, specialist ateliers such as Berluti and Loro Piana maintain traditional craftsmanship expertise, while emerging acquisitions await future development. This strategic diversification enables a self-contained regenerative system where luxury's ephemeral appeal circulates within the organization's boundaries rather than migrating exclusively to external competitors.

By contrast, Kering implements a more concentrated approach with a deliberately limited roster of fashion-forward properties. Their methodology prioritizes creative revitalization, as demonstrated through transformative reinventions like Gucci's rebirth under Tom Ford's direction and later Alessandro Michele's vision. While delivering exceptional results throughout the 2010s, recent performance fluctuations, particularly at Gucci, illustrate potential vulnerabilities in strategies overly dependent on creative leadership and cultural currency.

Richemont has architected its portfolio around mastery in "hard luxury," primarily watches and jewelry, anchored by prestigious houses like Cartier and Van Cleef & Arpels alongside specialized horological maisons such as Jaeger-LeCoultre and IWC. Their strategic emphasis centers on exceptional heritage preservation and technical craftsmanship rather than seasonal fashion cycles, positioning their properties as "timeless" rather than temporally defined.

Independent maisons offer illuminating counterpoints to conglomerate approaches. Hermès and Chanel have crafted proprietary methodologies that deliberately resist conventional evolution patterns. Hermès adheres to calibrated, incremental advancement rather than aggressive expansion, maintaining unwavering commitment to exceptional craftsmanship standards, deliberately constrained production volumes, and intergenerational value preservation.

Chanel maintains its private ownership structure while exercising meticulous distribution oversight, notably declining fashion e-commerce despite industry trends, based on their conviction that physical retail experiences constitute an irreplaceable luxury component. This deliberate limitation enables preservation of perceived exclusivity alongside substantial commercial success.

These contrasting organizational approaches illuminate diverse methodologies for navigating luxury's evolutionary trajectory. Despite structural differences, all successful luxury enterprises recognize that managing contradictions, rather than attempting to eliminate them, constitutes the essence of effective stewardship. The most sophisticated organizations neither resist nor lament the evolutionary cycle but instead strategically leverage it, sometimes deliberately accelerating specific developmental phases to establish market advantages while simultaneously insulating their most valuable assets from premature dilution.

Amber light bathes the circular forecourt of Gucci's Florentine headquarters as evening approaches. Chauffeur-driven vehicles arrive in steady procession, delivering fashion journalists and retail executives gathered from across the globe for the upcoming collection debut. These surroundings of cultivated luxury obscure an astonishing transformation. Just three decades prior, this venerable house had descended into such disrepute that sophisticated consumers deliberately avoided its products.

The early 1990s witnessed Gucci transformed into luxury's foremost cautionary example: once-coveted horse-bit loafers and distinctive bamboo-handled bags appeared on discount retailers' shelves, while the previously prestigious signature adorned mass-produced accessories from inexpensive neckwear to drugstore keychains. By 1993, financial deterioration had become so severe that Investcorp executives removed Maurizio Gucci, grandson of the founder, following his unsuccessful rehabilitation attempts.

What followed became the template for modern luxury revitalization. The appointment of Tom Ford as creative director and Domenico De Sole as CEO initiated a dramatic transformation. Their comprehensive strategy addressed every aspect of the business: creative direction, pricing, marketing, distribution, and manufacturing. Perhaps most crucially, they recognized that Gucci's damaged perception required not incremental improvement but complete reinvention.

Ford dramatically shifted the aesthetic from classical to overtly "sexy and glamorous," targeting younger, fashion-conscious consumers rather than traditional luxury clients. The team lowered average prices by approximately 30% to realign with competitors, improving perceived value while broadening the customer base. Distribution control proved essential to rebuilding exclusivity, with the team drastically reducing wholesale partners and focusing instead on directly operated stores.

The strategy proved extraordinarily successful. Gucci transformed from near-bankruptcy to one of the world's most influential and profitable fashion houses. What makes this revival particularly instructive is that it relied not on returning to some mythical golden age but on strategic reinvention that acknowledged market realities while respecting brand essence.

What unites successful revivals is their multi-dimensional approach. They don't merely change logos or launch new products; they fundamentally restructure their businesses while creating new brand narratives that acknowledge heritage without being constrained by it. Perhaps most fascinating is the psychological dimension of these transformations, what might be called "strategic brand amnesia," the ability of consumers to forget or re-contextualize negative associations when presented with compelling new narratives.

These phoenix brands demonstrate that luxury's cycle is not deterministic. While patterns repeat, strategic intervention can alter trajectories. Brands can rise from the ashes of dilution through deliberate revitalization, but only when that strategy addresses the fundamental tensions of luxury rather than merely changing surface elements.

Florence's Palazzo Pitti houses a meticulously preserved Gucci bamboo-handled bag from 1947, ceremoniously unwrapped by white-gloved archivists from acid-free tissue. Adjacent galleries display Tom Ford's boundary-pushing velvet suits from five decades later. This curatorial juxtaposition would have bewildered the original craftspeople who fashioned that inaugural bamboo handle: the concept that within one generation, their creations would witness a complete evolutionary sequence: meteoric ascent, precipitous decline, dramatic reinvention, renewed prominence, subsequent stagnation, and another artistic metamorphosis.

What took Dior decades, the journey from founder's vision to excessive licensing to revitalization, now unfolds in compressed timeframes that can dizzy even industry veterans. The acceleration of luxury's cyclical pattern stems from a confluence of forces that have fundamentally altered how brands evolve and how consumers engage with them.

Digital platforms and social media have transformed luxury from distant admiration to constant visibility. Instagram created a global stage where luxury consumption became performance art, privileging the most recognizable signifiers and inadvertently rewarding the loudest luxury statements rather than subtle quality markers. This visibility dramatically compressed the exclusivity-to-ubiquity timeline. Before digital platforms, a luxury item might take years to transition from rarified discovery to mainstream awareness. Today, a single viral moment can catapult a product from obscurity to omnipresence within weeks.

Ownership structures exert powerful influence on cycle velocity. Publicly traded luxury groups face quarterly earnings pressure that can drive decisions prioritizing immediate growth over long-term brand equity. The contrast with private ownership is stark: Chanel's refusal to sell fashion online despite digital retail's explosive growth reflects the freedom provided by private ownership to resist short-term market pressures.

Financial democratization has created entirely new cycle dynamics. The explosive growth of luxury resale platforms has dramatically expanded access to previously exclusive products, accelerating the product lifecycle as items move more quickly from primary to secondary markets. Meanwhile, Buy-Now-Pay-Later services reduced both practical and psychological friction in the acquisition process, while the investment narrative surrounding certain luxury goods has shifted purchase motivation from personal enjoyment to potential appreciation.

Generational dynamics add another layer of complexity. Different age cohorts experience luxury cycles from distinct vantage points, creating parallel but asynchronous perceptions. Baby Boomers might recall Gucci's original craftsmanship and subsequent dilution, Generation X witnessed Tom Ford's provocative reinvention, Millennials experienced the brand primarily through social media, and Generation Z encounters Gucci with no memory of its previous incarnations.

The cumulative effect of these accelerants has been to create what some observers call "micro-luxury cycles," shorter, more intense periods of rise and fall than those experienced by previous generations. A craft-focused brand might emerge, gain recognition, expand too quickly, compromise on quality, and experience consumer rejection within years rather than decades.

Yet amid this acceleration, the fundamental pattern remains remarkably consistent. The tension between exclusivity and accessibility, between craft integrity and commercial scale, between heritage authenticity and contemporary relevance: these contradictions continue to drive luxury's cyclical evolution, even as the timeframe compresses and the players change. The wheel turns faster, but its essential mechanism remains unchanged.

Conclusion
The Perpetual Tension

The pale winter sunlight gilded Stanford Shopping Center, casting long shadows as I adjusted my Hermès scarf. The "Fleurs de Giverny" pattern, a tapestry of crimson, azure, and emerald blossoms that seemed to bloom across the silk, retained its vibrancy a decade after I'd first unwrapped it from that signature orange box.

My fingertips traced the hand-rolled edge, feeling the subtle ridge where artisans had meticulously folded and stitched the hem. With each wearing, the scarf revealed new secrets: miniature flowers nestled among larger blooms, whisper-delicate leaf patterns previously unnoticed, the alchemy of colors that shifted with movement and light.

Outside the Loro Piana boutique, a pale green parka caught my eye, the shade of spring's first leaves, a soft fluorite hovering between mint and sage. Through the window, the fabric's subtle luminescence suggested something transcending ordinary rainwear.

Inside, reality shifted: the gentle perfume of fine wool and leather, hushed acoustics, and attentive yet unobtrusive staff. The sales associate, noticing my interest, approached with warmth.

"It's our Evan parka," she said, already retrieving it. "Would you like to try it on?"

The moment it touched my hands, I understood its commanding price. What appeared to be simple silk was a technical marvel: Habutai silk treated for water resistance, creating fabric impossibly lightweight yet substantial, with a velvety suppleness that responded to touch like something alive. As I slipped it on, the parka settled with perfect balance, the metal-tipped drawstrings adding just enough weight to create impeccable drape.

"It's extraordinary," I murmured, while discreetly checking the price tag that confirmed my suspicion, stratospherically beyond my reach. "Though I wonder about its practicality in California's climate."

"True luxury isn't about practicality," the associate replied with knowing insight. "It's about possibility."

As I reluctantly returned the parka, my hand instinctively moved to adjust my Hermès scarf. The juxtaposition crystallized: this decade-old silk conveyed the identical essence as the Loro Piana parka: exceptional craftsmanship, obsessive detail, materials selected and treated with reverence. Both embodied profound understanding of how fabric should embrace skin, how colors should dance in light, how every element should serve both function and beauty.

Walking through the shopping center, I passed storefronts bearing names that had dominated earlier chapters of luxury's narrative: Louis Vuitton, Cartier, Gucci, Chanel. Their windows showcased familiar codes: interlocking Cs, monogrammed canvas, bamboo handles. Yet alongside them stood newer names, Brunello Cucinelli, The Row, Gabriela Hearst, brands emphasizing materials and craftsmanship over obvious logos, quality over recognition.

In a climate-controlled archive beneath LVMH headquarters lies a leather-bound guest book from Christian Dior's first couture show in 1947. The elegant signatures, fashion editors, society women, industry insiders, document the moment his "New Look" transformed postwar fashion. Nearby rests a 1970s advertisement for Dior-branded household linens, a physical relic from the period of excessive licensing that nearly destroyed the brand's prestige. A few shelves away, sketches from John Galliano's theatrical revival of the house in the 1990s reveal yet another chapter in the brand's evolution.

These artifacts, spanning decades of Dior's history, tell not just one company's story but luxury's eternal narrative: a continuous cycle of creation, expansion, dilution, and rebirth driven by a fundamental tension that cannot be resolved, only managed. This tension, between the exclusivity that defines luxury and the growth that businesses naturally seek, ensures that luxury's evolution will continue as long as humans desire both specialness and success.

The cycle begins with creation: a founder's vision translated into exceptional products through superior craftsmanship and materials. Christian Dior's revolutionary silhouettes, Guccio Gucci's fine leather goods, Louis Vuitton's innovative trunks, each represented a genuine advancement in their category, winning devoted followers through inherent quality rather than marketing. This creation phase naturally limits scale through the constraints of handcraft and the founder's direct involvement.

Success breeds expansion as founders and their successors seek growth. Initially, this expansion maintains quality while reaching new markets or categories. But eventually, the pressure for continued growth, whether from shareholders, family members, or simple ambition, leads to compromises. Production scales beyond craftspeople's capacity, distribution extends to less prestigious channels, and licensing provides revenue without direct oversight. Each individual decision seems reasonable, but collectively they begin to erode the very exclusivity that made the brand desirable.

Dilution follows as the brand becomes increasingly accessible and visible. The distinctive becomes commonplace; the special becomes standard. Finally, rebirth occurs, sometimes through extinction and replacement, sometimes through strategic revitalization. Bernard Arnault's revival of Dior established the template: regain control through license cancellation, reinvest in product quality and innovation, reestablish exclusivity through controlled distribution, and reconnect with the brand's original creative essence while making it relevant to contemporary consumers.

What makes this cycle both predictable and seemingly inevitable is that it emerges from contradictions inherent to luxury itself. True luxury requires scarcity, whether natural (rare materials, limited production capacity) or artificial (deliberate supply constraints, controlled distribution). Yet business success traditionally demands growth, more units sold, more markets entered, more categories covered. These opposing forces create a perpetual tension that pulls luxury brands toward democratization even as it threatens their foundational exclusivity.

Jean-Noël Kapferer termed this challenge "abundant rarity," the paradoxical requirement to be both desired by many but owned by few. How can a brand appear exclusive while selling millions of units? How can it maintain craft quality while meeting Wall Street growth expectations? How can heritage values survive industrial scale? These questions have no permanent solutions, only temporary balancing acts that inevitably tip toward one extreme before correcting toward the other.

Digital transformation has not eliminated this tension but accelerated and amplified it. Social media platforms compress the timeframe between exclusivity and ubiquity, while online availability removes physical barriers to access. Financial democratization through resale platforms and payment services further accelerates the accessibility phase. Meanwhile, the pressures of public ownership drive growth imperatives that can force compromises in quality and exclusivity.

Yet amid this acceleration, opportunities emerge for brands that understand and strategically manage these tensions rather than being passively carried by them. The most sophisticated luxury groups now deliberately maintain brands at different stages within their portfolios, allowing excellence to migrate within their ecosystem rather than escaping entirely. Some independent houses have established business models that deliberately limit growth to preserve exclusivity, demonstrating that commercial success need not require constant expansion.

The future of luxury unfolds not as a single narrative but as multiple parallel stories, each responding to these fundamental tensions while being shaped by distinct cultural contexts, consumer values, and business strategies. As the current market correction unfolds, several trajectories emerge that suggest how luxury's next chapter might evolve.

The established luxury conglomerates face their most significant strategic reassessment since the 2008 financial crisis. After years of extraordinary growth heavily driven by price increases, accounting for 80% of the sector's expansion between 2019 and 2023, groups like LVMH, Kering, and Richemont confront the limits of this approach. As McKinsey notes, "luxury leaders will need to conduct a holistic, strategic reset and play the long game, rather than rely on quick fixes to address their most pressing challenges."

This reset likely involves rebalancing between mass luxury and craft-focused offerings. LVMH's recent portfolio adjustments suggest recognition of this need, with increased investment in houses like Loro Piana and Berluti that maintain stronger craft credentials while simultaneously exploring new premium experiences through ventures like the Cheval Blanc hotel collection.

Regional luxury houses emerge as significant guardians of craft tradition. In Japan, brands like Tsuchiya Kaban and Hender Scheme have gained international recognition for exceptional leather goods that emphasize handcraftsmanship and material quality. In China, houses like Shang Xia point toward a revival of Chinese luxury traditions reinterpreted for contemporary consumers. These regional houses benefit from cultural authenticity and craft heritage that Western luxury often claims but rarely sustains at scale.

Independent luxury houses following the Hermès model of controlled growth and craft emphasis represent another guardian category. Young, founder-led brands like The Row, Gabriela Hearst, and Brunello Cucinelli have established business models that prioritize quality over expansion, maintaining exclusivity through deliberate supply constraints rather than prohibitive pricing.

Technology creates both threats and opportunities for luxury's future. While digital platforms have accelerated change, they also enable direct connections between craftspeople and consumers that weren't possible in previous eras. The growing use of blockchain for authentication, digital product passports that document provenance, and made-to-order manufacturing enabled by advanced logistics could collectively create new forms of exclusivity and scarcity.

Sustainability imperatives represent perhaps the most profound force reshaping luxury trajectories. The 2018 controversy surrounding Burberry's destruction of $38 million worth of unsold inventory highlighted practices once common but increasingly untenable. For future guardians, sustainability may represent not just ethical necessity but a new dimension of luxury itself, products that embody responsibility toward materials, makers, and environment.

Perhaps most intriguing is the possibility that brands might consciously design for tension management from their inception. New luxury entrants with knowledge of historical patterns could potentially create structures and strategies that allow for sustainable growth without the dilution that traditionally accompanies scale.

Ultimately, luxury's eternal tensions ensure not just the continual rebirth of individual brands but the perpetual renewal of luxury itself. The essence doesn't disappear; it migrates, seeking vessels that can temporarily contain the paradox of exclusivity and desirability before moving on when that balance inevitably tips. This migration creates space for new creators, new interpretations, new expressions of craft and quality, ensuring that luxury remains forever ancient and forever new.

For consumers, understanding these patterns offers perspective on the seemingly revolutionary changes in luxury consumption. What appears transformative to each generation, the current migration toward craft-focused independent brands, sustainable luxury, or quiet luxury, represents merely the latest turn in a pattern that has repeated throughout luxury's history. The specific vessels change, but the underlying desire, for specialness, for distinction, for connection to human craft and creativity, remains remarkably constant.

For brands, recognizing these tensions provides strategic clarity. Rather than fighting against inevitable contradictions, the most successful luxury houses embrace them, designing business models that accommodate paradox rather than denying it. They understand that maintaining luxury's essence requires deliberate tension management, balancing growth with exclusivity, innovation with heritage, accessibility with aspiration.

My hand drifted once more to the Fleurs de Giverny scarf, appreciating anew its perfect weight, the precise printing that revealed new details even after years of wear. What endures from luxury's evolution is not just the objects themselves, still crafted with exceptional skill and materials, but the memory of how they made us feel: the pride of first acquisition, the pleasure of appreciating fine details, the sense of participating in traditions that stretch back generations. These emotional imprints persist even as the luxury landscape evolves, reminding us of what emerges when craftsmanship, exclusivity, and desire exist in perfect equilibrium.

The essence isn't gone. It simply migrates, seeking new vessels that can momentarily contain luxury's inherent contradictions. As I left the shopping center, the winter sun caught the threads of my scarf, illuminating the intricate pattern of flowers with unexpected brilliance, a reminder that true luxury transcends trends and time, connecting us to both craft traditions of the past and the enduring human desire for something extraordinary, something that feels, however fleetingly, like magic.

About The Author

Karina Vunnam is a Stanford-trained economist, researcher and author whose work examines how cultural systems, psychology, and economic forces shape human behavior and desire.

Born in Mumbai and raised across continents, Karina's journey from the streets to Stanford University informs her nuanced understanding of status, aspiration, and cultural capital. Her economics background provides the analytical framework for examining how luxury functions across different societies and economic strata.

Her other work includes *Debt by Dysfunction: The 2033 Fiscal Crisis Hiding in Plain Sight*, a statutory audit of America's converging entitlement and debt crises; *The World Is Always Never Ending*, exploring how historical cycles provide perspective on modern anxiety; and the Mumbai Street Siblings children's book series. She writes about systems thinking, cultural analysis, and the patterns that shape collective behavior at KarinaQueries.com and on Substack at karinaqueries.substack.com.

Bibliography

Books and Monographs

Arnault, Bernard. *La Passion Créative*. Plon, 2001.

Belk, Russell W. "Possessions and the Extended Self." *Journal of Consumer Research*, vol. 15, no. 2, 1988, pp. 139-168.

Berry, Christopher J. *The Idea of Luxury: A Conceptual and Historical Investigation*. Cambridge University Press, 1994.

Boltanski, Luc, and Arnaud Esquerre. *Enrichment: A Critique of Commodities*. Wiley, 2022.

Bourdieu, Pierre. *Distinction: A Social Critique of the Judgement of Taste*. Harvard University Press, 1984.

Bruzzi, Stella. *Undressing Cinema: Clothing and Identity in the Movies*. Routledge, 2012.

Currid-Halkett, Elizabeth. *The Sum of Small Things: A Theory of the Aspirational Class*. Princeton University Press, 2017.

Day, Dapper Dan. *Dapper Dan: Made in Harlem*. Random House, 2019.

Flügel, J. C. *The Psychology of Clothes*. Hogarth Press, 1930.

Joannes, Paul. *Louis Vuitton: The Birth of Modern Luxury.* Abrams, 2021.

Kapferer, Jean-Noël. *Kapferer on Luxury: How Luxury Brands Can Grow Yet Remain Rare.* Kogan Page, 2015.

Kapferer, Jean-Noël, and Vincent Bastien. *The Luxury Strategy: Break the Rules of Marketing to Build Luxury Brands.* Kogan Page, 2012.

Lipovetsky, Gilles, and Elyette Roux. *Le luxe éternel: De l'âge du sacré au temps des marques.* Gallimard, 2003.

Martin, Richard, and Harold Koda. *Haute Couture.* The Metropolitan Museum of Art, 1995.

Mazzeo, Tilar J. *The Secret of Chanel No. 5: The Intimate History of the World's Most Famous Perfume.* Harper, 2010.

McCracken, Grant. *Culture and Consumption II: Markets, Meaning, and Brand Management.* Indiana University Press, 2005.

Okonkwo, Uché. *Luxury Fashion Branding: Trends, Tactics, Techniques.* Palgrave Macmillan, 2016.

Pasols, Paul. *Louis Vuitton: The Birth of Modern Luxury.* Harry N. Abrams, 2005.

Postrel, Virginia. *The Fabric of Civilization: How Textiles Made the World.* Basic Books, 2020.

Thomas, Dana. *Deluxe: How Luxury Lost Its Luster.* Penguin Press, 2007.

Tungate, Mark. *Luxury World: The Past, Present and Future of Luxury Brands.* Kogan Page, 2009.

Turner, Victor. *The Ritual Process: Structure and Anti-Structure.* Aldine Publishing Company, 1969.

Journal Articles

Adam, Hajo, and Adam D. Galinsky. "Enclothed Cognition." *Journal of Experimental Social Psychology,* vol. 48, no. 4, 2012, pp. 918-925.

Ahuvia, Aaron C. "Beyond the Extended Self: Loved Objects and Consumers' Identity Narratives." *Journal of Consumer Research,* vol. 32, no. 1, 2005, pp. 171-184.

Berger, Jonah, and Morgan Ward. "Subtle Signals of Inconspicuous Consumption." *Journal of Consumer Research*, vol. 37, no. 4, 2010, pp. 555-569.

Berthon, Pierre, et al. "Aesthetics and Ephemerality: Observing and Preserving the Luxury Brand." *California Management Review*, vol. 52, no. 1, 2009, pp. 45-66.

Catry, Bernard. "The Great Pretenders: The Magic of Luxury Goods." *Business Strategy Review*, vol. 14, no. 3, 2003, pp. 10-17.

Dion, Delphine, and Eric Arnould. "Retail Luxury Strategy: Assembling Charisma through Art and Magic." *Journal of Retailing*, vol. 87, no. 4, 2011, pp. 502-520.

Dubois, Bernard, and Patrick Duquesne. "The Market for Luxury Goods: Income versus Culture." *European Journal of Marketing*, vol. 27, no. 1, 1993, pp. 35-44.

Dubois, Bernard, and Claire Paternault. "Understanding the World of International Luxury Brands: The 'Dream Formula'." *Journal of Advertising Research*, vol. 35, no. 4, 1995, pp. 69-76.

Eckhardt, Giana M., Russell W. Belk, and Jill Avery Wilson. "The Rise of Inconspicuous Consumption." *Journal of Marketing Management*, vol. 31, no. 7-8, 2015, pp. 807-826.

Festinger, Leon. "A Theory of Social Comparison Processes." *Human Relations*, vol. 7, no. 2, 1954, pp. 117-140.

Fournier, Susan. "Consumers and Their Brands: Developing Relationship Theory in Consumer Research." *Journal of Consumer Research*, vol. 24, no. 4, 1998, pp. 343-373.

Godey, Bruno, et al. "Social Media Marketing Efforts of Luxury Brands: Influence on Brand Equity and Consumer Behavior." *Journal of Business Research*, vol. 69, no. 12, 2016, pp. 5833-5841.

Han, Young Jee, Joseph C. Nunes, and Xavier Drèze. "Signaling Status with Luxury Goods: The Role of Brand Prominence." *Journal of Marketing*, vol. 74, no. 4, 2010, pp. 15-30.

Hennings, Nadine, et al. "The Complexity of Value in the Luxury Industry: From Consumers' Individual Value Perception to Luxury Consumption." *International Journal of Retail & Distribution Management*, vol. 43, no. 10/11, 2015, pp. 922-939.

Ho, Harrison C. Y., and Jacky W. C. Wong. "Disassociation from the Common Herd: Conceptualizing (In)conspicuous Consumption as Luxury Consumer Maturity." *Consumption Markets & Culture*, vol. 25, no. 3, 2022, pp. 254-270.

Holt, Douglas B. "Does Cultural Capital Structure American Consumption?" *Journal of Consumer Research*, vol. 25, no. 1, 1998, pp. 1-25.

Joy, Annamma, et al. "M(Art)Worlds: Consumer Perceptions of How Luxury Brand Stores Become Art Institutions." *Journal of Retailing*, vol. 90, no. 3, 2014, pp. 347-364.

Kapferer, Jean-Noël. "Abundant Rarity: The Key to Luxury Growth." *Business Horizons*, vol. 55, no. 5, 2012, pp. 453-462.

Kapferer, Jean-Noël. "The Artification of Luxury: From Artisans to Artists." *Business Horizons*, vol. 57, no. 3, 2014, pp. 371-380.

Kastanakis, Minas N., and George Balabanis. "Between the Mass and the Class: Antecedents of the 'Bandwagon' Luxury Consumption Behavior." *Journal of Business Research*, vol. 65, no. 10, 2012, pp. 1399-1407.

Keinan, Anat, Ran Kivetz, and Oded Netzer. "The Authenticity Paradox: When the Human Touch Becomes a Liability." *Harvard Business School Working Paper Series*, no. 17-038, 2016.

Keller, Kevin Lane. "Managing the Growth Tradeoff: Challenges and Opportunities in Luxury Branding." *Journal of Brand Management*, vol. 16, no. 5, 2009, pp. 290-301.

Lynn, Michael. "Scarcity Effects on Value: A Quantitative Review of the Commodity Theory Literature." *Psychology & Marketing*, vol. 8, no. 1, 1991, pp. 43-57.

Makkar, Manpreet, and Siang-Fung Yap. "Emotional Experiences Behind the Pursuit of Inconspicuous Luxury." *Journal of Retailing and Consumer Services*, vol. 44, 2018, pp. 222-234.

McCracken, Grant. "Culture and Consumption: A Theoretical Account of the Structure and Movement of the Cultural Meaning of Consumer Goods." *Journal of Consumer Research*, vol. 13, no. 1, 1986, pp. 71-84.

Nedungadi, Prakash. "Recall and Consumer Consideration Sets: Influencing Choice without Altering Brand Evaluations." *Journal of Consumer Research*, vol. 17, no. 3, 1990, pp. 263-276.

Nelissen, Rob M. A., and Marijn H. C. Meijers. "Social Benefits of Luxury Brands as Costly Signals of Wealth and Status." *Evolution and Human Behavior*, vol. 32, no. 5, 2011, pp. 343-355.

Thomson, Matthew, Deborah J. MacInnis, and C. Whan Park. "The Ties That Bind: Measuring the Strength of Consumers' Emotional Attachments to Brands." *Journal of Consumer Psychology*, vol. 15, no. 1, 2005, pp. 77-91.

Truong, Yann, Rod McColl, and Philip J. Kitchen. "New Luxury Brand Positioning and the Emergence of Masstige Brands." *Journal of Brand Management*, vol. 16, no. 5, 2009, pp. 375-382.

Vigneron, Franck, and Lester W. Johnson. "Measuring Perceptions of Brand Luxury." *Journal of Brand Management*, vol. 11, no. 6, 2004, pp. 484-506.

Wilson, Robert. "The Psychology of Vicarious Luxury Consumption." *Journal of Consumer Psychology*, vol. 30, no. 3, 2020, pp. 543-559.

Yeoman, Ian. "The Changing Behaviours of Luxury Consumption." *Journal of Revenue and Pricing Management*, vol. 10, no. 1, 2011, pp. 47-50.

Zajonc, Robert B. "Attitudinal Effects of Mere Exposure." *Journal of Personality and Social Psychology*, vol. 9, no. 2, 1968, pp. 1-27.

Zane, Danielle Mantovani, and Jonah Berger. "How the Perceived Effort of Acquisition Influences Product Valuation." *Journal of Consumer Research*, vol. 44, no. 6, 2018, pp. 1364-1378.

Industry Reports and Publications

Bain & Company. *Luxury Goods Worldwide Market Study.* Annual reports, 2015-2024.

Bain & Company. "Luxury in Transition: Securing Future Growth." January 2025. https://www.bain.com/insights/luxury-in-transition-s ecuring-future-growth/

Boston Consulting Group. *Global Luxury Consumer Report.* Various editions, 2019-2024.

Deloitte. *Global Powers of Luxury Goods.* Annual reports, 2018-2024.

LVMH. *Annual Reports and Financial Statements.* 2015-2024.

McKinsey & Company. *The State of Fashion.* Annual reports, 2018-2025.

McKinsey & Company. "The State of Luxury: How to Navigate a Slowdown." January 2025. https://www.mckinsey.com/industries/re tail/our-insights/state-of-luxury

Media and Digital Sources

Business of Fashion. Various articles on luxury industry trends, 2015-2025.

Christie's. "Hermès Handbags: A Collecting Guide." Accessed April 2025. https://www.christies.com/en/stories/hermes-handbags-colle cting-guide

Financial Times. Luxury business coverage, 2018-2025.

Vogue Business. Fashion and luxury industry analysis, 2019-2025.

Wall Street Journal. Luxury market reporting, 2015-2025.

Corporate and Institutional Sources

Chanel. Corporate communications and annual reports, 2015-2024.

Hermès International. Annual reports and investor relations materials, 2015-2024.

Kering Group. Annual reports and sustainability communications, 2015-2024.

Louis Vuitton. Brand heritage and manufacturing documentation. https://en.louisvuitton.com

Richemont. Annual reports and maisons documentation, 2015-2024.

Digital Culture and Social Media

Instagram. Platform data and luxury brand presence analysis, 2010-2025.

Reddit. Luxury consumer community discussions (r/LuxuryReplicas, r/LuxuryLifeHabits), 2020-2025.

TikTok. Luxury manufacturing and authentication content analysis, 2020-2025.

Interviews and Primary Sources

Anonymous interviews with luxury industry executives, conducted 2024-2025.

Consumer interviews with luxury purchasers across demographics, conducted 2020-2025.

Field research at luxury retail locations, Paris, New York, and Shanghai, 2023-2024.

Note: This bibliography includes the most authoritative and frequently cited sources from the original research. Additional sources and detailed citations are available in the complete research documentation. All web sources were accessed between December 2024- May 2025 unless otherwise noted.

www.ingramcontent.com/pod-product-compliance
Lightning Source LLC
Chambersburg PA
CBHW071544210326
41597CB00019B/3109